Desirée Hetzel

Moving Lives – Cultivating with Climate Change in Vanuatu

EnvironmentalAnthropology | 10

Editorial

The series **EnvironmentalAnthropology** publishes studies that are based on ethnographic methods, reflect emic perspectives and contribute to environmental theory building. The series is based on a broad concept of the environment, which includes both the social, human-made and the "natural" environment. With this broad thematic scope, the series maps the diversity of culturally specific lifeworlds and practices worldwide. The series also aims at bringing together ethnological studies with an environmental focus and to promoting dialogue within interdisciplinary and international debates. In this way, the writings published in **EnvironmentalAnthropology** make unique contributions to pressing environmental issues of the present day.
The series is edited by Eveline Dürr, Frank Heidemann, Oliver D. Liebig and Martin Sökefeld.

Desirée Hetzel works with ni-Vanuatu climate activists and political representatives, and with women, men and children in the village communities of Dixon Reef on Malekula and Siviri on Efate, two islands in the South Pacific state of Vanuatu. Such intensive collaboration has contributed to ethnographic details on the links between gardening and climate change in Vanuatu.

Desirée Hetzel

Moving Lives – Cultivating with Climate Change in Vanuatu

[transcript]

Revised doctoral thesis from Ludwig-Maximilians-Universität München (Germany), 2022.

The research, on which this book is based, has been funded by DFG (German Research Foundation, grant number: 298643416). Further fieldtrips were financially supported by the European Union Horizon 2020 research and innovation programme FALAH (Family Farming, Health and Lifestyle in the Pacific, Marie Skłodowska-Curie grant agreement number: 873185). The production of this book has been supported by the Open Access Fonds of Ludwig-Maximilians-Universität München.

Bibliographic information published by the Deutsche Nationalbibliothek
The Deutsche Nationalbibliothek lists this publication in the Deutsche Nationalbibliografie; detailed bibliographic data are available in the Internet at https://dnb.dnb.de

transcript Verlag | Hermannstraße 26 | D-33602 Bielefeld | live@transcript-verlag.de

Cover design: Maria Arndt
Cover illustration: Desirée Hetzel
Printing: Elanders Waiblingen GmbH, Waiblingen
https://doi.org/10.14361/9783839407080
Print-ISBN: 978-3-8376-7766-9 | PDF-ISBN: 978-3-8394-0708-0
ISSN of series: 2629-415X | eISSN of series: 2747-3597

Printed on permanent acid-free text paper.

Contents

List of figures

Acknowledgments – Tok Tankiu

My first visit to Vanuatu was in 2015, when I met young enthusiastic ni-Vanuatu in the capital of Port Vila. They were active in their fight for climate justice and concerned for the safety of their families residing on the many islands of Vanuatu. They directed me to investigate the thoughts of people in rural areas on the topic of climate change. My initial thanks, therefore, go to the Vanuatu Climate Warriors for those first discussions and directions.

I am grateful to everyone in Vanuatu who agreed to contribute to my research and therefore this book. Individuals have opened doors, given guidance, made critical statements and offered constructive comments. Particular thanks go to all the women and men of Dixon Reef and Siviri villages, who I had the pleasure of accompanying on numerous visits to their gardens – thank you for your patience and open-mindedness! It is not easy to teach an anthropologist about everyday life and render the ordinary once again extraordinary.

Mi wantem talem tankiu long ol man, woman mo pikinini long Dixon Reef mo long Siviri. Tankiu blong support blong yufalla! Bigfala Tankiu i go long late principal Jif mo fildwoka Joachim Kaibaba blong Dixon Reef. Hemi bin wantem contributem long ol risej, from hemi telem risej hemi wan wei blong documentem ol samting wanem i happen tedei. Bigfala tankiu i go long famili blong mi long Dixon Reef. Fulap taem oli spendem wetem mi, hemi bin wan bigfala kontribution long buk ia. Tankiu long ol mama blong Dixon, oli bin lanem evri lil samtin long mi, tankiu blong support blong yufella!

Tankiu tumas long ol man, woman mo pikinini long Siviri, mo long Chief Atavi blong Siviri blong strong interest mo save. Mo, wan bifgfalla tankiu i go long famili blong mi, hu bin welkam mi evri dei mo no bin taid long ol discussion.

Tankiu long ol mama blong Siviri wetem open hart mo wais words, tankiu blong support blong yufella!

The Vanuatu Cultural Centre has the central institution in the country to have supported this research. Many thanks go to Henline Mala for immense administrative help! I am also grateful to the members of the National Advisory Board on Climate Change in Vanuatu for their continuous engagement and facilitation of this climate change research.

Arno Pascht and I started this research project together and he accompanied me through all stages of my dissertation writing, helping me to realise this book through invaluable advice and critical discussions. My special thanks go to Arno, a constant source of encouragement!

I further want to acknowledge Eveline Dürr for her dedicated academic guidance and Magnus Treiber for his academic support. I would also like to show appreciation to the editors of the 'Umweltethnologie' series for gathering research insights together and making publications possible.

Members of the Oceania working group of the DGSKA (German Association for Social and Cultural Anthropology) have given me great assistance through academic exchange, inviting me for talks and advising me to continue with my work.

This book could not have been realised without the many individuals who have dedicated their precious time. I would like to thank the following people for reading, commenting, editing and for generally supporting me (in alphabetic order): Rosa Dümlein, Valerie Hänsch, Marianne Hartan, Sergio Jarillo, Rebekka Kanesu, Robin Rieprich, Julian Schmischke and Nadine Witte. Additionally, I appreciate all comments given within the doctoral colloquium and through various external conversations. For giving this book final language editing, I am indebted to Suzie Maine, my copyeditor.

Last but not least, I would like to thank my friends and family for their unconditional support. Writing a book requires friends and family to bear a lot while listening to the same stories over and over again.

My 2016–2019 fieldwork took place in the framework of the research project 'Localising Global Climate Change Policies in Vanuatu: Reception of Knowledge and Cultural Transformation', funded by DFG (German Research Foundation, grant number: 298643416). Further fieldtrips were financially supported by the European Union Horizon 2020 research and innovation programme FALAH (Family Farming, Health and Lifestyle in the Pacific, Marie Skłodowska-Curie grant agreement number: 873185).

During my last visit to Vanuatu in 2023, I discussed these chapters with some of my research partners. A lot has happened since then – babies have been born, friends and families have died, there have been several further cyclones, people have rebuilt houses and replanted gardens. Community lives change. Ni-Vanuatu remain critical of their lives and continue to move on.

Tankiu tumas – Thank you – Danke!

Preface

This study is part of a growing number of ethnographies that address the effects of climate change in Oceania. It draws on 13 months of fieldwork, mainly on the west coast of Malekula, in the Dixon Reef area, but also including perspectives of interlocutors of the village of Siviri on the main island of Efate. In contrast to dominant media representations, which more often than not show various scenarios of 'vulnerability' of people living on islands, this book examines the ways ni-Vanuatu understand climate change in their own ways. Taking politically-driven climate change projects as a starting point, the focus is on 'mekem garen' ('make the garden'; unless stated otherwise, all translations are from Bislama), and the study argues that gardening is much more than a horticultural practice. Rather, mekem garen refers to an ensemble of practices for making sense of climate change and includes both social and environmental dimensions. Gardens are conceived as places of encounters and intersections, where different knowledges and ontological assumptions meet – such as local gardening knowledge and scientific climate change terminology. This is particularly the case when adaption programmes are conducted in order to foster food security in Vanuatu. In this vein, Desirée Hetzel skilfully analyses how cultivation and climate change come together in multi-layered interactions of people, plants, paths, hills, soil and so on. In this process, mekem garen becomes central to making sense of climate change by creating what Desirée Hetzel calls 'climate change worlds'. Mekem garen is a constantly evolving practice, taking on new influences and reaching beyond the environmental realm. Indeed, gardening is seen as a way of building relations and fostering community. With these insights, Desirée Hetzel's work offers a novel approach to gardening in the Anthropocene that results from encounters in climate change projects and provides insights relevant beyond the Pacific Islands.

Eveline Dürr, December 2024

1 Introduction

Figure 1: Map of Vanuatu with research sites marked

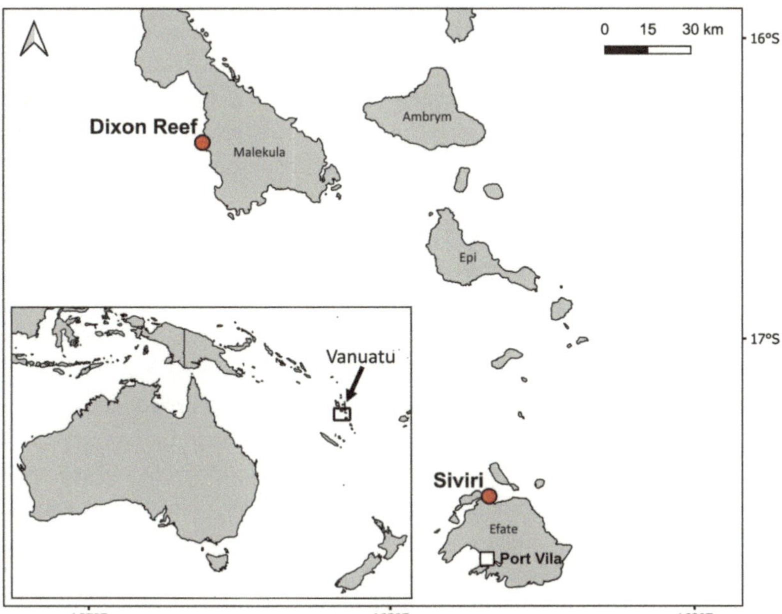

D. Hetzel

Our hands and feet covered in dirt, we were sitting at the side of the garden areas, on the top of the hill overlooking the plateau. Jenny and I had worked there most of the day. The sun had long since passed its zenith, but it was still burning on our heads. Until that point, we had been removing weeds around pineapple plants and planting countless maize kernels and manioc stalks, so-called 'hands' of manioc.[1] Now keen to find some shade, we hid underneath the finger-like leaves of the manioc plants. From our vantage point on the hill, we had a good view over the huge garden sites, cultivated by several families of the village of Dixon Reef. This was a stately area, around the size of a football pitch. However, the boundaries were difficult to discern, as the cultivation area of one family merged directly into that of another so that the garden areas stretched across the entire plateau and over the next green slope. Looking around, I was able to identify a wide variety of crops – banana,[2] taro[3] and tomato[4] – as well as some smaller pits with yam[5] vines ranking up. Also, at this time, maize[6] plants formed an impressive arrangement, planted sequentially over a number of weeks to ensure an interrupted period of cultivation. Maize was one of the main food crops at that time, since it is a successful crop in extremely hot conditions and there had been an unusually long dry period between 2015 and 2017, known as El Niño. Villagers in Dixon Reef on Vanuatu's island of Malekula had been working through this prolonged drought and the problems it had caused, especially for yam, the most important food and ceremonial crop.

I turned to my companion, Jenny, a young mother who grew up a little further north along the coast of Malekula and since her marriage, had been living in Dixon Reef. I had been accompanying her on her daily garden trips over the past couple of months: "Do you think nowadays you face more problems when doing your gardening?", I asked. I wondered whether the current dry spell would be something Vanuatu horticulturalists worried about, especially since the prominence of climate change discussions in the country more widely. She looked into the far distance, thought for a moment and then answered: "What do *I* think? In my opinion, now *everything* changes. *We* too used to do things differently. Before, other plants were planted, and if something didn't grow well, we had our methods. Today we just do it differently. And, now the times are also different and we have to do our best to go on."[7]

---

1 Manihot esculenta

2 Musa ssp.

3 Colocasia esculenta

4 Solanum lycopersicum

5 Dioscorea ssp.

6 Zea mays

7 Quotations in the national language Bislama or the village languages Novol and Nasarian for Dixon Reef, and Nguna for Siviri, have been translated by the author into English for the sake of readability.

She was obviously irritated by my asking her opinion. Female horticulturalists from the islands of Vanuatu are usually quite shy to speak out. Her family lived quite a distance from national decision-making in the capital, Port Vila, further south on the island of Efate. However, Jenny gave me an important lesson: ni-Vanuatu[8] gardeners consider their lives and gardens to be undergoing diverse changes, mutually and constantly re-shaping both communal lives and cultivation practices. Over the course of many garden days and equally many conversations about climate change, I came to understand that environmental changes as well as changes in communal lives are two parts of the same process and are considered together by ni-Vanuatu to constitute the phenomenon called climate change. This notion is intertwined with how people interact with their environments in a flexible manner, and furthermore how they create and reshape their lives. Therefore, climate change can never be considered to be one or the other, separating social from environmental, but is rather better considered to be a single process encompassing both elements. Put another way, rather than taking differing perspectives on material matters of a predefined phenomenon, such change becomes part of the daily practices of cultivation and world making of the people of Vanuatu. Being themselves a part of the matter of climate change, they consider themselves to be actors in the creation of current realities. This book aims to explore processes of entangled change which moves the lives of horticulturalists, showing how cultivation is practised as a way of making sense of these all-encompassing transformations and a way for ni-Vanuatu gardeners to move their own lives forward.

In the course of this book, I describe and analyse an ensemble of practices for making sense of climate change in Vanuatu. I refer to these composed practices as *mekem garen*. Mekem garen is a Bislama expression I first heard when my host father in the village Dixon Reef set off to the cultivation sites outside the village, readying his bush knife, shouldering a spade and enthusiastically declaring that "hemi taem blo mekem garen" (it's time to make the garden). That day, he headed toward the garden areas to take care of his new yam garden plots. As a first attempt, this Bislama[9] term can be loosely translated into English as 'making the garden(s)'. While 'A New Bislama Dictionary' refers to

---

8 The term 'ni-Vanuatu' is the self-designation of the indigenous populations of Vanuatu. Only ni-Vanuatu lived in Dixon Reef at the time of my research.

9 Bislama is a Neo-Melanesian English-lexifier pidgin-creole and was introduced as the language of traders. It is now one of the national languages of Vanuatu.

'mekem' as a verb translated as 'make', mekem is a very familiar Bislama composition and can also be translated as 'take', 'behave', 'engage among many others'; while 'garen' can be referred to as 'food garden' (Crowley 1995). This expression, I argue, hints at a current development, not disruptive but rather transformative in several aspects of the ecological, economic and social elements of life. First, I take the vocal Bislama composition mekem garen as framing for a Vanuatu practice of creating climate change worlds, where gardening is becoming politically intertwined with forms of so-called adaptation measures. Herein horticulturalists in rural Vanuatu become climate change actors. Second, I will take mekem garen as a way of viewing horticulture in its practical process-oriented approach and rethinking dichotomies between environmental and social situated in the Anthropocene. Third, mekem garen becomes a methodological approach of collaborative cultivation in fieldwork, co-creating gardens and knowledge between my interlocutors and my anthropological research partner.

I consider ni-Vanuatu horticulturalists' practices to be essential for grasping gardening as flexible and multidimensional. In connection with this, I pose the following questions: how do cultivation and climate change come together in these complex interactions of mekem garen? Through this, what are the approaches of horticulturalists as climate change actors in times of change? I follow adaptation practices introduced by NGOs and connected to the cultivation of Vanuatu's 'aelan kakae' (island food), the locally produced food of the islands of Vanuatu. I trace ni-Vanuatu practices of everyday cultivation while understanding and creating what my interlocutors called klaemet jenj[10] (Pascht 2019). The Vanuatu garden thereby exceeds being a mere site of representation of how environmental changes materialise and how people perceive these shifts, instead becoming a communal ontological meeting point of my interlocutor's climate change worlding.

For this, in the anthropology of climate change,[11] others have started important points of discussions. As one of the first, Peter Rudiak-Gould acknowledged people in Oceania as participants in making sense of climate change as much as they are observers of its consequences, reliant on international committees for their definitions (Rudiak-Gould 2011). Understanding that local residents in Oceania are participants in shaping international

10 Arno Pascht (2019) refers to klaemet jenj as the localised but new concept of climate change.

11 As defined by Crate and Nuttall 2009.

discourse rather than simply provers of external predefinitions becomes an essential part of this.

> When it comes to climate change it is insufficient to assume and ascribe the scientific account of the causes of global warming – and to only then look to culture after the fact as a resource for adaptation or else a basis for vulnerability. Instead, their predisposition is to look beyond this Eurocentric folk-model and academic convention and to anticipate that Pacific peoples will have shifting and multiple explanations. (Crook and Rudiak-Gould 2018, 5)

Talking about climate change also includes the production of new concepts, by being involved in modes and practices created through scientific and localised encounters (Hastrup 2016). For Oceania, Rudiak-Gould emphasised that this phenomenon is both experienced and integrated within discourses about future scenarios, allowing local communities to build their own notions of climate change. In order to understand how people operate in their daily practical activities, not only through patterns of weather and climate, such discourses also interact with explanations, information and projection (Rudiak-Gould 2011). Other scholars write in line with this argument and describe practices in connection with climate change as informed by global narratives and political strategies (Ourbak and Magnan 2018; Rudiak-Gould 2013) and the interaction with natural scientific explanations of climate change (Pascht 2019). Publications like 'Thinking like a climate' (Knox 2020) re-direct our view towards these combinations of people acting with weather phenomena and thinking with the benefit of both experiences and scientific knowledge. In Hannah Knox's opinion, people are not only concerned with climate change effects in the form of weather phenomenon, but also of matter and explanations and scientific contextualisation (Knox 2020).

What then happens in and through Vanuatu gardening? This haptic praxis of creating environments and communities and the settings of scientific environmental change lead to a requirement for new explanations for the climate change phenomenon. Mekem garen becomes central to making what I refer to as 'climate change worlds' (see Chapter 2). Herein mekem garen forms an approach, constantly evolving, taking on board new influences, hinting as to how people see themselves as involved in these changes and supporting what Rudiak-Gould calls 'beyond the environmental' (Rudiak-Gould 2016). Discussions about climate change are very often of institutional origin and suggest a general understanding of concepts and environmental transformations, that can be either accepted or rejected by actors in global arenas or localities (Hulme 2009). However, what I have learned from my ni-Vanuatu interlocutors is that this clear thinking runs up against realities where people navigate their thinking and actions through different contexts. This challenged my own thinking and hopefully will do the same for readers about current implications of a globalised climate change narrative. I want to contribute to the approach to this local and global crisis of our time by presenting a joint work of diverse understandings, by exploring how *life*, living together with humans and other-than-humans, is transformed and also re-created at the same time. Following my interlocutors on the Vanuatu islands of Efate and Malekula, there is also the reminder that this is not always about local people adjusting their lives but also a process based on hard-working pragmatism and flexible work in facing new challenges.

In my research, I especially engaged with people living on the west coast of Malekula, most of whom spend their lives in the Dixon Reef area. Additionally, I refer to other research partners in the village of Siviri on the main island of Efate, and to the work with political representatives and residents in Port Vila.[12] At the time of my research, the village communities of Dixon Reef and Siviri had been involved in adaptation projects for almost a decade, balancing national political implications and their own everyday cultivation. Over the following chapters, I will outline how participants acted in their cultivation practices following their workshop experiences and discuss the so-called 'heavy impacts' on horticulture. Explanations, statements, descriptions and practices of my interlocutors stand hereby always in relation to their village communities. Even while stating their own opinions, conversation partners in the villages referred to other equally important practices and explanations of others. Sometimes people are named and details of their lives are mentioned. When referring to either sensitive issues or more general understandings among my interlocutors, I sketched out scenes and discussions and grouped together participants, sometimes referring to the village communities as a whole. In some depictions, I have taken the liberty of merging biographies and changing names. This is not to say, of course, that everyone thinks the same

12 This research was part of the project 'Localising Global Climate Change Policies in Vanuatu: Reception of Knowledge and Cultural Transformation' (Grant number: 298643416) together with Arno Pascht, funded by DFG (German Research Association, as the main Funding Agency in Germany). This project considered livelihood practices in urban, peri-urban and rural communities in Vanuatu, both on Efate and Malekula.

– village members' perspectives differ according to a wide variety of factors including age, gender and social status. Furthermore, this is not a normative stance to show what has to be done, but it rather shows the range of relevant discussions and activities. All the people I have worked with over the years have contributed to this book – a book which discusses climate change in Vanuatu as a local example of a regional fight by island nations and Pacific Islanders to find ways forward in times of crisis, but also productive transformation in global matters. The topic is current climate politics in Vanuatu in reference to cultivation practices and how this draws attention to thinking anew about Melanesian everyday gardening in the Anthropocene. This contributes to a growing anthropological study of climate change.

1.1 An Island State in Times of Climate Change

Vanuatu is a republic in the South Pacific. As part of Oceania, it forms one part of the region of Melanesia.[13] The Y-shaped archipelago of Vanuatu numbers 83 islands, of which 63 are inhabited (Radcliffe et al. 2018). Those islands cover a total area of 12,190 km² (Mückler 2010, 162). Vanuatu is divided into six provinces: Malampa, Penama, Sanma, Shefa and Torba. Malekula is part of the northwestern province of Malampa, and on Efate in Shefa province the capital Port Vila is located (Vanuatu Project Management Unit 2024). Unlike the low-lying atoll islands of Micronesia, which have been gaining prominence in international climate forums because of sea level rise (Lazrus 2012), the islands of Vanuatu are "made up of Tertiary and Quaternary extrusive volcanic rocks and raised reef limestones, and Recent alluvium" (Pierce 1999, 150). In the discussions about climate change in Oceania, the islands of Vanuatu complement the picture by including the perspective from Melanesia.

With independence from the French and British condominium in 1980, the previously named 'New Hebrides' were re-named Vanuatu, for 'our land forever' (Adams and Foster 2024). Vanuatu became a parliamentary democracy and efforts to return the land to the traditional land owners increased (Clarke et al. 2013; Farran 2002). The majority of the population of indigenous ni-Vanuatu lives in lineage structures connected to the land of their ancestors. Over the last

13 Oceania was divided into three regions, Polynesia, Micronesia and Melanesia, by European explorers and cartographers (Tcherkézoff 2003). Although these denominations have often been criticised, they are still used by people in Oceania in most contexts.

century, missionaries and colonial administrations have led to compounded villages bringing together several clans or nasara.[14] Since independence, these villages have been included in regional and country-level government structures. Furthermore, population numbers have increased rapidly, and thus Vanuatu is a very young nation in the double sense. The share of population of those aged 15–29 totals 39% (Vanuatu National Statistics Office 2017, 1–3). Today's adults and adolescents born after 1980 contribute to a sense of national identity and now also strive for a new national climate movement (Hetzel 2016). They additionally shape the picture of the urban areas of Luganville on Espiritu Santo and the capital of Port Vila on the main island of Efate (Kraemer 2020). Although the urban population continues to grow (especially due to an increasing birth rate), 78% of the total population of 300,019, as of 2020, live in rural areas (Vanuatu Bureau of Statistics 2022, 2). As for the preliminary report for the agricultural census in the country of 2022, 225,023 agricultural household members live in rural areas (MALFFB 2022). The rural population is mainly concerned with agricultural production and is perceived as the backbone of the country's self-sufficiency in times of crisis (FAO 2020, 7). In turn, concerned with wider environmental issues, urban sites have become important junctions for knowledge and action being brought to the islands. This also provides younger ni-Vanuatu town residents with a new expert role, forming urban narratives on environmental transformations and striving to transmit information on key concepts and phenomena such as the greenhouse effect, global warming and sea level rise.

Such discourses are framed in English or French and then disseminated in the lingua franca, Bislama (Hetzel and Pascht 2017). Although there are still up to 100 vernacular oceanic languages spoken in Vanuatu (Lynch and Crowley 2001), people complain about a decline in traditional language use because more and more communication is conducted in the pidgin language, Bislama. Today, people in the area of Dixon Reef speak several languages but Novol and

14 Nasara may be described as patrilineal clans which were located as discrete groups in the interior of Malekula before relocation. Bratrud mentions that in Vanuatu it also refers to a historical place and typically to the ceremonial (dancing) ground (Bratrud 2011, 18; Lannoy 2004, 15). My Dixon interlocutors confirmed this when they explained that nasara for Dixoners is primarily the ceremonial ground which is the original place of the origin of the group. Nasara is a Bislama expression of relatively recent origin (Lannoy 2004, 261, 284).

Nasarian are the main indigenous languages (McCarter and Gavin 2011; Walworth et al. 2021). In Siviri, as in most places of Northern Efate, people speak Nguna (Schütz 1969).However, Bislama is the language to connect the islands from north to south. Today, urban and political communication mainly depends on Bislama expressions, especially when it comes to national working schemes like climate change programmes. Bislama is used for official communication, but also connects with new topics and technologies (Vandeputte-Tavo 2013). NGOs or governmental organisations working in rural areas conducts their workshops in Bislama, including climate change workshops. English terms are translated into Bislama, 'climate change' becomes 'klaemet jenis' or 'klaemet jenj', creating new common expressions but also novel conceptualisations (Pascht 2019). Referring to Bislama terms is also seen as (creative) engagement with international scientific terms, which are brought together with cultivation methods.

These workshops are based on a scientific discourse that is, for example, referred to in reports like that of the FAO (the Food and Agriculture Organization of the United Nations), which considers Vanuatu as extremely vulnerable to climate change-related adverse impacts and thus for the production of food (Allen 2015; FAO 2008). The Government of Vanuatu was among the first nations in Oceania to introduce the topic of climate change and the then Prime Minister, Ham Liñi, initiated the National Adaptation Programme for Action (NAPA) in 2005 as a "a country-wide programme of immediate and urgent project-based adaptation activities in priority sectors, in order to address the current and anticipated adverse effects of climate change, including extreme events" (NACCC 2007, 7). Since then, the political environment for climate action has become prominent and two bodies have been introduced: The National Advisory Board on Climate Change and Disaster Risk Reduction (NAB)[15] and the Department of Climate Change as part of the Ministry of Climate Change Adaptation, Meteorology, Geo-Hazards, Energy, Environment and Disaster Management, which also coordinates climate change policies.[16] These bodies work closely together with other ministries[17] to focus on disaster risk reduction and general (infrastructural) support for agriculture and community life, preparing the country for the decades ahead.

15 NAB 2021b

16 Government of Vanuatu, Department of Climate Change 2021

17 e.g. Ministry of Agriculture, Livestock, Forestry, Fisheries and Biosecurity (MALFFB 2021)

A decade after the initiative of the NAPA, tropical Cyclone Pam was considered one of the first indicators of anticipated climate-related challenges: on the night between the 13th and 14th of March 2015, Vanuatu experienced a category 5 storm, which went down in meteorological history, "as one of the strongest cyclones ever recorded in the South Pacific Ocean" (Gutro 2015, n. pag). This storm came from the northeast, heading directly over the central and southern islands, its strong winds affecting the whole country. Cyclone Pam hit the main island Efate with full force – there were several episodes of flooding, erosions in the coastal sections and power cuts for days afterwards (Rey et al. 2017). I witnessed this event during my first stay in the capital, Port Vila. After we had made it through the stormy night, getting up in the morning to see trees upside down and roof parts scattered, people in town, after an initial brief shock, immediately set about initiating recovery, health and food provision measures. Although the urban population faced financial problems after the storm (ibid.), what worried them much more were their relatives in the rural areas, on the many islands of Vanuatu. There, Cyclone Pam had not only destroyed houses and coconut plantations, but also garden crops. Images of green islands and white sands could no longer be met because of defoliated or destroyed trees and beach areas that had been turned over during the storm. This tropical cyclone also marked a turning point for the international press and Vanuatu received increased attention as being under threat of climate change.

Due to its categorisation as a Small Island Developing State (SIDS), Vanuatu is one of the countries in which issues of climate change are said to have "a very tangible impact" (United Nations Office 2021). Looking at natural science prognoses, the country is expected to be exposed to increasing natural hazards such as cyclones, earthquakes and floods over the next decades. Climate projections give several prognoses for weather events: rise of mean temperatures, more extreme rain events after which droughts might occur and cyclones intensifying but becoming less frequent. Ocean acidification and coral bleaching will further progress as well as changes to extreme weather events, although it is not certain whether these will be in enhanced or reduced form (CSIRO 2014). Cyclone Pam led to a short but intensive wave of reports about the consequences of anthropogenic environmental changes and the so-called vulnerability of small island states, citing Vanuatu as a worst-case example. On the one hand, this implicitly reproduced a narrative of what Carol Farbotko calls the 'wishful sinking' syndrome (Farbotko 2010), in which island states are reduced merely to their land size and instrumentalised to show the effects of global warming with intensifying weather phenomenon and sea level rises.

Vanuatu has been identified as vulnerable to extreme weather and pictured as a country that lacks resilience due to inhabitants' perceived inability to act on their own behalf (ibid.). On the other hand, the aftermath of Cyclone Pam also underlined a self-empowering narrative of ni-Vanuatu politicians about the country's capability to establish networks for adaptation across the country. During COP 27 in Morocco (in 2022), the then Climate Change Minister of Vanuatu, Ralph Regenvanu, sitting in the German pavilion next to Germany's foreign minister, emphasised the immense work of his country to consider and mitigate the effects of climate change, concluding with a mention of the huge financial burden which his country must bear and the financial compensation required from the international community as a result. These two narratives of vulnerability and self-empowerment culminated through this stormy event and, in Vanuatu, especially food gardens became connecting points for the discussions.

Since 2015, Vanuatu's politicians have been working rigorously to achieve international climate justice while also working on adaptation and mitigation measures within the country (Wewerinke-Singh and Salili 2020). Discussions about a problematic future have become matters of present concern. For years, agricultural programmes had ensured the adaption of cultivation methods, introducing new strategies and methods for soil preparation. Prognoses and analysis of 'extreme weather events' are embedded in a discourse approach to adaptation measures happening directly within the village communities (McNamara and Prasad 2014). On our way to an Agriculture and Food Security cluster meeting in late March 2015, I sat on the back of the truck and talked with one of the co-workers. Over the years, she had been involved in various relief efforts by international organisations and was now, after the storm, busy with the initial supply of food and distribution of seeds. This young ni-Vanuatu university graduate, who was volunteering in the food distribution cluster, identified Cyclone Pam as *the* proof of climate change: "Now we know what climate change looks like. This is what we have been preparing for all of these years." Measures for disaster risk reduction were intensified after this event.

For political actors in Vanuatu itself, Cyclone Pam marked simply another step for lives that have to change and are continually changing. Tropical cyclones of lesser intensity are somewhat common in Vanuatu, forming part of the annual weather cycle known to uproot root crops and pick apart the leaves of plants, but also bringing rain and enriching the soil (Russel and Horvat 2023). At the same time, flooding can be expected (Deo et al. 2021), causing crops to stand in water for days and, as my village interlocutors liked to put it, start to 'stink'. When I asked them what to do in the case of uprooted or flooded harvests, they recommended immediately rushing towards the gardens once the winds had calmed down, saving what could be saved, replanting uprooted banana plants as well as every other root crop and then moving on to replant as fast as possible. Methods of dealing with cyclones and maintaining food security are well-known across the country. Even though people in rural communities have recently noticed a decline in their own efforts and an increasing dependency on disaster relief (Warrick 2021), new movements are also trying to pass on previous knowledge. The technique of harvest and replant was also proposed directly after Cyclone Pam, by the government and the specially formed Agriculture and Food Security Cluster to all communities across the country. Due to the severity of the storm, village communities were additionally supported through the distribution of seeds, planting material and processed food, such as rice or canned goods (McDonnell 2020; Wentworth 2020).

Beyond this political and media narrative about the storm, for many villagers, the drought that followed posed more difficulties. I left Vanuatu a few weeks after Cyclone Pam in April 2015, leaving my urban research partners in a busy but positive mood when it came to repairs of houses and food supply services. However, when I returned in October 2016, the El Niño drought persisted and people had become exhausted from the constant heat. These two related events became a test for the countrywide designed adaptation methods, in that people often chose to amend what they had been taught, and led to discussion about how to approach cultivation in challenging times among horticulturalists in the villages and beyond (see Chapter 4). Brochures and short animated videos explained El Niño and La Niña as the warm and cool phases which bring either sunny periods (El Niño) or extensive rainy events (La Niña) as part of the Pacific climate pattern of ENSO, the El Niño-Southern Oscillation (Chowdhury et al. 2007; Kelman 2019, 406; Power et al. 2013). When a prolonged El Niño period between 2015 and 2017 caused the rainfall in Vanuatu to drop sharply, people were already informed about scientific explanations and the whole country started discussing events in meetings, media and climate change awareness programmes. In the villages of Dixon Reef and Siviri during this time, my interlocutors were less worried about storms but quite exhausted by the constant sunny and hot working days. During my first visits, the chiefs immediately pointed towards their community's lost yield. Shrugging their shoulders about minor governmental and non-governmental organisations making food deliveries from ships, they remarked that yam was both too small for consumption and not plentiful enough to leave as planting material for the next cultivation cycle. Climate reports described the combination of both events within one year as having posed particular problems: "The impacts of this year's El Niño event have made it doubly difficult for some people to recover. Many island communities have been struggling with serious food and water shortages caused by drought-like conditions." (Red Cross Red Crescent Climate Centre 2021, n. pag.)

I spent many hours between 2016 and 2019 with island communities, in Dixon Reef working with people in their garden areas, and additional months in the village of Siviri on Vanuatu's main island, Efate. Both communities had been selected to become sites for climate change adaptation programmes, as they were located in parts of the islands with low rainfall and where cultivation continues to play a decisive role in everyday life, albeit with different dynamics. Dixon Reef is a village of around 450 inhabitants. People live in nuclear or extended families in several houses, including small kitchen houses and sleeping houses, along the western coast of Malekula. In Siviri, located in the north of the main island of Efate, the approximately 400 inhabitants live at the seafront or along the ring road with direct connection to the capital, Port Vila. Over the past 10 years, they have started to bring their gardens either closer to their houses, to combine cultivation with wage labour in town or elsewhere on the island, or used plots scattered over the whole island, using their cars to visit the plots, mostly at weekends with their whole family. Dixon Reef gardens, however, lie outside the village and Dixoners have to walk some distance to reach their cultivation plots. In terms of changes to the way of life of ni-Vanuatu, agriculture plays an important role (Hetzel and Pascht 2019). Moving gardens, or rather cultivated areas, has become one approach in both places in these uncertain times (Chapters 4 and 5). These communities have not only become interested in being part of several workshop programmes to tackle climate-related issues in cultivation, but when my colleague Arno Pascht and I first visited both communities, they enthusiastically agreed to work with us to further talk about these topics. Although there were other social and economic concerns in the communities, the topic of climate change had already found its place in their view on how to ensure future supply with their own food.

1.2 Vanuatu Climate Politics

Over the years, the term food security[18] has been expressing the main concerns for many Pacific countries encountering changing environments. Various political actors aim towards food security and helping people to become 'resilient' to climate change.[19] Challenges for global agriculture through intensification of environmental hazards are one of the main results of the IPCC (Intergovernmental Panel on Climate Change) report (Mbow et al. 2019) and have been picked up for Vanuatu's farming system by the FAO (2013). The National Adaptation Programme has focused on conducting agriculture and food security projects (Maclellan 2015).

Ni-Vanuatu and their gardens form a key cultural and economic connection.[20] Even though fishing, animal husbandry and arboriculture hold complementary roles, horticulture stands out as both important for securing food and being part of ceremonial life, creating island landscapes at the same time (Calandra 2017; Mondragón 2018). For people in Dixon Reef and Siviri, fish and seafood make only a supplement or temporary cash product, as it is either not available every day or people do not fish on a daily basis. What they do is cultivate multiple garden parcels along the coast and inland. 'On the islands', ni-Vanuatu mostly live on what they grow in their gardens. Horticul-

---

18 The term 'food security' refers, in the context of international development, to people having access to enough food that they do not starve and that malnutrition is prevented. Countries dependent on agriculture and exposed to 'climate extremes' are considered to be at risk of food insecurity (Boliko 2019, 5–6).

19 For a critical approach to the concept of resilience, see McDonnell 2020. She explains the different origins of the term and its use in development discourse describing the 'strengthening' of people when facing environmental hazards (McDonnell 2020, 57). For further context, see Chapter 2. NGOs with whom we have had contact used the term 'resilience' in order to explain what people in rural areas needed in order to face climate change. I therefore use this term due to its use in climate change measures in Vanuatu following the Vanuatu Adaptation Program. "The program has developed the central concept of 'resilience' as a framework for action, to build capacity to respond to shocks and stresses and adapt to uncertain futures. This concept is illustrated in this report by two case studies – one focused on agriculture and food security projects in an isolated rural island; the other at the international level, as the government and people of Vanuatu intervene in global climate negotiations." (Maclellan 2015, 5)

20 Aside from fisheries, cultivation of food crops remains the biggest sector in the country and is considered to be one of the main targets of climate change adaptation, since for many people it is the main method of securing their livelihood (FAO 2008).

ture is characterised by shifting cultivation, as it is widely practised all over the Pacific, "to be the archetypal form of traditional agriculture in the tropics […]. In the Pacific Islands, it is found on almost all high islands and raised limestone islands where at least some secondary forest or productive grassland savanna remains" (Manner and Thaman 2013, 342). Supply for locally produced food through cultivation is considered to be increasingly under pressure so one of the foci of climate change forecasts is Vanuatu's rural population and the consequences for the horticulturalist farming system (CSIRO 2014; FAO 2016). Furthermore, Olivia Warrick states that the reasons are manifold and "attributed mainly to less robust subsistence agricultural systems and increasing dependency on external resources namely disaster aid, imported goods, money and knowledge" (Warrick 2021, 6). Since 2012, teams of national and international humanitarian agencies have developed a nationwide programme to address climate change (McDonnell 2020, 58). The resulting overarching programme was given the Bislama title 'yumi stap redi blong klaemet jenis'[21] ('We are ready for climate change') (Pritchard 2017). For agriculture, they especially promoted the adaptation of cultivation methods and developing new strategies, including the installation of home gardens next to the house. In this way, cultivation could be moved from 'the bush' closer to people's homes and could therefore supplement a new diet with vegetables which need closer monitoring (Maclellan 2015, 26). Consequently, numerous projects were designed. Along the coast of western Malekula, several villages underwent the same workshop schedules and consequently new forms of home gardens could be found in every single one. Dixon Reef first became a role-model for applying new strategies for cultivation, until the El Niño event when the gardens were left alone and the discussion about how to approach gardening in times of crisis took another turn (Chapter 4).

Through climate politics in Vanuatu, indigenous gardening is matched with ideas of climate change adaptation, and this has far-reaching consequences. Carlos Mondragón exemplified that new encounters in climate programmes on the Torres Strait islands in northern Vanuatu bring up and create new narratives: information about sea level rise shifted local perceptions of fluidity between ocean and land, in that the water takes land but also gives some of it for free, to a stark fixation on the shapes of islands and also

21 There does not exist a consistent writing form for the phrase 'climate change' in Bislama. I therefore refer to each document's spelling or the pronunciation of the people I worked with.

human communal settlements, including land use for gardening. Given the annual fluctuation of seawater and sea level, suddenly the water was marked as a threat, taking away land (Mondragón 2018). Reports of environmental degradation depict humans as merely reacting but Mondragón argues that knowledge regimes of adaptation programmes must be made transparent and must also rethink approaches that consider the agency of ni-Vanuatu. This would reflect on ni-Vanuatu human-environmental relations as processual and undergoing continuous alterations, especially when it comes to moving houses and gardens to other locations and therefore working with shifting land and sea (ibid.). The construction of food *in*security hints also at a history of island lives exposed to external influences, very often critically traced from colonialism, then globalisation and the opening to world markets, and finally influences through global warming with higher risks of extreme weather events. Often, this is described as causing food insecurity, in the form of self-organised and independent supply with local resources on the decline (Allen 2015, 1344; Campbell 2015, 1320).

This raises the question of how people living in Oceania are perceived by the international community. For the islands, where adaptation measures are meant to support horticultural practices, some examples paint a picture of far greater self-sufficiency. For example, Matthew G. Allen, working with communities on Malo, one of the outer islands of Espiritu Santo in the northern part of Vanuatu, emphasised local strategies for preventing food shortages. These strategies include selling cash crops and moving sometimes beyond 'traditional' food cultivation and preservation techniques, the consumption of imported foods rendering food supply more consistent and diversification giving more flexibility against economic changes (Allen 2015). For the author, these strategies are no less effective and thus disprove the "food insecurity narrative", which "entails a denial of agency on the part of Pacific Islanders" (ibid., 1341).

Nevertheless, or precisely because new things are met with curiosity, the open-minded village chiefs of both Siviri and Dixon Reef have also motivated their people to attend food security workshops investigating newly-introduced cultivation methods. This has opened spaces of thinking anew about what is done in terms of cultivation. Chiefs wanted their communities to take part in workshops because they were interested and valued new perspectives entering the community. When I attended my first workshops, a few years into the adaptation programmes, and the project manager, an engaged and practical-minded ni-Vanuatu woman from town, invited people for another session, the community hall in Dixon Reef continued to fill. Very experienced gardeners of all ages explained that it was interesting to share thoughts about current challenges. It did not seem to be a contradiction for them to use offers embedded in a discourse of progressiveness for their own purpose. However, during one workshop, a discussion heated up when the project manager expressed concern and wanted to know why participants were not following the exact strategies shown. One of the elder men simply commented: "Because we also have our way of making the gardens." In the following chapters, I will detail this process – how new forms of cultivation become a comprehensive practice and integral part of mekem garen. Seeing how practices on the ground should be influential to policies, in the context of such implementation, people had chosen their own path to transform practices using their own means. At the same time, they want to be involved in new practices. It therefore also becomes essential to see the realities of everyday lives in which climate change adaptation programmes are a part now and how people navigate this – critical but also creative in the context of such programmes.

Through these programmes, villagers became part of Vanuatu climate discourses and practices. Furthermore, on a national level, Vanuatu gardening has become embedded in a self-declared national fight against climate change with rural self-sufficiency becoming quite central. As Maëlle Calandra explains, the entanglement of gardens and people on Tongoa, in central Vanuatu, has become once again the backbone for difficult times and the creation of new ways of dealing with challenges. She describes how the states of garden, crop or cultivar loss after Cyclone Pam started discussions about the severity of the event, which they then call 'disasta' (disaster). Calandra also underlines that it is another take to see how people operate with new concepts in their own environments, bringing in processes of change, instead of analysing the effects of predefined disastrous events (Calandra 2020). The way in which ni-Vanuatu work the ground and new discourse around the subject also brings changes to what they are doing and how they talk about current globalised narratives. A novel stance on Vanuatu gardens in the Anthropocene must include methodologies for dealing with disasters and their conceptualisation, but it also must also yet again look at what a garden is and what it means for local people when we are talking about climate change.

1.3 Reconsidering Vanuatu Gardening in the Anthropocene

Anthropological work on gardens in Melanesia has shown both that they are not solely about food cultivation and that gardeners are creating identities and communal lives (Bolton and Mitchell 2021; Calandra 2017; Nombo, Leach and Anip 2021; Rio 2007b). Bronislaw Malinowski brought Melanesian gardening to the centre of anthropological attention in his famous study on the coral gardens of the Trobriand Islands. He described the Trobriand gardeners' practices of working in their gardens as skilful ways of categorising the environment into untouched bush and cultivated land, making a landscape that both represented how the gardeners work and at the same time the individual becoming a part of the community by learning how to be a gardener (Malinowski 1935). Taking this relational approach even further, Philippe Descola (2013), in his very prominent example from the Americas, argues for dissolving the opposition between nature and cultural practices, showing the diverse relations between people, animals and plants. In his example, the Achuar people, living between the borders of Peru and Ecuador, did not aim to transform plants with their actions but rather showed that their work led to building up and maintaining certain relations. Descola refrained from analysing Achuar practices as transforming pre-defined categories of wild into domesticated, because people themselves do not undertake these distinctions, but rather think in terms of relations, mirroring blood relatives and relatives in marriage in their interaction with plants and animals (ibid., 6). Descola refers to Marilyn Strathern and how people in Papua New Guinea, where horticultural ways of living do not manifest a distinction between wild and domesticated, live in the absence of a concept of the natural environment (Strathern 1980). He compares these thoughts with the garden world of Amazonia, illustrating his narrative through the gardening conceptualisations of how to understand entanglements of humans and non-humans (Descola 2013, 62–70). In both cases, it is not the human who decides how the surroundings should look and domesticate them, but rather a constant enabling of the blossoming of relations between humans and more-than-humans and their surroundings.

The practices of Melanesian gardeners have been described as bridging concepts of culture and nature, including plants, animals and spirits, into a wider network of place-making. In Vanuatu, the collaboration with crops was intended to create genealogical connections to their father's and mother's relatives – taking gardens as social performances (Rio 2007b). The cultivation process does not create a distinction between these those practices; rather, it encourages a holistic approach to gardening. Instead of viewing these cultivation and genealogical practices as mutually exclusive, it is possible to consider them together as a means of producing food and enhancing communal life: "Taro and Yam do not grow by themselves. They are always part of and embedded in, other relationships. Just like people" (Nombo, Leach and Anip 2021, 368). This also shows that the crops of the garden are embedded in cycles of ritual and practice as more than just food or cultural objects. Gardening itself is associated with ceremonial exchanges and rites of passage. These practices are also influenced by seasonal changes and weather events.

Current examples for Vanuatu show that those relational practices are performed and thus re-constituted in ceremonies, also in context of ecological crisis. Not long after Cyclone Pam and El Niño, people in Tanna, one of the southern islands of Vanuatu, staged a performance called the nieri. It was made with and from numerous newly harvested taro plants, reviving both the gardens after adverse weather events, as well as the social relations that are enacted alongside this (Mitchell 2021). Mitchell interprets this as important for both younger people to connect to activities and for their relationships with the elders: "This cyclone crystallised, for a new generation of Tannese, the multiple ways in which the lives of islanders and food gardens are entwined through sustenance, sociality and spirituality" (Mitchell 2021, 433). As she also emphasises, however, a huge ceremony at that point also showed the strength of the joint work of plants and people. Cyclones can only be faced by taking care of gardens and through this of people (ibid., 437). "Gardens allow people to fulfil social obligations by connecting them to a web of spiritual and material processes" (ibid., 443). Something similar happened in Dixon Reef. The year following the El Niño event, I accompanied some of the younger men on their garden day, were looking for a yam tuber to harvest. Sent by their families to gather the biggest crops for presentation at the next wedding ceremony, the young men were aware of their irreplaceable roles in this. The yam harvest of long tubers, reaching far into the ground, meant strong physical work. When we arrived at the side of the garden plots, one of the young men, being on his way to becoming the next chief of the village, explained that they had planted some of the yams they had received from their elders there, placing them in a separate spot next to the other garden parcels. Two boys took it in turns to dig up this yam with spades. They stood in the hole up to their shoulders in order to remove the entire length of the yam tuber. This team effort was rewarded when they finally uncovered a yam measuring approximately 1.7 metres in length, wrapping it around a tree branch to carry it back home. Back in the village, my host father admired the yam and posited that he expected many more ceremonies this winter. This was the first time after Cyclone Pam that they had managed to gather enough for exchange in marriage ceremonies. Such ceremonies are of importance to fulfil reciprocal relations and also re-produce persons per se (Rio 2007a). In the following weeks, we harvested some more impressive yams and on one day I took one of these yams on my shoulder while my host family took a photo, feeling the weight of this garden crop and also feeling the importance of this accomplishment for my interlocutors. They managed to contribute to important cultural events from their own gardens, proving that they could both overcome the dry period and take part in forming kin relations.

Recent social science literature on climate change generally also challenges dichotomies of natural causes and social effects, human action and natural reaction (Hulme 2010, 2015). Additionally, the idea of the Anthropocene thus further blurs dichotomies of environmental and social and cultural (Chua and Fair 2019). In the time of anthropogenic climate change, markers of human influences in the form of more extreme weather events and changing land- and waterscapes inflict challenges for all everyday matters of lives. Amelia Moore calls for anthropological research in 'Anthropocene spaces', where the 'conjunctures' of those ideas that anthropogenic alterations again bring new implications for social and ecological live on this planet must be addressed through research. The author brings the island state of the Bahamas into the picture to show how those islands have attracted new international attention and are reimagined through the idea of the Anthropocene. Doing research in such contexts is to understand how these several medial and political globally connected discourses represent the idea of the Anthropocene (Moore 2015). Turning again to Vanuatu and the gardens, I follow Maria Paula Diogo and colleagues, who suggest that ethnographic approaches to Gardens and Human Agency in the Anthropocene (2019) "use the conceptual apparatus being developed within discussions on the Anthropocene to revisit and reassess former concepts associated with gardens and landscapes as localities where nature and culture converge and interbreed" (2019, 6). While all of these above-mentioned examples of Vanuatu certainly illustrate how gardening is about more than the environmental, they also concentrate on performative expressions, special moments of ceremonial encounters. That brings me to the question of what happens in the quotidian works of gardening in Vanuatu, in those moments of the Anthropocene in between performative events.

For Vanuatu, being brought into the politics of the Anthropocene means that gardens and gardening are set into new narratives in which the everyday practices of food production are politically discussed as practices change for horticulturalists in and with their environments. As Vanuatu gardening in the 21st century becomes involved in climate change discourses, it is framed as a main economic basis for self-supply and cultivation and at the same time is labelled by governmental and non-governmental initiatives as a form of adaptative approach to ensure future lifestyles. How do these garden works become aggregations of negotiation of the Melanesian way of life? I take a closer look at what happens in the daily routines of gardening when it is put in the context of adaptation programmes and politics. Gardens and gardening are therefore not only an indigenous ni-Vanuatu practice but also reflect global matters. This includes the everyday practice as embodied work and how gardening in Vanuatu in the tradition of anthropological work can also be considered alongside matters of the Anthropocene. Sarah Pink considers gardens "as a process" (Pink 2012, 20), thinking in unbounded places towards a practice, "considering how it is not simply something that is done to and in gardens" (ibid., 96). Pink tries to see how garden work is processual in a double sense: as an experience, sensory bodily work that changes the environment, and at the same time how the garden itself can be known (ibid., 94). With my approach of mekem garen, I look at cultivation and communal work to understand what climate change is for ni-Vanuatu in rural areas, in the context of Vanuatu gardening with ideas set within the Anthropocene. This Melanesian practice of working for community and place therefore provides a lens for visualising new ways for future living. Furthermore, this practice is negotiated in relation to future imaginaries (cf. Bryant and Knight 2019) since adaptive measures are designed to aim for a liveable future on the islands (Chapter 6). Vanuatu gardening therefore becomes also a process that stands for more than simply a local example and the gardeners are more than simply the recipients of practical knowledge to be implemented.

1.4 Researching Mekem Garen

This book is part of a growing body of anthropological research on climate change, which is bringing together local activities in matters of planetary environmental crisis. Many scholars researching anthropological climate change encourage ethnographic work as engaged research to make others aware of local issues and their specific perspectives (Crate 2011; Eriksen 2020; Goodman 2018). Others bridge the activist or political claims of local actors (Barnes et al.

2013; Krause 2021). Listening to the many voices in this climate crisis, research is challenged at various levels. Especially in Oceania, opening up the topic brings up Pacific Islander's strivings for emancipation, political independency and justice (Chao and Enari 2021). Sophie Chao and Dion Enari create awareness that what is at stake for island communities is not only their life on the islands, but that they also have to assert themselves against hegemonic knowledge and praxis regimes (2021). My anthropological research plays a part in this. In Chapters 2 and 3, I will explore my interlocutors' engagement with some of those hegemonies, aiming to show that this is characterised by their original approaches of current issues and new conceptualisations of climate change. These new creations have resulted from interested engagement with the adaptation programmes rather than rebellion against them.

In Chapter 2, I describe this as 'climate change worlding' and show that this is ontological work that brings up different climate change worlds – contradicting or complementing, overlapping and defining each other. This contributes to the contextualisation of many and diverse political climate change practices. I aim to understand human action and interaction in the context of climate change as an all-encompassing phenomenon. This ethnography presents an example from the South Pacific and, with it, hints to broader global considerations. This is in line with Crate's definition of 'climate ethnography' as "ethnography for the world" (Crate 2011, 185). Michael Bollig points to a need for a change of perspective when he states that "while the sciences have focussed on the losers of climate change", ethnographic research can "show that there are winners of (the politics of) climate change" (Bollig 2018, 87), or at least that people deal with climate activities on their own terms and have their own ways of explaining what is happening and how to act accordingly. Jerome Whitington proposes "that 'climate change' designates a problem domain rather than a set of authoritative facts [...] and stipulates that research must remain open to ontological difference" (Whitington 2016, 7). What Whitington calls ontological differences, I also call ontological assumptions, which work in 'worlding practices' (Blaser and de la Cadena 2018; see Chapter 2). As Arno Pascht and Eveline Dürr remarked in their introduction to an edited volume about environmental transformations in Oceania, this is not searching for the truths, rather it represents an interest in interpreting current activities (Pascht and Dürr 2017, 103) in order to understand the processes of climate change from daily activities and encounters, by including indigenous conceptualisation as one part of the picture.

I recognise that doing social science and anthropological fieldwork raises colonial heritage and therefore current fieldwork needs to attend to hierarchies of knowledge production. Acknowledging one's part in these studies means for many scholars following matters of care about the important stories research partners develop together (Daswani 2021, Declercq and Ayaka 2017). The process of fieldwork is a lot about learning, in various contexts, from, but especially with, people. This also includes unlearning what I brought with me from my institutional, personal and societal background. My research partners were the local experts in this, but in our work, we tried to open up shared spaces for learning. This meant for everyone involved finding ways of communicating what is experienced about current changes. This work has been characterised by various forms of learning through aspects of mekem garen: participating in adaptation workshops, gardening with my interlocutors and research partners, discussing gardening approaches, reflections with NGO and governmental representatives about food security, academic exchanges about Oceanic agriculture and climate change. Just as making a new garden includes a process of working together with humans, plants, soil, the weather and climate, my fieldwork included various forms of learning together with my research partners, in team research and through wider exchange in Vanuatu and Europe. Taking these frameworks and the work of gardening into the methodological process brings together physical labour and cognitive work.

During one of our almost daily conversations in Dixon Reef, the local teacher was searching for ways to explain current important variations in cultivation: "You know, all these questions you ask, we can't answer them, just live it and you'll see." My daily work opened up many contexts to see, but even more to interact with. Martin Sökefeld describes working with people during social science fieldwork as a form of interaction, thus they become 'Interaktionspartner', partners in this interaction, and fieldwork becomes a social process of communicating and acting together (Sökefeld 2007). Especially insular lives in the wake of the environmental crisis in Oceania, like Katerina Teaiwa emphasises, are formed by various connections spread in time and space, to land, sea and the ancestors. This mobilises communal action to 'Remember, Recommit, Resist' (Teaiwa 2018). Most of the people I have worked with see their own perception and actions beyond their own cosmos and island lives (Chapter 4). In this book, I don't specifically single out individual interlocutor's knowledge but want rather to emphasise my learnings through our interactions. I have then tried to put into words my hope that this can be followed by a wider interested community. Furthermore, these expressions witness cultivation and life at a certain critical time in my interlocutors' lives as they move them forward. Hence, in my writing I refer to learning I experienced through discussions with several people and when describing points of discussions, I generalise or combine several discussions for the purpose of my interlocutor's anonymity.[22]

I accompanied people in Dixon Reef and Siviri walking through their environment and gardening in different spots along the coast and over the hills, in order to gain a "multisensorial embodied engagement" with my interlocutors and their environments (Pink 2009, 25). Experiencing and talking at the same time made it easier for me to ask questions and allowed people to interact by showing what they meant when answering my questions. Living and working together, practical participation in their everyday lives (Ingold 2011) and working with the senses was integral to the research. This was supplemented by various interview methods, which included conversations during work and on the way to our gardening days. These included 'go-along interviews' (Kusenbach 2003) and the visualisation of gardening methods as a basis for joint analysis. When I could not follow villagers on their working days in the bush, we developed walking maps of their movement, which render routes and practices visible for those who were not physically present. This method was inspired by other ethnographic mapping methods in social research (Clark 2011; Powell 2010). This method of 'walkabaots' (walks) was developed together with my research partners during our time in the village (see Chapter 5)

Furthermore, this book is a result of team research together with my anthropology colleague, Arno Pascht. During our months of both joint and individual stays in the village communities, we were complementing insights and findings – what Erickson and Stull name 'witnessing together' – and then discussing findings, sharing field notes and debriefing as key elements of team research (Erickson and Stull 2011). This special from of anthropological research included tandem and individual fieldwork over a period of 13 months from October 2016 to April 2019 on the island of Malekula and on the island of Efate. This followed my own three-month research project in 2015 on climate activism in Port Vila (Hetzel and Pascht 2017). This research collided with Cyclone Pam in 2015 which had an impact on further work, focusing on specific horticultural practices in connection to adaptive measures. The research design for the

22 Living together in the villages was also characterised by explaining anthropological work. Publications and anonymisation options were discussed in all interviews.

team research then envisaged a longer-term period of fieldwork for both researchers at more than one site. We worked in three places in Vanuatu, one urban and two rural. Dixon Reef and Siviri were contacted because they attended workshops in climate change programmes with a focus on agriculture over a longer period of time. This follows an approach to team fieldwork that includes working on the same topic but through the perspective of different members working with different groups or sites, events or time periods (Mackinem and Higgins 2007). Arno Pascht and I had different phases of individual stays, joint discussions and presentations and evaluation. This led to individual stays in the communities, joint meetings with partners such as NGOs and the National Advisory Board for climate change and several meetings between individuals in the communities. In addition to discussing interviews and observations, we considered our own experiences to be part of the fieldwork data (Luhrmann 2010). This included following a full gardening cycle, setting up our own new yam garden and taking on board the expertise of various visitors through instructions, taking this as an affective experience: "emotional reactions, sensory experiences, gut feelings and other embodied sensations" (Turunen et al. 2020, 6). During the period of fieldwork, I relied on experiences being shared as well as separate, with diverse kinds of expertise. I thereby follow an understanding that knowledge is both situated in and influenced by locations (Haraway 1988). During my fieldwork, working with my interlocutors in the garden plots, working with plants and soil, exposed to all weather elements, these experiences demanded incorporation into my work.

When interviewed about his own approach, anthropologist Andrew Scott further proposed approaching fieldwork as a communal learning process, "to attend to what your consultants in the field find puzzling and problematic. What are they preoccupied with or struggling to understand or trying to cope with? What do they wonder about?" (Golub 2014, n. pag.) In the context of climate change adaptation projects, one set of central questions posed by the people who discussed approaches to gardening is reflected especially in 'the case of the abandoned home gardens', small garden plots which were initiated in workshops as safety nets for adverse weather events and climate alterations. They included working in one spot, with specified methods of soil preparation and irrigation (see Chapter 4). In these home gardens, ontological assumptions about gardening came together. All the people involved, NGO representatives and villagers, were irritated by discussions that arose about whether the small home gardens were apt methods to secure livelihoods and why villagers left them behind during the El Niño event. This guidance through research by moments that might be a source of irritation not only for myself but also for the people I worked with, can be grasped through Anna Tsing's concept of 'friction', in which, through interaction, something new is created. "Attention to friction opens the possibility of an ethnographic account of global interconnection." (Tsing 2005, 6) I pay attention to friction additionally in order to arrive at insights about the topics of my research. I thereby take mekem garen as a Vanuatu practice in the tradition of the constant evolution of knowledge, crops and exchanges with other islands entangled in current climate change activities, including and making new practices. This becomes a way of seeing climate change worlding in its daily routines as a constant process of transformation.

I have put many of these learnings, in situ and in many conversations, into written words. These words will always stand in relation to the many thoughts of the people I have worked with on the topic of climate change.

1.5 Outline of the Book

In Chapter 2, I refer to current discussions of climate change in anthropology and social science research in Oceania, which primarily request, in line with demands from Pacific Islanders, the political and scientific communities to recognise residents of Oceania as actors in the climate change process on every level (Crook and Rudiak-Gould 2018; Farbotko 2010; Lazrus 2012). This demand also runs through a consideration of the issue of climate change as both global and local and leads to the question of who is defining climate change and how it is approached (Hastrup 2018; Hulme 2009). I approach this dynamic of global and local actors through a discussion of, on the one hand, a combination of reception and observation studies (Rudiak-Gould 2012) and, on the other hand, my engagement with encounters in adaptation projects (Pascht 2019). In capturing encounters as potentialities for the creation of something new, I withdraw from considering climate change as a translation from international to national 'ideas' (de Wit, Pascht and Haug 2018). In contrast, I discuss my frame as a production of this global idea at different localities in interactions. I use approaches that take these productive elements into account: Tsing's contribution of 'friction' (2005) and the contribution by de la Cadena and Blaser (2018), who refer to 'worlding practices'. I additionally refer to an approach that is led by ontological questions and ontological assumptions (Holbraad and Pedersen 2017).

Chapter 3 introduces 'worlding practices' in Vanuatu and Dixon Reef. It shows climate change reception in dialogue with urban narrratives, giving insight into discrepancies between what people say and act upon in urban political contexts and what is enacted on the community level. Following Rudiak-Gould's views on climate change as "beyond the environmental" (2016, 261), my interlocutors showed that they refer to both environmental and social changes simultaneously in their conversations about the climate. I argue that people engage with discourses based on natural science, distribute responsibilities between industrialised nations as well as their own actions and have a progressive approach to climate change expressed in their everyday cultivation practices. What they call 'envaeromen' (environment) is influenced by human action in terms of social connections as much as anthropogenic actions. New horticultural practices form a part of climate change for external actors, but also for people in Dixon Reef. The external actors assert that climate change must be addressed through agricultural adaptation strategies. However, everyday Vanuatu gardening is not restricted to food security, for the people of Dixon Reef.

Chapter 4 is the first of three chapters in which I concentrate on encounters of people in connection to gardening practices. It commences with the interactions of villagers and representatives of the Food Security programme over the home gardens – a method for immediate and permanent gardening close to the kitchen. Encounters in the project are characterised by what I call 'ontological friction' (Tsing 2005; Blaser 2009, 2013). I take this ontological friction as a starting point but also present how, through this friction, people living in the Dixon Reef area have indeed worked out practices of gardening in times of change. The case of the abandoned home gardens as the fulcrum of my considerations leads the way to further explorations into gardens and gardening. This is the first chapter in which I ask what gardening is and means for the people of Vanuatu. Further engagement with garden practices through literature in Vanuatu (Barrau 1958; Calandra 2017; Rio 2007b; Walter et al. 2007) and through ethnographic description show that in Dixon Reef, practices of diversification and constant renewal exist alongside each other. People never concentrate on one location for their gardening, but either plant different kinds of plants and varieties together or the same kind of plants in different places. This flexible approach to gardening is my first insight into the definition of gardening in Dixon Reef, and is, in my interpretation, at the same time a valid approach to climate change.

Due to this praxis of cultivating different kinds of plants and planting in different locations, in Chapter 5, I concentrate on gardening through movement. I give ethnographic insights into the work of a gardening day and show how people do their gardening not at one locality but by being in motion. This chapter discusses the conceptualisation of the garden as a place by referring to the social science literature on place (Cresswell 2014; Pink 2012) and approaches to the Vanuatu concept of 'ples' (Bolton 1999; Hess 2009; Rodman 1992). This leads me to further question whether we should consider gardening as place-bound or interpret it as practices of movement. I discuss social science literature about place and practice and complement it with the phenomenological approach taken by Ingold, to which I refer due to his introduction of terms such as 'wayfaring' (Ingold 2007) and 'taskscape' (Ingold 1993). I adopt from this the ideas that practices come first and that gardening is a way of making the environment through movement.

Chapter 6 considers the notion that people in Dixon Reef, through their everyday practices of gardening, also create social relations. Since climate change is a future-oriented topic, this chapter takes gardening as a way of making sociality towards the future. I refer to literature on both sociality (Long and Moore 2012; Strathern 1988) and future (Bryant and Knight 2019; Rollason 2014), both in general terms and for Melanesia in particular, in order to frame the topic of sociality in gardening for the future. Furthermore, I show that people in the Dixon Reef area see gardening as a way of building relations. Although they explain that gardening and sociality are both imposed by change and do this through looking back and looking ahead (Hau'ofa 2008), they also emphasise that the everyday practice of gardening is important for the sheer fact of being alive in a community. People want to do everything they can to ensure that this praxis, although in changed form, will continue in the future.

2 Worlding Works - Climate Change Communities

Oceania is a region of transformation, and both international politics as well as actors in the region not only live *with* but also "live climate change" (Crook and Rudiak-Gould 2018, 1). This includes a wide range of actors being connected on different levels: from politicians, activists such as Pacific climate warriors, citizens of every island state, in urban areas and in villages. All have something to say and act upon, "shedding light on the 'foreshadowed problems' of climate change" (Goodman 2018, 342). In 2018, in a video message Ralph Regenvanu, then Vanuatu's Climate Change Minister, addressed both the members of the Climate Vulnerable Forum and the global players of industrialised countries, accusing them of still betting everything on fossil fuels. He described Vanuatu as having a contrasting approach, being a player in this global network with unrestricted dedication to climate politics, showing an exemplary approach to the climate crisis: despite being among the countries most affected by global warming, despite contributing little to global emissions, people in Vanuatu make exemplary efforts to combat climate change (Woonton 2018). What this also shows is involvement locally in global climate politics, which also contrasts the representation of global discourses of local vulnerability. Climate change practice, however, is very often framed by approaches of politics to vulnerable communities to render them more resilient to anticipated or current ecological and economic challenges. In this chapter, I deploy this tension of, on the one hand, acknowledging people on the ground as being affected by changes and, on the other hand, those same people still being able to reflect on such changes in a productive way. Village communities, like those of Dixon Reef and Siviri in Vanuatu, are included in this policy of forward-looking practices, but the role they play is viewed differently in literature and in political practices. This includes forwarding narratives of people on the ground perceiving changes, realising adaptation measures or indicating changes of weather patterns. In the following, I will explore how social science climate change research in Oceania and beyond give relevant framings for climate change practices in Vanuatu. I further reflect on the role of villagers and suggest how we can approach the actions of local people as a kind of climate change worlding, simultaneously learning more about the impact climate change on the ground.

Although scholars have argued against attributions such as 'the victim slot' and framings of vulnerability, which keep island nations small and their actions insignificant (Farbotko 2010; Lazrus 2012; Orlove et al. 2014) and further distract from the real culprits of the effects of climate change (Hughes 2013), these attributions are still prominent in climate change discourses about Vanuatu, as well as across the whole Pacific region (and surely beyond). Accordingly, scholars working in the region ask to acknowledge people in Oceania to tell their own 'Oceanic philosophies' and bring them "to the frontline of social scientific theorization" (Crook and Rudiak-Gould 2018, 2). This can be done by looking at the "knowledge practices" (ibid., 4) of Pacific Islanders, how they deal with discourses and practices in order to open up possibilities of understanding (cultural) encounters with new forces. However, the sole designation of dealing with climate in terms of the natural that strikes back and people having to cope, is criticised as reductive. With this, "Pacific people are framed as the 'subject' of disaster responses, especially in the context of climate change. Representations of local Pacific communities in the wake of disasters reveal a particular polemics attached to depictions of agency." (Ballard, McDonnell and Calandra 2020, 10)

Literature in social science about climate change in Oceania moves within this field of tension between the seriousness and urgency connected with climate change on the one side and the self-assertion of the people on the other. So-called Small Island Developing States being challenged by the effects of anthropogenic climate change, especially rising sea levels, higher intensity of storms, salinisation of the soils, coral bleaching and fish dying, and Pacific Islanders' ways of dealing with this, are central topics (Barnett and Campbell 2010). Mike Hulme states that, "Small islands frequently are given merely symbolic value as icons of vulnerability to climate change." (Hulme 2010, 561) Furthermore, their critical voices are not yet being taken equally seriously in international political discussions (Klöck and Fink 2019). However, on recognising islanders as important actors in global discourses and practices, many suggest that we learn along with the strategies of people in island states and their daily interactions with national and international actors in climate change encounters (Crook and Rudiak-Gould 2018; Farbotko 2010; Lazrus 2012, 2016; McNamara and Farbotko 2017).

This approach does not mean that there are no differences or difficulties arising between the island states. The year 2021 marked a break when several Micronesian countries left the Pacific Islands Forum, due to internal differences and feelings of underrepresentation, including within matters of climate change (Carreon and Doherty 2021). Not every country in Oceania faces the same problems and politicians of low-lying atolls are concerned about land loss whereas Vanuatu's islands are mostly high volcanic islands and accordingly this issue is not a priority. Thus, island nations are not completely unified in terms of addressing issues due to climate change. This diversity must also be addressed (Lata and Nunn 2012, 170–71). At the same time, climate framings in the individual countries and how people talk about related issues can change over time and under different governments (Hermann and Kempf 2019). Other examples show that inhabitants of such countries can be less concerned than expected because islanders know how to deal with changing patterns and thus are rather irritated by climate politics (Bønnelykke Robertson 2018). It is also important to note that Vanuatu has similar challenges to other countries, especially when it comes to developing common strategies around climate change. I will concern myself with activities in the context of adaptation projects and focus on what happens and what is created in this intensive cooperation between NGOs and village communities and how it came about that Dixon Reef became a climate change site. This chapter describes global and local dynamics in their entanglements. Actors in Vanuatu are connected to people on other islands not least through the wider struggles of the Pacific Islands region. They live in a time when the concepts of climate change adaptation, mitigation and resilience influence their practices and discourses.

2.1 The Narrative of the Vulnerable Islands

For some years, the world risk report, published by an alliance of international development agencies, has put Vanuatu at the top of the list of the most vulnerable countries in terms of disaster risk and consequences of climate change (Mucke, Kirch and Walter 2019). Political measures in the country are designed to help people develop resilience to environmental hazards in situ. In the many conversations during my fieldwork, the topic of migration as a strategy to escape from the impacts of climate change was neither made prominent nor categorically excluded. Governmental and non-governmental organisations in Vanuatu, however, maintain their focus on climate change adaptation and other protective measures.[1] This goes in line with a wider approach to the adverse effects of global warming:

> At present, the impact of climate change on society is primarily framed in terms of adaptation, vulnerability and resilience. They are translated into political measures and adaptation projects, which are implemented at the local, national, regional and transnational level. (Klepp and Chavez-Rodriguez 2018, 8)

The authors also refer to the article by Michael T. Bravo (2009), which goes on to say that such frames are needed for the creation of a global climate crisis narrative, being responded to by certain action; even though this could include alternative responses for diverse context (Bravo 2009, 259).[2] Following this narrative, international media and policy documents as well as some scholars draw a picture of islands in Oceania as being located at the frontline of climate emergencies and at the same time having to face the fact that their futures are threatened by severe problems – or even that such lives are 'doomed' (McNamara and Farbotko 2017). Scholars working in the Pacific often work against this metaphor of the 'small vulnerable islands'. Focusing on people's 'vulnerability' of the catastrophic consequences for the environment of Pacific Islanders has been criticised repeatedly "as to paint whole countries or people as the passive victims of 'natural' forces, thus occluding the geo-political origins of the climate change crisis" (McDonnell 2020, 58).

Carol Farbotko labels this discourse as being influenced by the Western 'gaze' on the Pacific Islands. She explains that this 'wishful sinking' (Farbotko 2010), represents waiting for islands to disappear in order to have proof of climate change, and is merely a reflection of what Europeans think of islanders living far away and secluded from global interactions. They become the 'canary in the coal-mine' to explain that this projection only serves the global community, serving as a warning sign if the islands are really sinking down (which they are not, being flooded rather than sinking) (ibid., 53–54). "The disappearing islands thus embody not a located tragedy of importance in itself but a mere sign of the destiny of the planet as a whole." (ibid., 54) This criticism has not only

1 In contrast to perspectives of other Pacific Islanders, for example those of Kiribati (Hermann and Kempf 2019), the Marshall Islands and Tuvalu (Constable 2017) or Chuuck (Hofmann 2016), all of which are Micronesian countries.

2 These terms are accepted in this discourse without considering their (political) origins and the contexts in which they are renegotiated (Goldman, Turner and Daly 2018, 4).

been levelled at the Eurocentric treatment of Pacific Islanders, it also applies to interaction with other indigenous people who do not participate in global negotiations but who are those who will deal with irreversible changes and therefore provide early evidence of the effects of climate change. Communities around the world become at the same time poster children and victims in the arena of political discussions on climate change (Crate 2008; Roncoli, Crane and Orlove 2009). Bravo writes in the same vein that Arctic environments and lives of Arctic people are depicted as "an early warning system of environmental change" (2009, 257). Critical voices stress that local communities in many places are only considered as the experts within their localities and thus can only react to weather changes or environmental changes. This international discourse relies on a vulnerability narrative of global North-South imbalances and are considered as victims who need to be helped, mainly by deploying the development strategy known as adaptation (de Wit, Pascht and Haug 2018, 10; Arnall, Kothari and Kelman 2014).

The topic of Pacific Islanders' vulnerability has been targeted for dissolution by taking into account alliances across the Pacific. By referring to Epeli Hau'ofa's perspective on Oceania and his idea of a connected and empowered region as a 'sea of islands', Heather Lazrus emphasises the strength of those connections also in times of wider transformative forces (Hau'ofa 1994; Lazrus 2012). This renewed kind of 'world enlargement' (Hau'ofa 1994), draws a counter-image to the smallness of Pacific Islands: "Regional alliances and networks of island communities allow them to harness this argumentative resource by having a significant presence in international climate arenas." (Lazrus 2012, 292) One example of this is the Alliance of Small Island States (AOSIS) representing the Small Island Developing States at UN assemblies. Moreover, many scholars working on climate change topics in Oceania have considered the active engagement of their research partners with political discourses (Kempf and Hermann 2014) as well as actions connected to the so-called 'materialisation' of climate change such as storms, droughts and rising sea levels (Rubow 2013). The activist group of the Pacific Climate Warriors expect others to recognise that they are not victims of the circumstances. To the 'resisting the doomed fate' narrative (McNamara and Farbotko 2017), they have responded with the slogan to keep on 'fighting not drowning' (Fair 2018). While I was working with them in Port Vila, the Vanuatu Climate Warriors repeatedly emphasised their motivation to deal with anticipated problems of climate change for the whole country and taking up their responsibility in their new roles as young urban climate 'experts' (Hetzel 2016; Hetzel and

Pascht 2017). In terms of Vanuatu's rural communities, Olivia Warrick stresses that such communities also take an active part in discussing climate change, arguing that the use of the concept of vulnerability itself should be questioned because people do not see their activities as a reaction to biophysical hazards (Warrick 2011). Therein lies the critique of political measures for climate hazards and consequently new emerging strategies and discourses of people on the ground have to be considered. For the events connected with Cyclone Pam, Siobhan McDonnell writes in her analysis about approaches to community activities that organisations should see local agency and resilience not "to return to the status quo" but that they should recognise transformative action on the ground (McDonnell 2020, 57). Further underlining this processual approach, Amiria Salmond writes about Pacific Islanders showing the ability of 're-building ships at sea' – i.e. taking something they have known for a long time and reworking it – considering what they want from the past and combining it what they aspire to for the future (Salmond 2017).

International discourses on climate change involve Pacific Islanders on different levels and make them part of a wider engagement with its information and approaches (Fache, Dumas and Ramon N'Yeurt 2019; Hermann 2018; Hetzel and Pascht 2019; Kempf 2019; Moesinger 2019; Newell 2018; Pascht 2019; Rubow 2013, 2018; Rudiak-Gould 2011, 2012). Governmental, non-governmental and both urban and rural communities are also shedding light on how people act in the context of political topics of mitigation or adaptation (Barnett and Campbell 2010; Filho 2013, Klöck and Fink 2019).[3] In Vanuatu, political and development actors concentrate on the three concepts of adaptation, vulnerability and resilience as triangulated to make future lives for ni-Vanuatu possible.

3 Studies on mitigation concentrate on carbon projects such as REDD+ and climate communication (Babon et al. 2014; Pascoe 2021; von Seggern 2021). Adaptation studies include topics of food security (Campbell 2015), coastal protection (Gesing 2019; Mimura and Nunn 1998; Piggott-McKellar et al. 2015), rainwater catchment due to soil salinisation, infrastructure and weather warning systems and conservation of reefs by planting corals (Kumar 2020). There is also considerable literature on migration, where the concept of 'climate refugees' plays an important role, and where the question is raised whether or not migration should be seen as adaptation (Boege 2016; Hermann and Kempf 2019; Hofmann 2016; Moesinger 2019; Nakayama, Drinkall and Sasaki 2019). For ni-Vanuatu, migration and leaving their islands behind is out of the question (Perumal 2018) and thus designating migration as an adaptive strategy places further stress on the lives of community members (Craven 2015).

McDonnell further writes that, especially when it comes to disasters considered to be a direct effect of climate change, resilience comes into play for measures of governmental and non-governmental organisations: "resilience is deployed as a strategy to overcome the vulnerability of communities in the wake of 'natural' disasters" (McDonnell 2020, 56). However, this does not problematise "disaster responses which see the 'community' as a space to be acted upon by outsiders" (ibid.). Resilience is mainly met and improved upon by adaptation measures, especially for the agricultural sector. Therefore, publications about climate change concentrate on key actors in the context of adaptation in those political measures (Clarke et al. 2019; Walshe et al. 2017; Warrick 2011).

Studies of adaptation focus on how these projects work and how community members perceive them (Clissold and McNamara 2020; Granderson 2018; Orlove 2009; Walshe et al. 2017; Warrick 2021). Some question the conception of such projects due to their use of Western termini, approaches and goals (Warrick 2011). By doing this, they make us aware of the different impacts which 'adaptation' as an operative term can have on local communities (Orlove 2009) and ask for more informed interactions in climate change adaptation involving people in communities as the developers of these methods (Walshe et al. 2017). Adaptation as a concept has recently been critically analysed by Klepp and Chavez-Rodriguez who draw attention to political aspects of adaptation methods and the concept of adaptation itself (Klepp and Chavez-Rodriguez 2018, 3). In their case study of Kiribati, they describe socio-economic changes due to climate change adaptation discourses and politics (ibid., 2). Explaining that scientific discussion has de-politicised climate change adaptation, they call for the refocusing of social science onto power dynamics and the consequences for local people (ibid., 11–13). Adaptation as a linear term that takes the environment and humans as reactive and thus the possibility of "the adjustment in natural or human systems in response to actual or expected climatic stimuli or their effects, which moderates harm or exploits beneficial opportunities" (IPCC 2007, 27) becomes problematic. Nevertheless, in Vanuatu, adaptation projects also create spaces in which participants encounter the topics around climate change. Until now, the focus of studies has been the effectiveness of these projects which is often measured by how important explanations are perceived and changes in the environment are observed (Clarke et al. 2019; Walshe et al. 2017). However, all of these studies are mainly interested in what lives look like when adaptation measures are implemented. This leaves the way open to see what happens in these projects in a more holistic way, when looking at examples of how villagers come into contact with this climate information in connection to their daily work and how they get involved in the projects. These initial moments of being involved in adaptation projects also shows what motivates villagers and what makes them aware of the subsequent practices.

2.2 Becoming a Climate Change Community

Figure 2: The village of Dixon Reef

D. Hetzel

When I first came to Vanuatu, villagers in the Dixon Reef area had been involved in the adaptation programme for cultivation for several years: climate change was a topic everyone could talk about, drawing on the several workshops, village meetings, conversations with relatives in town or for the younger people, from what they had heard in school. Villagers pointed to changes along the coast and the effects of the dry spell, explaining what they had learned in terms of soil preparation or planting methods. Inside Dixon Reef, another smaller compound of Lerambis was founded by some people who became part of the Presbyterian church and split off from Catholic Dixoners. Although divided by congregations, they were all attending the climate change workshops together. Furthermore, relatives from the neighbouring village of Blacksand were also happy to join in the discussions on this topic. This led to ongoing work with the programme's project manager with all of these people over a longer period.

The village of Dixon Reef with its 450 inhabitants[4] is located in the west of the island of Malekula, in the northwest of Vanuatu. The area directly faces the open sea. When I spent my days in the village, we often sat on the beach looking over the ocean in the direction where we expected Australia to be. The houses of the village community of Dixon Reef stretch along the beach directly exposed to the west winds and sheltered from rain by the precipitation slope from the east, which had already caused rain in the higher centre of the island. Villagers used to tell me that "Dixon is a dry and sandy place." Especially along the beach where the several houses were built, people kept emphasising, there was hardly a hummus layer to grow anything. From the village shores, it takes two hours to reach the next town by boat, which operates a few times a week, because there is no road connection. The principal chief of the village was a well-connected man and a fieldworker for the Vanuatu Cultural Centre, who had built his Nakamal[5] right on the beach where passenger and transport boats dock, and who was always ready to receive people and news. Around 2010, he responded to a call from various NGOs, who asked communities to take part in their programmes. He heard about a workshop series for agriculture and thought it would be helpful and, above all, interestingly novel for the families in his village, and thus placed his community on the list. Dixon Reef was accepted onto the Climate Change and Food Security Programme 'kaikai blong laef' (Food for Life) from 2012 onwards under the leadership of an international NGO, which held workshops and consultation visits to the village several times a year. Dixon Reef was included in the programme because of the constant dry environmental conditions and additional elements which fit other criteria such as economic factors: cash crops are mainly coconuts for making copra, where people separate coconut flesh from the fruit by hand and then dry it on blast furnaces, and cacao, both sold in situ to passing ships. Some also began to plant kava (piper methysticum) a few years ago, a pepper plant of which the roots are used to produce the well-known beverage also called kava.[6] All these sources of income were not only subject to crop fluctuations, but also to extreme price fluctuations and people lived mostly off what they grew in their

4 This number is subject to seasonal fluctuation and around Christmas time and the subsequent holiday season it increases significantly for months.

5 Nakamal (Bislama) today denotes the meeting place for drinking kava, but is also the ceremonial dance and meeting place.

6 Kava is used as a ceremonial drink in some parts of Vanuatu and is now sold all over Vanuatu in so-called 'kava bars' or nakamal.

numerous garden parcels. The programme implementers were quick to note that residents' gardens were located up to two hours' walk away from the village, and therefore access was not possible at times such as storms. Areas for cultivation were distributed over kilometres, along the coast, inland, up the mountainsides and beyond, meaning that there was a wide area in which people moved for hours during their gardening day.

Malekula[7] in the western part of Vanuatu is an island of Malampa Province in north-central Vanuatu. It is the first island of the northwesterly branch of the archipelago (Layard 1942, 3). Malekula is the second largest island of Vanuatu, at 167° E and 165°S, 88 km long and 48 km at its widest (Larcom and Beierle 2002). The origin of the name Malekula is disputed, as no reference to this name is found in any of the current languages. 'Mal' refers to 'people', but also sometimes corresponds to place (Goodenough and Ivens 1933; Layard 1942, 8). Pedro Fernandez de Quiros, a Portuguese explorer, claimed to have first written about the island of Malekula in the 17th century, and it was then only visited again in 1774 by Captain Cook (Goodenough and Ivens 1933, 209). The island became an Anglo-French Condominium of the New Hebrides in 1906 (Larcom and Beierle 2002), and then in 1980 part of the new nation of Vanuatu. Large parts of Malekula are francophone, first through the French mission, and then through the influence of the French part of the condominium. Although it has no active volcanos, as exist in other parts of the archipelago, Malekula is a volcanic island, with large rivers, densely forested in the inner parts and fertile inland (Barrau 1958, 35; Cheesman 1933). With the exception of the northern part of the island, in the rest of Malekula, the higher mountains stretch from north to south, dividing the island in half, and are responsible for people mostly travelling by boat when they wish to travel from one of the communities in the east to one in the west. At the time of my fieldwork, the regional government was trying to build a road through the mountains to connect those two sides of Malekula, most importantly the regional economic centre of Lakatoro (Rousseau 2012), connecting the people living at the coast with the inner island. William Goodenough, in his research in the 1920s, described people in Malekula as being divided into two groups "the salt-water men and the bushmen", with the latter having had lesser contact with missionary endeavours

7 There are different spellings: Malekula on the one hand and Malakula on the other, which is probably due to the different pronunciations depending on the region. I will follow the first spelling used by Layard and others.

(Goodenough and Ivens 1933, 210). Dixon Reef, on the contrary, is a newly composed village,[8] founded in the 1950s, when the French Catholic missionaries asked several kin groups, the nasaras, to join together. Through this, people from the inner part of the island were brought down to the shores. It is a type of settlement which is found in many places across Vanuatu, in which Christian missionaries brought people together and founded new village communities, first administered by the missionaries and in the condominium, then integrated into the democratic structures of the new republic. With the conversion to Christianity, people were motivated to move down to 'school' and thus attend church. All of the Dixoners' bubu (ancestors) and some elder people who still remembered the time before the missionaries lived up in the mountains and were thus what were referred to as 'men of the bush' (men of the bush) (Bonnemaison 1974). A consequence of their relocation to the coast is that today only a few inhabitants of Dixon Reef are 'traditional landowners' of the land in that area. The others have to ask the traditional landowners' permission if they want to use land for horticulture or building houses. Although now living close to the coast, subsistence agricultural techniques from living inland were brought with them. Villagers still spend little time fishing, while horticulture remains their main activity for food supply. This is supplemented by small-scale livestock farming, of chickens, a few pigs per family and very few cattle. People in Dixon Reef area refer to themselves as gardeners and they value their work in the garden over other daily activities. When working in their own garden on week-days, my interlocutors referred to being very self-sufficient and having fulfilling days. On Sunday and holidays, gardening paused and people undertook some on-shore fishing or looked for crabs. As the women explained to me from the very beginning, no one would ever conduct gardening on a church day as they regard everything connected to the gardens as work.

Dixon Reef is made up of several patrilineal clan groups. Marriage is predominantly virilocal, which means that women in Dixon Reef often grew up on different islands in Vanuatu. This part of Malekula, the population in the southern region, call themselves Smol Nambas. The name refers to a type of penis sheath worn by the southerners and marks the difference from the Big Nambas in the north-west of the island (Farran 2010, 15; Regenvanu 2005, 43). With the foundation of the village community, people first named it Tavendrua (in the indigenous language Novol/Nasarian, for a bird and a turtle laying their

8 The composition of the village of Dixon Reef corresponds to the one called by Bratrud "a typical Melanesian 'composite society'" (Bratrud 2011, 3).

egg in the same nest), which is also found on some maps. In everyday conversation, however, the name of the present reef took over, naming the village after a man called Dixon. Due to their history and connections to several places on Malekula, many people have close kin relations to villagers of the next village called Blacksand, a few kilometres north along the coast. This also means that people in the area of Dixon Reef are multilingual, but Novol and Nasarian are the main autochthonous languages spoken (McCarter and Gavin 2011; Walworth et al. 2021). General communication, e.g. during village courts, often takes place in Bislama, as do all meetings and workshops with people from outside the community. Furthermore, everyone in this region is francophone and services in the Catholic Church are also held in French.

At the time of my research, every family cultivated crops in several gardens, hours' walk away from their houses. Since there was only one motorised vehicle in the whole community and most of the time no fuel to run it, let alone roads to use, people walked most of the time. Gardening is therefore a practice that involves walking and hence being on the move. Leaving the village, one would first cross underneath the high coconut trees, and nowadays the coconut and cacao plantations take up some space, with gardens being pushed further away from the houses. To enrich their planting, people used the technique of shifting cultivation, a horticultural technique without irrigation but rather seasonal shifting of purpose-built pits (Manner and Thaman 2013, 342). The slash and burn technique has undergone frequent critique by the Vanuatu Department for Agriculture who are attempting to deter people from burning organic material, because it causes further CO_2 emissions and is therefore harmful to the climate. Accordingly, Climate Change and Food Security programmes promoted preparation of the sandy soil next to kitchen houses with permaculture methods to make it more fertile – one of the more important methods to ensure vitamin-rich nutrition. The workshops also touched on explanations of cause and effect, greenhouse gases and global warming.

After Cyclone Pam had flooded garden areas and uprooted banana plants and was then followed by the dry spell, the development organisations were pleased that they had invested time in training adapted and alternative agricultural methods which could, in their eyes, equip villagers for those kinds of crisis. This was also the case in the village community of Dixon Reef. Here, 'home gardens' next to the villagers' houses were planted in the expectation that they would provide people with good support in times of crisis, as was the case from 2015 onwards. During this dry time, however, people began to act on their own terms, at the same time reflecting on their own garden practices (Chapter 4).

They decided to be part of climate change practices set up by organisations and followed up on those programmes in their own ways. They were trying to make sense of current changes and so finding explanations for causes and possible ways forward was part of this (Chapter 3). Nevertheless, villagers thought it was important to attend the workshops, and were still interested in discussing current changes. In one of the conversations with a young woman who divides her time between Blacksand and Dixon Reef and tried to be part of the workshops from the beginning, she took a critical view of the programme, which sets strong guidelines for gardening practices: in her view local people should be more involved in developing strategies. Nevertheless, she thought it was important to discuss climatic changes.

2.3 The Intersections of Local and Global

An anthropology of climate change "has embraced contrasting and potentially conflicted understandings of the human condition and the human dimensions of climate change" (Baer and Singer 2018, 13). It has also brought about some insights into how to approach those dimensions and "research today focuses on the consequential engagement of local worlds with global processes and structures" (ibid., 9). One main aim here should be to dissolve the existing juxtaposition of 'global' and 'local' in the sense of a conceptualisation that is used in political forums and refers to global processes that have an impact on these localities.

Until the 1990s, the natural sciences were mainly concerned with climate projections for the future, monitoring and modelling transforming environments and finding solutions. By the beginning of the 2000s, it became increasingly clear that anthropogenic climate change must also include the human (social and cultural) perspective (Crate 2011). Climate change was first conceptualised by representatives of natural science, drawing on local examples of environmental change, but it was further discussed on the international political level and marked the beginning of far-reaching practices: environmental shifts were labelled with ideas of global climate change, discussion reaching from international forum to single countries. However, there is uncertainty surrounding the issue of why we 'disagree about climate change' as a whole (Hulme 2009) and the question is raised as to whether or not this top-down approach will bring us an understanding and bears the critique of hierarchies of defining the concept of climate change. This interaction regarding climate measures and agendas takes place within a 'science-policy bubble' and with a certain radiance, of course, but not with a superimposition on the local processes. Exchange outside the bubble is orchestrated with conceptual framings in the form of guidelines, negotiations, agreements and policies (Barnett and Campbell 2010, 561; Hastrup 2016), setting the tone for further action.

Concerning these dynamics, Susan Crate describes anthropological research and outlines two dominant approaches: first, local research and second, research on global negotiations and discourses. While the second deals mainly with human rights and security concerns, e.g. 'climate justice' (Crate 2011, 182–83), the first is more concerned with the local effects of environmental changes due to global climate change – impacts on local weather forecasts, adaptation processes and resilience, as well as disasters and resource management are major fields of research (ibid., 179–81). Here, the four 'axioms' outlined by Roncoli, Crane and Orlove, which show how people deal with climate change, can be found again: perception, knowledge, assessment and responses (Roncoli, Crane and Orlove 2009, 88). Ideas related to this, such as 'adaptation', have been understood in recent literature as a 'travelling idea' (Czarniawska and Sevón 2005) and thus as a production of different actors operating at different scales (Weisser et al. 2014). Weisser et al. are concerned with how translation processes work across different localities (after Callon 1986, 201). The authors refer to translation as a way to "not act according to the script of a single global idea, but that they [local communities] appropriate or modify parts of that script and also invent new ones" (Weisser et al. 2014, 112). De Wit, Pascht and Haug explain that with the 'idea of climate change', we refer to a set of various concepts, models and representations that comprises of scientific information about climate change, [...] undergoes continuous translation by an array of translators such as scientists, journalists, governments (2018, 3).

This idea then is "the fruit of continuous interfaces and coproduction between highly interdependent and multiple constituencies" (ibid., 6). To take this further, people not only translate ideas in their own perception by including incoming information, but also through encountering those ideas and concepts in different contexts and over time. In a sense, this creates a new definition of climate change – not as something that is included in people's current explanations, but as a continuing process of creating climate change definitions. As O'Reilly et al. call it, "particularly as the problems and solutions of climate change are both borne, in large part, in marginalized bodies, communities, environments, and regions" (O'Reilly et al. 2020, 16). These climate change encounters, in diverse contexts where people come together in their creative potential, are what create climate change.

Rudiak-Gould added another aspect by emphasising the importance of what he calls 'reception studies', an attempt to understand how people around the world receive and shape discourses through local conditions, practices and discourses. With relation to the Pacific region, he stresses that Pacific Islanders as participants in discourses about climate change are aware of information that is distributed through different media (Rudiak-Gould 2011, 2012). He distinguishes this from equally important observation studies, which he defines as: dealing with "frontline and indigenous communities [who] become aware of global warming through first-hand observation of local impacts", which ignores "scientific discourse of global anthropogenic climate change" (ibid. 2011, 9). He concludes that narratives of an uncertain future are influenced by what people have heard or read in the media. However, what people discuss is also influenced by what is observed on the ground or, put another way, people search for signs of what they have heard and thus are more attentive to new information about it (Marino and Schweitzer 2016; Moesinger 2019; Rudiak-Gould 2013). In order to think with perception and observation as equally important and mutually interacting, it makes sense to address observation and reception together, and ask what climate change becomes for people in Vanuatu.

Observations as well as discourses are local as well as global. Local, as Kirsten Hastrup also notes, are all 'observations' because they take place on the ground (Hastrup 2016). There is a difference whether an individual is retrieving information from experiments conducted by scientific experts or those of ordinary people of the type I encountered in the village. "All kinds of knowledge are equally located and equally based in observation and analysis." (ibid., 41) And they are global, because they are embedded in an exchange that revolves around the topic of climate change:

> If the concept of climate change is based on assembled knowledge from a variety of sources, each individual, group, culture, and society assembles it both from the immediate surroundings and from other people, television features, Internet communication, and scientific reports. (Hastrup 2016, 43)

In the context of climate change projects, similar processes take place. Both observation of the different actors involved and scientific information of natural science are included, as well as further explanations of localised expertise.

In order to move even beyond a reception studies approach, I consider climate change as a process in those encounters and interactions, influenced by both observation and reception. This also means that "climate change is nothing if not global, even if backed by located observations and weather-events" (Hastrup 2016, 41). Global communication is greater than ever, which allows localities to move closer together, and which makes global flows a topic of discussion (Appadurai 1996).

Projections for future transformation due to global warming bring localities closer together – what happens in the Arctic is relevant for every other part of the globe – and brings a new level of awareness of connectedness. Hastrup indicates that the pressing questions of the time we live in are at once caused and can be answered by 'planetary connections', giving inspiration for local realities and speaking of matters that concern the global community. This includes the notion that local knowledge is important to explore because it speaks not only for local problems, since local topics everywhere also speak for universal 'truths' (Hastrup 2018). Geographer Mike Hulme argues in a similar way that climate change asks us to adopt a "cosmopolitan perspective" (Hulme 2010, 562). By referring to Beck's 'cosmopolitism' (Beck 2008), he concludes that: "Although borders persist, they are weakened and people, capital, brands and ideas flow more freely than before. It is a world of fluid heterogeneity, where scale becomes transient and Cartesian space easily subverted." (Hulme 2010, 563), as a spectrum of parts that, when put together, create a cosmopolitan picture. He also emphasises the construction of a climate change discourse and criticises global players for regarding processes in different localities merely as different materialisations of climate change, instead of recognising local populations as active participants in discussions about the concept itself (ibid.). In the Pacific region, places are connected beyond the scope of regionalism (Fair 2020).

These intersections can only be understood in terms of their mutual influence (Hastrup 2018). Hastrup also refers to Anna Tsing's work (2005) on global friction as forms of global discourses – of interactions of different actors in global discussions about conservation, in which the results of these interactions are open-ended. Here difference, according to Tsing, is crucial: "Difference can disrupt, causing everyday malfunctions as well as unexpected cataclysms." (Tsing 2005, 6) She further elaborates that "[b]oth global knowledge and knowledge that travels around the globe are improved by dialogue across difference" (ibid., 81), making researchers aware that neither is the global necessarily homogenous, nor is the local necessarily heterogeneous. "By letting the global appear homogeneous; we open the door to its predictability and evolutionary status as the latest stage in macronarratives." (ibid., 58) What happens in this process, during the dialogue between local and global, by reception and observation? I want to substantiate this through an ontological approach that recognises "ontological pluralism that can suggest the possibility of different futures" (O'Reilly et al. 2020, 17). I now turn to the more general theoretical approaches, considering them to be equally important worlding practices.

2.4 Worlding Climate Change

While a natural scientific lens claims for universality, with an answer from social science to scrutinise the interpretation, translation or perception of this concept made through the encounters, I want to redirect this process to the productive moments and refrain from an unidirectional process of learning about climate change. Work by Martin Holbraad and Morten Axel Pedersen helps here because in their 'ontological'[9] research approach, they focus on people's 'ontological assumptions' in order to find new ways to understand the use of and creation of concepts (Holbraad and Pedersen 2017, 15). This includes an openness for "conceptual redefinition" (Holbraad 2009, 80). I take inspiration from this approach by asking "ontological questions to solve epistemological problems" (Holbraad and Pedersen 2017, 5) and transfer them into the area of climate change studies. Accordingly, I consider climate change as an evolving conceptualisation of what happens referring to materialities, practice and knowledge to consider what happens when different people interact with adaptation programmes through ontological assumptions. This goes beyond the interpretation of a predefined phenomenon named climate change

9 Holbraad and Pedersen trace the genealogy of the ontological turn mainly to the publications of Roy Wagner, Marilyn Strathern and Eduardo Viveiros de Castro (Holbraad and Pedersen 2017, 26). There are many authors who have contributed to what we today call in anthropology the ontological turn and quite different approaches can be distinguished (Holbraad and Pedersen 2017; Salmond 2014). This book is mainly influenced by aspects of the representatives of the so-called recursive approach and by the political ontology approach developed by Mario Blaser, Marisol de la Cadena and others. However, I am not concerned with presenting different ontologies, but agree with Holbraad, Pedersen and Viveiros de Castro when they write about their view on working ontologically: "The anthropology of ontology is anthropology as ontology; not the comparison of ontologies, but comparison as ontology." (ibid., n. pag.).

in different localities (Holbraad 2009, 82) and against a search for its materiality in the 'real world' where climate change is only represented differently (Henare, Holbraad and Wastell 2006, 10). As this process might have conflicting or surprising elements, it also means that you have to endure a certain ontological pluralism (Goldman, Turner and Daly 2018). This means that people have different ontological assumptions regarding climate change, referring both to their observations and their discourses. In their view, research in social science should take those enacted climate change worlds seriously, bringing in more than illustrative aspects but also insights for expanding how we operate with climate change as a concept (ibid.). Other scholars have tried to capture what local people refer to when talking about climate change or accompanying practices (Burman 2017; Hastrup 2011; Rosengren 2018) in their "radically different understanding of climate change" (Burman 2017, 923), in scientific and everyday contexts.

Dan Rosengren shows, in his research with the Amazon indigenous Matsigenka people and migrants from the Andean highlands in Peru, that climate change discourse depends on categories such as weather and climate, which are themselves underlying ontological differences. Rosengren elaborates that local people find different causes for a full riverbed, for example, ascribing responsibly to a range of factors not limited to the amount of recent rain (Rosengren 2018, 610–12). While the *colonos* migrants regard climate change as responsible for constant rain, the Matsigenka do not follow this causal chain, but "according to Matsigenka people, it rains more frequently because there is much water in the rivers (*kimoárini*) and another when there is little or no water in them (*shiriagárini*)" (ibid., 612). Rosengren argues that it is necessary "to take ontological differences seriously and acknowledge that in given situations, opposed and competing discourses can exist in parallel" (ibid., 610). However, concentrating on differences is only one part of the work. As Amiria Salmond puts it, this becomes "ontological innovations in action" (Salmond 2017, 221). This elaboration is not bound to certain groups, in the sense of being attributed, but always arises through interaction between groups. It is not my aim to consider individual perceptions of what climate change is, but rather to consider it as a co-production (Hastrup 2011) and approach this as "worlding practices" (de la Cadena and Blaser 2018, 6). Therein everything connected to climate change becomes 'worlding practices'[10]. I borrow this expression of

10 I use 'world' or 'worlds' following Henare, Holbraad and Wastell (2006), who turn away from an epistemological representation, in the sense of world view. Rather, they con-

'worlding practices' from Marisol de la Cadena and Mario Blaser (2018) who advocate a so-called 'political ontology' approach. For them, ontological differences might lie at the core of political encounters[11] (Blaser 2009; 2013; 2014). Their approaches explicitly address the encounters of different ontological assumptions and consider the resulting processes of these encounters. An example of such a result is "'misunderstandings' that occur in settings where attempts are made at integrating Indigenous and modern scientific knowledge" (Blaser 2009, 11). Blaser concludes that "these misunderstandings happen not because there are different perspectives on the world but rather because the interlocutors are unaware that different worlds are being enacted (and assumed) by each of them" (ibid., 11). While the focus of this example is on misunderstandings, I will take those as part of creative processes of encounters and making worlds – 'worlding practices'. Thinking outside the 'one-world world' theory, where everything is tailored according to one world view (Law 2015) the focus is on "heterogeneous worlding practices that come together around dissimilar interests in common" (de la Cadena and Blaser 2018, 6). These worldings are neither spatially nor temporally fixed but are "constantly coming about through negotiations, enmeshments, crossings, and interruptions" (ibid., 6). In the context of adaptation programmes the 'worlding practices' now become climate change worlding practices in this work. Climate change is worked out by people I have worked with and by myself. 'Worlding practices' are creative moments, which have the same potential as what Tsing calls 'friction'. These ontological misunderstandings (Blaser 2009), which I also refer to as 'ontological friction' (see Chapter 4), can become 'productive misunderstandings' (Tsing 2005). This may also be regarded as an "experiment" for "rethinking climate change" (Salmond 2017, 221).

---

sider the conceptualisation of worlds that are not place-bound but lie in the 'things' with which people interact (ibid., 12–15).

11 Political ontology explicitly deals with the interaction of different ontologies (Blaser 2013) and is thus useful for this research in which climate change sites are characterised by the interactions of different actors. This also moves in the direction of what Holbraad, Pedersen and Viveiros de Castro call 'politics of ontology' (2014), following "the idea of an ontological self-determination of peoples" without "supporting ethnic essentialism" (ibid., n. pag.).

2.5 Conclusion

Asking ontological questions[12] gives us insights into statements and practices that seem contradictory at first glance. When working in the garden and talking about both observed and narrated changes, people considered social changes to also be part of this phenomenon (Chapter 3). A focus on how to make sense of current shifts in the lives of villagers enrolled in adaptation programmes bring them in a context of both global and local ideas. It has to be considered in what people do and say in their daily lives and what they express to be part of what we call 'global climatic change'. In this chapter, I have shown that the call for an actor-based stance from the anthropological climate change literature about the Pacific region goes beyond people as representatives of current changes. This includes diverse voices and practices, which give insights apart from the simplified and misleading 'sinking island' narrative.

Ni-Vanuatu in Dixon Reef look back at a history of being involved in political and cultural changes. As other village communities in Vanuatu, they have been involved in forming new kinds of living and working together. Now the villagers have become part of these processes of the Anthropocene through enrolling into adaptation programmes – and did this because they were interested in being included in the new spaces. This also indicates that they were actively starting to shape these climate encounters themselves. However, while seeing how people acted and their explanations for such actions, I do not want to extent the literature's request for actor-centredness solely through another example of climate change adaptation in Vanuatu. Rather, this book becomes a contribution to the search for connection practices of the local and the global, using an approach that seeks worlding practices. In this way, it moves beyond translation processes, from the international level to single localities, and considers the interactions which in themselves might create something new, not as a version of the idea arising, but as something that contributes to it.

This offers an interpretation of ways in which people produce their climate change worlds and how they act within them. Furthermore, it also intends to initiate further reflection through interpretations of why people act the way they do in the context of diverging ontological assumptions, and tries

12 In order not to reify different 'ontologies' (Henare, Holbraad and Wastell 2006; Holbraad 2009), I use the adjective or adverb 'ontological' to stress the processual character of climate change worlding.

to offer inspiration in terms of rethinking and 're-constructing' (Holbraad and Peterson 2017) climate change (O'Reilly et al. 2020). I further encourage reconsideration of a topic scholars and politicians have now discussed for decades, viewed through the theoretical lenses above and using as a case study a long-standing anthropological topic for Melanesia, namely gardening. Mekem garen, as ni-Vanuatu practice, presents these collaborations of different actors, in a changing Vanuatu in the 21st century, in which it does not present the ideas of climate change, but processes of worlding climate change. In this, as Amiria Salmond has put it, Pacific Islanders are trying to create something new by reworking the known. This also means that mekem garen provides new approaches to gardening that result precisely from these encounters in climate change projects.

3 Of Heat, Politics and Gardening

One afternoon, I was sitting underneath a tree on the beach in the middle of Dixon Reef village, watching the children play in the shadow. It was an exceptionally humid afternoon; people had done their garden work in the first light of day in order to stay at home in the afternoon, taking care of housework, minor reparation work and preparing their evening meals, but also taking a rest from the exhaustingly hot day. I had felt the heat rising for days to the point where it was impossible to stay indoors, even though most Dixon houses at that time were made of bamboo and the rooves made of leaves and perfectly equipped for tropical temperatures. At these moments, I tried to find a breeze at the seafront, like the others, seeking some rest. Hanging out there also gave me the chance to catch up with people. Unsurprisingly they were talking about the weather: because people were complaining about the sun and the endless days without rain, I had started to mark the weather over the previous days in my diary. We had reached ten days without any clouds, and my notes showed that we had already endured a month without any relief. "San i strong" (the sun is hot) had already become part of our greetings, with a quick protective hand movement to the head. This was in the first few months of 2017, when people were going through what they would call an exceptional time. Usually, I was told that it should have been the season of 'Lewutau' (in Novol/Nasarian, meaning everything is green), when everything grows because of daily rains, and the ground would be soaked and roads and paths transformed into rivers (as I then experienced in 2019). However, in 2017 it did not rain much. That day at the beach, Marie-France, one of the mamas, pointed me towards their perceived changes: "Before, we could walk in the sun and as younger people we played volleyball in the sun, no problem. But now you don't want to be in the sun anymore because she is too strong." She laid down on the bench next to me to feel the breeze, which felt more like looking into an oven, but at least one could feel some air on the face. She sighed as she lay down and covered her face with her arm. "It's really hot", she murmured alternately in Novol and in Bislama.

I heard this sentence many times, women running to fetch umbrella or push me underneath a tree when they felt that I was too exposed to sunlight. What they referred to were their bodily experiences to change. One of the neighbours joined us in the shade and agreed with Marie-France: "Before, they sun was our friend, now it's getting hotter and we won't know what it will bring in the future." However, in the same way as residents in Siviri village, they emphasised that the sun also brought another harvest of mangos. Although the adults watched the trees in irritation, they still did not mind being able to harvest mangoes "all year round". This was also a change they attributed to matters of climate change. After all, having mangoes all the time cannot be all good, because there is a season for everything, and now this season should have started to change. "Nothing is the way it used to be", the men in particular grumbled. One evening after a hot day, one of the men expressed that he felt the change in his body:

> I used to feel that everything was fine with my body. We are fit for doing the work. But now I stay in the sun for a short while and already I don't feel able to work. As soon as the sun is gone, you go into the garden and you work, work, work. But when the sun is too strong, you say to yourself, no, you can only lie down, maybe you can get back to it in the afternoon.

Others, however, shook their heads and rather pointed to people who had become lazy – identifying this as the reason why they work less in the garden rather than changing weather patterns. Some explained that working in the garden on a daily basis was simply no longer the top priority and the week was dominated by all the tasks that had to be done in the village. This laziness and lack of activity was explained as being caused by and at the same time *being* climate change itself. In my host family, it was discussed how people created climate change in being less active than before, which also brought changes to their community life. Younger Dixoners agreed with their elders that they, as the younger generation, were far too occupied by new technologies such as mobile phones and the Internet, using their money and time to communicate only in their rooms or hanging out at the beach at night to talk to friends and go online. When I asked what this has to do with climate change, one of the boys answered: "This new technology makes us move less, and climate change makes everything new come to us and then things change." In his opinion, this had an effect on all aspects of life.

The day following this short rest at the beach was a garden day and I went to work with one family, a young married couple and their child. I asked about the dry period and how they managed their gardening during this time. Again, I heard complaints about how difficult it had been to plant yam tubers over the past months, that the young leaves would be burnt by the constant sun. "This is because of what they call El Niño in the workshops." "And what is El Niño for you?" I wanted to know. "It is this time where there is only sun, this is what they [in the workshops] call part of climate change." The couple explained further that they had lost some yam at that time and that their bananas had not grown as expected, but that this year they would grow again. They had never seen a growing season like it. After expressing these concerns, they concluded: "But you have to try", underlining their own responsibility for making crops grow, showing that failure cannot be blamed on an environmental change causing them to have problems, but that rather their own approaches to these challenges was the critical factor. In the evenings after the sun set and we were back in the village, during my usual rounds passing by the kitchen-houses, Dixoners had their dinner or sat down for a chat, very often with a shell of kava. We again exchanged thoughts I had experienced during the sunny, and therefore exhausting, garden day. I was concerned with the questions – what can one do when there is this drought and what did they do? Since everyone was in relaxation mode, they just laughed and told me that they had switched on to other cultivars and other planting sites. "Malele bananas did not grow well, but others were fine." When some malele banana plants[1] do not bear fruits, they moved their banana gardens to the riverside. They assured me that to continue and diversify cultivation would be the only option.

During this time, villagers had been dealing with what they had heard in adaptation projects over the past couple of years, being part of climate discussions. I approached them as experts in their own terms, having interacted with governmental and international experts to create a climate change site, as explained in the previous chapter. In a similar vein, but working with the Makushi in Guyana, James Whitaker considers diverse climate change encounters with NGOs, eco-tourists and consultants, looking at the ontological framing of climate change among villagers underlining pluralism: "expressions indicate the heterogeneity of local ontological concepts (Whitaker 2018)

1 Kind of banana (Musa spp.) which is very common in Vanuatu (cf. Calandra 2017, 461).

as well as the influence of outsiders" (Whitaker 2020, 848). "Ontological heterogeneity" in connection with climate change between and also inside different groups have been noted by Whitaker (2020, 855), as well as other authors (Burman 2017; Rosengren 2018). Here, ontological differences become visible through interactions, especially when talking about global issues such as climate change (Rosengren 2018). This chapter deals with the question about how climate change urban narratives will meet everyday village lives. I then look at the solutions worked out by the villagers in these encounters: namely a concept that ni-Vanuatu living in the Dixon Reef area called klaemet jenj. I take this not only as a Bislama translation of climate change but also as a new concept (Pascht 2019). As Arno Pascht explains, considering these new concepts brings out new climate change nuances, localising global discourses and practices (ibid.). I will refer to relevant recent approaches in anthropology and geography to the study of Pacific Islanders' encounters and practices.

3.1 Differing Explantions

Many studies have intended to show how Pacific Islanders make sense of the new information they receive about climate change (Pascht 2019; Rudiak-Gould 2013), and how they live their lives according to the changes perceived and experienced (Bønnelykke Robertson 2018; Kempf and Hermann 2014; Warrick 2011). There is a wide range of perspectives in terms of how people in Oceania act upon or interact with change. 'Responses' are framed in 'mixed repertoires' of knowledge; meaning that argumentations could be influenced by Christian belief systems, traditional knowledge, economic interests or natural science (Rubow 2013). Cecile Rubow pronounces different approaches of Cook Islanders to 'repertoires' in 'enacting' cyclones, some connected to climate change, some not. For them, she stresses, this is not a contradiction – different explanations for what climate change contains are all seen as valid. Responses are often interpreted as framed according to one cultural framing, using one 'ideology' to explain destructive forces (Rudiak-Gould 2013). These examples underline that for people living in Oceania, assumptions about climate change differ. Responses may be context bound but several of them coexist simultaneously (cf. Calandra 2020). Furthermore, these ethnographic studies show that there are Pacific people (such as those on Kiribati) who completely reject climate change as a concept and focus on what they know. They do not acknowledge any drastic changes discussed on political levels, because for them uncertainty is already an 'existential condition' (Bønnelykke Robertson 2018). Moreover, there are younger people who fully embrace changing scapes of information as well as the acquisition of new information (Hetzel 2016).

All of these studies indicate that climate change worlds are diverse, and that people are negotiating them in their own terms. They also show that what might seem contradictory on paper does not feel contradictory for people on the ground. The authors have discerned a wide range of responses to discourses and practices connected to climate change in Oceania: rejection, adoption, co-existence of different kinds of responses and reception. Furthermore, all of the studies show that these different ways of dealing with climate change exist in response to a change in the environment, which possibly is also framed according to natural science discourse regarding the environment. Peter Rudiak-Gould frames this as reception of climate change knowledge of his research partners in the Marshall Islands. The author underlines that the Marshallese reception of climate change knowledge lies not exclusively within the 'environmental frame' of a natural science approach (Rudiak-Gould 2016). When people discuss climate change-related issues, they not only speak of environmental changes but also refer to a broader set of changes in their lives:

> Marshall Islanders do not usually speak about the existential threat of climate change within the environmental frame. It is spoken of as a crisis of tradition not a crisis of nature; the cause is understood to be the local adoption of foreign, untraditional, pollution artifacts. (Rudiak-Gould 2016, 265)

As he emphasises, Marshallese people include several aspects of life into their definition of what they call climate change. In this they see the causes for it in their lifestyle being influenced by external goods and thus form the argument that this leads them to further problems, both environmental and social (Rudiak-Gould 2013). This goes hand in hand with what Hulme suggests: that matters of climate change itself call for a rethinking of the categories used in global discussions around "global kinds of knowledge" (Hulme 2010, 559).

Turning to the sites of encounters, over the last few years, studies out of geography analysed adaptation projects in Vanuatu. These studies look at how ni-Vanuatu in rural communities deal with the content and useful implementations, and how they act regarding climate change-related issues and challenges already happening. The authors observe that most ni-Vanuatu in rural areas do not respond to questions in line with scientific explanations of climate change, which has further impact on the prescribed success of the project (Buggy and McNamara 2016; Clissold and McNamara 2020; McNamara and Prasad 2013; McNaught, Warrick and Cooper 2014; Warrick 2011). As these studies show, ni-Vanuatu are apparently not primarily concerned with scientific prognoses about climate change, nor do they talk about their experiences as solely directed in the framework of its definition (Clissold and McNamara 2020; Granderson 2018). During conversations with local community members on two islands of Vanuatu, Mota Lava and Tongoa, research partners of geographer Ainka Granderson addressed matters regarding all aspects and challenges of life. Granderson writes:

> Climate-related issues did not figure prominently. Limited access to water and sanitation, land disputes, youth delinquency (e.g. teenage pregnancy, marijuana use, disrespect of elders and traditions) and food insecurity were the major issues identified in villagers' assessments. (Granderson 2018, 485)

Other studies have additionally shown that concerns of people lie in interactions within the community itself. Members of communities indicate different kinds of changes and different causes for changes, both of which lie in contrast to framings following natural or environmental causes (Granderson 2018; Mondragón 2014; Warrick 2011). Granderson concludes that people see changes but do not "interpret climate-related impacts and risks as purely hydro-meteorological phenomena, and global climate change was only one of the many explanations for changes" (Granderson 2018, 492). However, her research partners did also talk about changes, which the scientific community would define as environmental, such as the experiences of "temperature extremes, greater variability in rainfall, and rising tides and sea levels" (ibid., 485). Granderson identifies these definitions of climate change as contradictory to the categorisation of natural science (ibid., 492). Similarly, geographer Olivia Warrick criticises the fact that international discourses on climate change use a "Western frame of reference, where nature and culture/society are separate entities and science and politics are disconnected" (Warrick 2011, 332). However, in my view these studies fail to acknowledge that people could actually communicate in terms of natural science. They use different explanations and therefore also acknowledge environmental explanations. Conversations can go in either direction, referring to diverse explanations and causes for the challenges that people experience. Hannah Fair concludes in her research that people in Vanuatu have different approaches to climate change, which can be differentiated into 'scientific' and 'not scientific' classifications.

"They highlight the potential for more-than-scientific yet not anti-scientific responses to climate change that are locally meaningful and morally compelling." (Fair 2018, 1) She calls this an approach of 'tufala save', a Bislama term which she translates into English with the term 'double knowledge', which can open potential channels for communicating climate change-related issues (Fair 2018, 2).

As I have already referenced, Carlos Mondragón describes how climate change information is integrated into the lives of residents and how people accept scientific discourses in towns and in rural areas. He shows, for the inhabitants of the Torres Islands, in northern Vanuatu, that climate change discourses arose in the area in the early 2000s. Previously, fluctuations in sea levels were considered as normal occurrences and people reacted with flexible housing on different areas of the island. He gives the example of an earthquake in 1997 which caused the sinking of part of an island and accordingly the flooding and destruction of coconut plantations. People interpreted this initially not as a dramatic event but as normal fluctuation. However, after various awareness workshops, the inhabitants of these islands have increasingly linked the flooding and the destruction of coconut plantations to rising sea levels and 'global warming' (Mondragón 2018). He writes: "Subsequently, some islanders began to associate the 'sinking' of their islands with sea level rise." (ibid., 20) This example from another region of Vanuatu shows that external parties try to make sense of local phenomenon and local people have largely accepted their interpretations. Mondragón states that in 2009, there was another earthquake that raised the islands by 200mm, so that the sea level sank again to the level of 1998. Coastal areas dried out, new vegetation returned, partly also as a result of new plantings of mangroves by the inhabitants (ibid., 18). This shows that people in different locations in Vanuatu may apply concepts connected to discourses about climate change based on natural science when talking about different kinds of changes.

However, according to the examples just given, ni-Vanuatus' statements regarding what we call climate change are obviously neither based solely on scientific explanations, nor are they without recognition of such scientific explanations. This means that climate change may be framed plurally. The authors named above give different interpretations – either they state that people integrate or gradually adopt those concepts or that people differentiate between different kinds of knowledge. After participating in adaptation workshops, my interlocutors, both in the Dixon Reef area and in Siviri, used terms connected with climate change discourses – e.g. environment changes, sea level rise, greenhouse effect, ozone layer etc. This may be interpreted as a change in their fundamental assumptions, as Mondragón assumed for the Torres Islands or as 'tufala save' as in Fair's interpretation. However, other studies rather underline that something new is created that draws on diverse sources. Local people's methods of dealing with challenges in cultivation in the village of Efate support the assumption that "[p]eople in Siviri not only know the term klaemet jenj, but they identify quite a wide range of recent developments with it. Klaemet jenj is not an abstract concept for them, but a lived reality" (Pascht 2019, 240). In Vanuatu, the climate change workshops wrap their climate change knowledge around the topic of cultivation and food, which political actors in town also considered as necessary to keep horticulturalists independent in growing their own food. This brings in different knowledges about what climate change can be.

3.2 Between Town and Village

Port Vila, the capital of Vanuatu, on the island of Efate, is the meeting point for international visitors, information about various topics, and thus equally for climate change information and policy efforts. As Port Vila represents a melting pot of people from all regions, ni-Vanuatu in town see themselves as mediators for the islands of Vanuatu, alongside NGOs and government programmes. Discourses and practices around climate change build bridges between town, peri-urban areas and rural areas on the main island of Efate and the other islands of Vanuatu. In this urban context, ni-Vanuatu born after 1980 are perceived as having a special expert role, having access to first hand news, and they see it as their task to pass on climate change information to their relatives on the islands (Hetzel and Pascht 2017). Statistics from 2009 show that Shefa province, where Port Vila is located, has the highest influx of people from other parts of Vanuatu (Johnson and Lenge 2012, 10). People move to the capital in search of education, jobs and the promise of a more varied and interesting life than in the village. Arriving in growing unplanned city settlements, many ni-Vanuatu become disappointed when life does not work out as expected, and young people are seen as a generation without jobs and with no connection to kastom[2] (Mitchell 2004).

Although economic improvement does not necessarily come with this new life, ni-Vanuatu in town nevertheless gain direct access to political discourse and information, including access to international information on climate change (Hetzel and Pascht 2017). When I spent time in Port Vila in 2015, it formed a space of information in the form of awareness workshops, information events and protests. People participated in self-organised climate protests, a local group of young people held boot camps for students and young adults to learn about climate action, and some of them followed the Pacific-wide movement to protest in neighbouring states like Australia – all in all, a growing movement at that time with ni-Vanuatu women and men in their 20s at the centre of it. This growing preoccupation with the future of the country has spread to other young people, and their interest has been matched with numerous opportunities to train as climate change educators or to integrate environmental issues into their education. Younger ni-Vanuatu living in town at that time were highly interested in talking about climate change, since they saw it as one of the most pressing issues of that time (ibid.). One motivation to collect as much information as possible for young ni-Vanuatu was to support their families. They also expressed concerns about their relatives relying on, in their eyes, uni-dimensional practices regarding weather observation for forecast and environment. Not knowing about the bigger picture of current changes made them concerned about leaving community members behind in their actions responding to climate change. The local group of the Pacific-wide activist movement, the Vanuatu Climate Warriors, decided after some years of national and international protest to concentrate on working in the country and pass on knowledge and information which could help ni-Vanuatu to understand what climate change really means for their lives – this they did by talking about climate change on their terms (Hetzel 2016). At that time a young woman being raised close to town explained:

> I think it's not best to follow nature, because now nature is dying and because of that climate change, or that thing […] we have to follow all that information […] people are giving out. Because if we follow nature, I don't know, we

2 In Vanuatu, kastom can have two different, but interconnected, meanings: on the one hand, it refers to ways of living in rural areas and on the other it forms part of a national 'collective identity' (Regenvanu 2005, 40).

> will be confused. Because climate change causes nature to die and if we put our trust and focus on our nature then we will be (...) confused. [3]

Scientific knowledge was seen here as key to a successful response to global warming and progress. Climate change for young ni-Vanuatu in urban areas meant the disturbance of weather and the changing environment and they assumed that adaptation to this was only possible through knowledge from outside. NGO representatives took the view that climate change would increase extreme weather events and concluded that ni-Vanuatu could not rely on their 'traditional' practices of 'predicting the weather' (also often referred to in the literature as 'traditional ecological knowledge' (McCarter and Gavin 2014a; 2014b). One of the Vanuatu Climate Warriors in Port Vila called these practices 'the forecast on nature', a nature that is no longer predictable, because of climate change. Although this is a quite drastic explanation, other ni-Vanuatu in town would have agreed with it as a general concept. The consensus was that climate change causes the environment in the country to change, and understanding and responding to this can only be conducted through scientific knowledge. Other narratives focus on religious explanations.

The conversation about climate change also entered churches and religious meetings in Vanuatu. In contrast to inhabitants of other countries, especially atoll countries, who see events depicted in biblical stories about disaster (e.g. the Noah story) as the cause of climate change or whose religious convictions result in climate change denial, ni-Vanuatu use religious discourse to encourage people to face disasters that are coming (Fair 2018, 9; cf. Timon, Kaunda and Hewitt 2019). Although not denying a scientific explanation, they would take their religious belief and make a "spectrum" (Fair 2018, 8) of both explanations for anthropogenic climate change. Similar to the scenario I described above among the young people in town, they would see the importance of spreading the word about climate change, enabling people to prepare themselves (ibid.). Concern that people in village communities might not be prepared was mixed with aspects of a development discourse of backwardness. Scientists and political actors in Vanuatu directly link challenges to life on the islands and information about climate change as directly linked with communities' life and agriculture. Urban discourse sees the future as marked by challenges. Climate change is viewed as a component of the environment

3 This was before Cyclone Pam affected the islands in March 2015 and the discourse around climate change impacts among the urban population intensified.

that can no longer be relied upon. Communities in rural areas thus become actors within these discussions by participating in climate change projects.

Young ni-Vanuatu joined a practice that tried to find solutions for people in rural areas. It was important for them to accumulate new knowledge in order to pass it on. This new knowledge they found in scientific approaches and explanations (Hetzel 2016). During my time in Vanuatu in 2015, climate change formed a topic of interest, which people were eager to talk about. Bringing conversations and actions forward, they formulated this as 'climate change awareness' and explaining scientific causes.

Efforts to disseminate scientific information on climate change in the country was a policy focus of the government in the early 2010s. In 2015, I talked to employees of the SPC/GIZ[4] (The Pacific Community/ Deutsche Gesellschaft für internationale Zusammenarbeit) and found that their extensive programme of disseminating scientific information on causes and effects of climate change aimed to bring 'awareness' to ni-Vanuatu not only in the urban area of Port Vila, but on all 'islands', as opposed to town. The coordinator of the project in the country at that time made clear that every person in Vanuatu had heard about climate change. The initiative 'mi save long klaemet jenis'[5] (I know about climate change), a cooperation of governmental and non-government actors, addressed ni-Vanuatu across the country. People wore T-shirts with the slogan in the villages, proof that they had participated. Shortly before I first came to Vanuatu, the government ran a programme of 'climate change quizzes', in which people all over the country were sent text messages with short questions related to scientific explanations in connection to climate change, and prizes were handed out to those who answered them correctly. However, one of the main measures was building up resilience among the villagers by running long-term projects, which not only included education about the effects of greenhouse gases and phenomena such as El Niño or La Niña, but also methods of adaptation for food security.

Recently, some official voices have also asked for a more inclusive and longer-term approach, based on cooperation between experts and communities on the islands, something that was actually followed up by the NGO

4 "The expanded SPC/GIZ 'Coping with climate change in the Pacific Island Region (CCCPIR)' programme aims to strengthen the capacities of Pacific member countries and regional organisations to cope with the impacts of climate change" (SPC 2010).

5 Writing of the Bislama term for climate change might differ, according to influences of English, French and local languages.

in Dixon Reef and the neighbouring villages. In an interview I conducted with one state employee, an expert in climate change adaptation, he told me that he had insisted that the programme should not overwhelm community members with more adaptation methods but that it should try to help them with scientific explanations about the effects of climate change and allow them to deal with it in their own way. He is one of the more critical voices who are not convinced that horticulture methods have to be improved by outside knowledge, but believes in people knowing what to do, when the time is right. However, and this in turn fits with the national political and urban discourse, he was convinced that one must continue to talk to people about what climate change can bring to the lives of village communities in the future and also in the present. Although the programmes may differ, national alliances of NGOs and governmental organisations continue to follow their wishes of building up resilience in rural areas. Political measures and initiatives are in no way coming to an end at this point. At the beginning of 2021, when European countries were busy dealing with the Covid-19 pandemic, in Vanuatu, a new climate change resilience programme was started. The initiative aims to inform all the people about climate change and possible mitigation and adaptation methods for agriculture, mostly concerned with what is called 'community resilience' (see Chapter 1).

Coming to the village, people in Dixon Reef explained: "We have klaemet jenj here now." The phrase has become part of the villagers' lifeworld and my interlocutors would refer to weather, plants and people when talking about climate change. Taking this Bislama expression on board also showed that people defined it in their own ways. People agreed on changes in their gardens, coastal erosion and coral bleaching. With this in mind, they agreed with arguments they heard in workshops that climate change is now a part of life. Unlike examples from some other Pacific countries where people were sceptical about the concept of climate change or denied its existence, or even said they had not heard of it (Bønnelykke Robertson 2018; Hofmann 2014), climate change in Vanuatu was marked as known and never denied. However, ni-Vanuatu also took on, and this corresponds with remarks made by scholars discussed above, the notion that changes in community life, such as concentrating more on businesses than on horticulture, also formed part of the changes of modern life. Therefore, projects in Vanuatu, as far as the western part of Malekula is concerned, have been not only about helping people to 'understand' what climate change is, but also included efforts to adapt their lives. People did not once reject the content of climate awareness events and reported that they found information gathered through workshops useful. The coordinator of the climate change project running in the village of Dixon Reef since 2012, a ni-Vanuatu woman who had grown up on Santo Island where she also had her house on her own property, explained to Arno Pascht and myself what climate change was for her and how she tried to convey this in the numerous workshops. Her explanations followed an argument, as described above, that the consequences of environmental changes would radically change the lives of the villagers. For her, climate change would not cause problems for people, but would heighten the intensity of storms and other weather phenomena. In her workshops, she aimed at participants recognising the consequences for horticulture and adapting garden practices to the conditions. This included explanations of weather conditions, such as El Niño and La Niña, the generation of greenhouse gases by industries, but also fire for shifting cultivation, or driving factors such as deforestation. When I attended the workshops, her reasoning ranged between personal responsibility and adaptation to the problems caused by others. Within this argumentation, the potential of one's own actions was nevertheless also made clear. After one of the workshops, she illustrated this as follows:

> All the time they [villagers] complain that there is no rain, at most 15 minutes a day and then it stops again. I told everyone not to destroy the forests. When there is enough forest, the weather is normal and then there is rain. The same is true for the bush. At the same time, no chemical fertiliser should be used, but compost and grey water for watering. All this helps.

Scientific explanations for climate change are linked here to local conditions and especially to agriculture. 'Adaptation' is one focus of initiatives, and continues to be one of the main political agendas. In Dixon Reef, the NGO which has been working with the people for the longest and most continuous period of time has tried to create a direct application link for gardening, learning the effects of global changes in their daily cultivation work while also apprehending what to do under new circumstances. While rising sea levels was not a problem with which people identified in Malekula, rising temperatures, on the other hand, was. As in Mondragón's example for the Torres Strait Islands, the emphasis of the project in Dixon Reef was mainly on adaptation, i.e. the introduction of new methods of agriculture as a way of solving the problem. At the same time, as the above statement by the project manager shows, local actions also had to contribute to reducing the impact of climatic changes. Accordingly, the workshops have focused on scientific explanations of climate change reasons and impacts, and then included strategies for taking action. Nevertheless, not everyone was happy with the contents of the workshops, especially with the methods to apply, but nevertheless they welcomed the guests and wanted them to share their experience of what they knew. They enjoyed attending workshops because they could learn about what was going on elsewhere in the country and beyond.

3.3 Making with Climate Change

When I asked people in the Dixon Reef area where they had first heard about 'climate change', most named the workshop of the NGO as their primary source. Next to the climate awareness and adaptation of cultivation workshop, people in Dixon mentioned school, radio and conversations with friends and family members passing through the village. As the topic entered the village from urban areas, it was discussed in the Dixon reef area in terms of being a problem emanating from the big industrial countries, which they must nevertheless treat in their immediate locality. In this sense, argumentation of damage to the environment and change in the community was considered simultaneously as a local and a global issue. Answers to my questions hinted to a conceptualisation of it as an all-encompassing theme of their current lives. In this they formed two important lessons to address current changes. The first was a novel stance on *envaeromen* (environment) combining terms of Melanesian respect for people and the surroundings, by also including climate change narratives into this. And second, during this they extended the gardening practices as something that deals with cultivating crops alone to a community matter of living together with human and more-than-human actors.

3.3.1 "Respektem envaeromen"

"It is because of what is happening in the big countries." At one of the interview meetings I had with a Marielle, a young woman, living with her mother in Dixon Reef, she explained to me that people in Vanuatu knew well that what was happening – the sun being hotter, higher frequency of storms, the ocean being unpredictable – this happened because of industrial infrastructures. "I think all this smoke is going up, plus the hole in the ozone layer is acting on that and there is El Niño that is too strong. Yes, I think that is the case." People often connected the phenomenon to places they had heard of but did not know themselves, as well as to processes outside their control. One of the older men summarised what he had learnt and experienced over the past years and then expressed great concern in this regard:

> Many tell us that it [climate change] is something that we just know will reach us. Then we say to ourselves, ok, other countries won't have problems with it, but we here in Vanuatu, it will reach us. We get everything that all the big countries have done.

This highlights the issue that although the causes of climate change lie with the large industrialised nations, ni-Vanuatu themselves must prepare to be directly affected. Although problems do not (only) originate in the Pacific region for my interlocutors, they must be addressed everywhere. What will happen is further unknown, but the fact that changes are coming seemed to be a certainty. It also resembles what Rudiak-Gould calls "industrial blame": considering the industrialised countries in the northern hemisphere as guilty with their lifestyle and machinery causing too many emissions, which then leads to consequences, including global warming, all over the world (Rudiak-Gould 2014, 366). Interview partners never denied that something is happening in large industrial countries (most locally Australia) which causes life to change for them. They even consider living in town in Vanuatu to be unhealthy, because of the traffic, soils that are covered by tarred roads and energy wastage through electric lights and other technologies, recognising that these elements have played a small part in the rising heat in Vanuatu. The women were always happy to see me in the village, because then I was no longer at the mercy of the dangers of the unhealthy city and could recover. "It's better you stay here and, the town is hot", my host mother in Siviri would shrug her head about paved roads and unhealthy food in the supermarkets. My companions in Siviri in particular pitied me when I had to make official trips to Port Vila and expressed their concerns about this lost environment. Town is considered to be an unsafe place, not only for physical health, also because of influences of a consumer lifestyle. However, in order to refrain from romanticising village life, it should be noted that other comfortable technologies of the town, such as television, electric lights and brick houses were very much welcomed and people admired those who made their life as urban brokers. For people in Dixon Reef, however, the new themes, new materials and changing weather were linked to connections to urban or international travellers entering the community from outside. People in the village of Siviri raised the same points. One of the younger men, waiting for his next trip to work on one of the bigger farms in Australia, pointed out that islanders would have to put up with this: "What can we do about what people are doing elsewhere?"

This only makes up one part of the argument. The other part is comparable with Rudiak-Gould's argument complementing the blame of Western countries: taking one's own actions into account. In his ethnographic example, Marshallese dealing with the topic of climate change do not see unilineal blame directed at industrial nations as the end of the story. They also reflect on their own life practices, in line with what the author calls "universal blame", where every person on the planet can be held responsible for what is happening to it (Rudiak-Gould 2014, 367). Similarly, official voices have called on ni-Vanuatu in urban residential areas to see how they contribute to CO_2 emissions through burning plastic and driving cars (Hetzel 2016). In Siviri, many of my interlocutors had access to a vehicle or at least used the bus on a regular basis. They took seriously the idea of cutting down the usage of cars since they also wanted to take responsibility for their actions. Although Dixoners do not use cars within their village, they argue in the same way, in the sense that they focus on their own agency. Here again, one of the younger females made a solid point:

> Yes, only we humans together, we have to try our best. Exactly that, we must not burn more plastic and try not to destroy everything around us. We must not cut down trees. When you plant your garden, don't burn it, just plant your food. […] Everyone can do something about climate change.

In Ralph Regenvanu's speech in front of the Climate Vulnerable Forum, we can see a reflection of this dichotomous argument: ni-Vanuatu see themselves as having a responsibility to contribute with their own doing, but only together, with the participation of all others, can current issues be addressed. They express this as an equally important distribution of responsibilities, in the sense that becoming aware of changes, starting to talking about them, also has to create further action. This also includes the notion that, although influence can vary in strength, collective action has the most impact.

This incorporation of shared ownership is in the case on ni-Vanuatu ability to act expressed above all in the practices around 'respektem envaeromen' (respect the environment). Officials of the agriculture department wanted to convince farmers to stop using fire for their horticulture and to refrain from the practice of slash and burn, also because clearing large trees and burning down organic material contributes to increasing emissions. In general, officials emphasised human activity as causing and contributing to climate change-related problems. Regarding the materialisation of climate change, I had many conversations with Augustina in Dixon Reef. During one conversation she mentioned:

> Yes, this strong sun is causing us problems, destroying our crops and flooding. We see the problems in the gardens and in the sea. The sea is rising and coming further and further into the country.

Human activities were what is supposed to 'spoelem envaeromen' (destroy/ruin the environment), whereas in order to work against this, one has to 'respektem envaeromen' (respect the environment). The 'New Bislama Dictionary' (Crowley 1995), does not list an equivalent for the English word 'environment'. In Novol and Nasarian, the indigenous languages spoken by people in Dixon Reef, there is also no vernacular translation for 'environment'. What people refer to, albeit with hesitation, which comes close to what they call 'environmen' in Bislama, can be translated as 'everything that is alive'. In their explanations this included plants, humans, animals, the hills and the sea. This circumscription of environment by my interlocutors can be compared to what Mondragón described as "humanized landscape". With this expression, he wants to emphasise on the one hand that people are the ones who shape their surroundings, in relation to it and on the other hand to differentiate Oceania environments from a natural given. He explains: "Such humanized landscapes give rise to forms of flexibility that are not always evident because they transcend narrow understandings of what constitutes indigenous adaptive capacities." (Mondragón 2015, 4)

For ni-Vanuatu, living with the environment also means working with plants and people, and thus also making their environment. In Dixon Reef, this included at times communicating with the bubu (ancestors) at tabu (taboo) places, where the 'spirits' of the bubu are located. Those places were everywhere around the village and further up the mountains. However, these places were contrasted with the general environment people had to care for in their daily lives. Tabu places were exceptional places in the environment, where only members of the nasara had access and often they were completely forbidden for women (Hess 2009, 129–31). Environment, however, was accessible to all women and men equally, and the responsibility of all. Here, the 'humanized landscape' became for Dixoners the environment in the context of climate change.[6] The chief of Dixon Reef explained to me his understanding of the word 'envaeromen' as: "Everything around us is environment. The trees, all the crops in the garden, the houses and you and me." Others agreed with that explanation, and included their daily activities. Building a house was interacting with 'envaeromen', while cutting down a tree was framed as 'spoelem envaeromen' – that is, the destruction of that which surrounds human beings. Humans interfere with part of the environment, but it needs to be kept alive in order for to maintain their own life. For my interlocutors, it became clear that they, as humans, also 'spoelem envaeromen'. On the other hand, destroying something in the environment is considered to be destructive behaviour of the worst kind. One example of 'spoelem envaeromen' Dixoners referred to was their experience with deforestation. Especially the men liked to tell the following story of the moment when they realised that their environment could be destroyed through money coming through big companies.

A few years earlier, a logging company began its work in the next bay to the south, where people usually made copra on their plantation and the slopes were still full of trees. The logging company promised to create opportunities for wage labour for the people. Since copra production is not always easy to plan and cash income depends on there being enough coconuts as well as on prices at the world market, people are happy to find new ways of increasing their cash income. On Malekula island, many villagers rely on making copra, to pay school fees for their children – one of the main responsibilities mentioned by parents. When I heard about the story of the logging company providing employment opportunities, I was first surprised that people spoke so negatively about it because after being supportive at the beginning, they soon became sceptical. One day, when I came down with a family from their hilltop gardens, Willisem and Denise, crossing this area every time they want to reach their impressive garden site on their own land, pointed at the path we had just followed. I could clearly see that this path had been much wider some time ago, larger trees stood at some distance and only low bushes grew in the immediate vicinity. On closer inspection, I could still see how the tyres of heavy machines had left their permanent marks in the ground. The couple shook their heads: "This is not good, look how they ruined everything." They did not like it and

6 The making of environment becomes the topic of Chapter 5. There I also refer to Arno Pascht and Eveline Dürr, who see environment as a relational process of making and becoming (Pascht and Dürr 2017, 9).

they referred to these activities as 'spoelem envaeromen'. "I say this because of all the trees. Our environment here, so all the trees, they bring the rain. If we then cut them down, there will be too much sun."

The men stopped working for the company for a number of reasons, partly because of poor working conditions but also because they were opposed to the felling of trees. "If everyone doesn't respect the environment and everything that exists, if all the trees fall and burn, it won't be good in the future. If El Niño, if it comes again, everything can be much worse." explained one of them. Of course, there were always some in the community who cut down trees in order to clear space, but most tried to not touch the large trees. Talking about climate change, men and women in Dixon Reef would make the connection between human activity and (also religious) narratives about life. Communities' actions are responsible for changes that can happen. My interlocutors also used terms that were distributed over different sources connected to climate change information. An intact 'environment' can help ensure that external causes like climate change do not affect anything else. 'Respek' for the environment was considered to be extremely important.

Lamont Lindstrom writes about the use of the Bislama term 'respek' among ni-Vanuatu today. This term was appropriated from the English word 'respect' into the Vanuatu Bislama. It became part of ni-Vanuatu language use in the 1990s through the interaction of ni-Vanuatu with pop culture. It mostly describes various forms of good interpersonal interaction (Lindstrom 2017). "They [ni-Vanuatu] bemoan respect's absence and they evoke disrespect to explain conflict and disappointment." (Lindstrom 2017, 3) Olivia Warrick (2011) learned in her research how ni-Vanuatu also connect 'respek' to matters of climate change: the community members on Mota Lava explained the topic of climate change as a loss of 'respek'. They explained that one expression of climate change is that of younger people losing respect for their elders and following a lifestyle which is dominated by consumer goods. In this case, 'respek' comes together with climate change in terms of social interactions among kin relations and community members. Dixoners use this to explain the proper way to interact between humans and the more-than-human world. They do also make this connection to climate change but combine it with another word they draw from new discourses: 'envaeromen'. While in workshops the word 'envaeromen' is used to describe on the one hand, the materialisation of climate change and on the other, the human impact to cause it – this brought a new nuance to the word 'respek'. In discussions about climate change, the term also referred to humans having to interact with everything including the environment in a way that ensures that interactions cause no harm. For many, this includes human interaction as well as their interaction with the non-human world. In this way, the behaviour in question is situated within a broader discussion about climate change, which considers the treatment of all living things. The effects and impacts of human actions are also considered together, both in terms of human coexistence with what they consider as environment as an animated landscape. I will elaborate further on this topic in the next section of this chapter. Here, climate change is an aspect that describes destructive human behaviour and how this behaviour may or may not be respectful.

3.3.2 Climate Change, Communal Life and the Gardens

In discussions about climate change, my interlocutors often mentioned changes in community life – in our conversation, many of them pointed me towards the recent shifting dynamics in their living together – in doing so, also practising self-reflection. Both older and younger people in the Dixon Reef area saw changes of lifestyle reflected in the increased and daily use of technical means of communication over the years. Younger ni-Vanuatu in particular are attracted by new technologies. One young man from Dixon Reef criticised his own generation for using the mobile phone, for calls, texting or using Facebook on the assumption that this would lead to their interacting less personally face-to-face. Furthermore, picking up the phone made them less motivated to travel, meeting relatives in other parts of Malekula because interaction was swiftly done from their own beaches. This brought up discussions in the family homes, where the parental generation expressed their concerns that younger people had become less interested in living together as a community, contributing to self-organised village life with running kindergarten or school, organising festivities or village gatherings, further learning the solidarities and respect in their agricultural work, because they retreat into their houses, absorbed by their phones.

Another aspect of changing community life that villagers in the Dixon Reef area increasingly mentioned was that individual families turned back to their kinship groups and focused less on the village community. This included complaints that nowadays community members are more concerned about their own benefits and keeping everything in the extended family – in contrast to thinking along lineage lines. If time was used so that individuals could afford material goods, less time remained for community work. Therefore, it was often said that work in the village, at the kindergarten or at school was considered too time-consuming (see Chapter 6). Individualism was to be considered a danger to community life and people complained that this contributes to climate change. When I talked to Thomas and Platine one afternoon, by making references to their own family life with their three children, the couple helped each other to frame their view on current changes. Thomas summed this up as follows explaining these connections by using the Bislama concept of klaemet jenj:

> I think klaemet jenj only follows all the traditions of our lives! It is indeed the case that we are losing all the ways of life and additionally kastom that we used to adhere to. Today we just do things differently. If we work only for money, then we eat rice. Ok, look, nowadays you go to the garden and then when you come back from the bush, we no longer eat what we grow there? Do you see what I mean? That's a big change! In the past, we used to work, when it was time to make copra [at the plantation], we would eat rice afterwards. For a festival, we ate rice. [...] We don't focus on our work anymore. So, it's not like it used to be. klaemet jenj is how we live our lives.

This statement combines causes with effects. Klaemet jenj, as Thomas put it, is and follows the way people live their daily lives. For both Thomas and Platine, the biggest loss for Dixoners was the way of life their parents were living decades ago, especially gardening and the consumption of the crops grown, which was often described as the ideal. This influences not only what happens in the village but it affects to the same extent community life and garden life. Klaemet jenj refers to living together in the community, and this is characterised by gardening. This includes not doing as much gardening as in the past, not eating the yield from the garden and thus not following the ideal of communal life (Chapter 6).

People living in the Dixon Reef area discussed the importance of gardening as producing their own 'aelan kaikai' (island food, cultivated crops) and criticised a growing reliance on highly processed foods, including rice, canned meat and canned fish. When Arno Pascht and I arrived in the village at the end of 2016, eating fresh and healthy food was one of the main concerns when talking about gardening. Since the adaptation programme running in the village had a focus on food security, the project leader was eager to have people eating their own cultivated crops, grown next to their kitchen houses. These home gardens were an approach designed to ensure a vitamin-rich nutritious diet.

However, in times of crisis, during the drought of El Niño, people resorted to a diet supported by imported rice, easily stored and ready to cook, supplemented by a few leaves, corn or pumpkin.[7] This approach by villagers led to discussion between the NGO and representatives from the community, which included topics around gardening, aspects of adaptation and, relevant at this point, aspects of good food. Even before this point, there had been numerous lessons on the classification of different types of food, a campaign that addressed the whole country: "Tri kaen kakae is a division of foodstuffs in Vanuatu, where foods are placed into three categories, kakae blong bildimap bodi or foods to maintain strength, kakae blong blokem sik or foods to maintain health, and kakae blong givim paoa or foods that provide energy." (Wentworth 2020, 81)[8] Ni-Vanuatu indicated that rice and tinned meat were one of the main problems causing illness. However, in many parts of Vanuatu, rice had become a staple food for huge parts of the population. Consumption of refined rice and other imported products (such as tinned meat and instant noodles) is now a serious health risk and an issue widely discussed in the country. Wentworth describes islanders as considering rice as something that helps during a short-term crisis, such as after Cyclone Pam, but not providing a long-term solution. Discussion about eating 'healthily' has already been integrated into NGO programmes and ni-Vanuatu discussed the risks of eating too much rice (Pollock 2017; Wentworth 2020, 81–2). Other movements such as the local Slow Food Festival, organised locally and held on a different island each year, also focus on local food. Here too, the importance of cultivation is seen as a transmission of knowledge of food preparation, and also as a basis for healthy eating (Willie 2019).

In Dixon Reef, people insisted that they would prefer 'aelan kakae' (island food) and that the consumption of rice was considered also to change life in general, beyond purely nutritional aspects. Klaemet jenj reflected this transformation in nutrition and the associated fast lifestyle based on consumption and less on cultivation. An elderly woman in Dixon Reef, who was considered to be an expert in cultivation, and who was therefore called 'Mama Agriculture' by the other villagers, warned against excessive consumption, suggesting that one had to be cautious of the use of rice, but can, however, eat it temporally.

---

7 There is a growing body of literature on how disaster food relief has affected peoples' taste and approaches to food security (cf. Ahlgren, Yamada and Wong 2014; Connell 2015; Iese et al. 2021).

8 The spelling of food as kakai, kaikai, kakae or similar is regionally different in Vanuatu.

She continued her thoughts: "Rice is the food of the 'white man' and it helped us a lot in the past and after Cyclone Pam, but now we return to our gardens." Since people immensely criticised the daily consumption of rice, while emphasising that they ate a lot of it, I followed up on this aspect. I noted the daily rice consumption of villagers. At the beginning of my research in 2016, which coincided with the time when my interlocutors were still dealing with the consequences of the El Niño drought, refined food and especially rice was eaten in every kitchen, mainly replacing root crops like yam, taro and cassava (20 out of 20 people asked ate rice as the main course). In 2019, almost two years after the El Niño drought, people in Dixon Reef still supplemented their diet with rice; however, meals contained mainly root crops (only one to three people out of 20 ate rice as a main course). At that point, my interlocutors praised the good quality of their food, the different flavours of yam and the excellent taro. The ambivalent attitude to these 'healthy' foods still prevailed, however, as rice was easy and quick to cook after long days at work.

This discourse included that the notion that people complained that they tend to take less care of their gardens compared to the past. When talking about klaemet jenj, people would refer to their garden crops and to the way they have changed, as this woman does:

> What I think, in my opinion, and I only compare today with the time before, all the crops carried well. In the time of the elders, you went to the garden and then you could dig out good taro, very good cassava, really big ones. But today, how everyone explains today, it's not like before again. Now everything changes.

Humans are considered as responsible for not following up their garden practice, or are seen as too lazy to work hard enough to generate the same yield as before. Life has changed and this can be seen in the humans' behaviour, in the environment and in the ways in which humans behave towards the environment. Just as the garden was important to people at the political level for food security, it was also important to people in Dixon Reef, but in a more multilayered way.

Political actors saw the gardens as a way to secure food today and in the future. Climate change programmes included efforts to achieve good nutrition and in general have been trying to communicate the value of home-grown food in recent years. For women and men in Dixon Reef, everyday gardening was also a matter of community life (see Chapter 6). Cultivation of food crops is seen as one of the key elements, both for a good life and with regard to the challenges posed by climate change, or to put this differently, gardening *is* expression and production of community life, and if it does not work, there is climate change. Thereby the villagers are connecting mekem garen, their practice of gardening, with climate change. The way to move forward for people in Dixon Reef also lies in the community. To the extent that humans are responsible for everything around them and their community life, they can act on climate change.

On another humid sunny day at the end of February 2017, I placed myself again in the shade at the seafront, and started talking to one of the men in order to discuss some difficult topics. We were talking for some time and my interlocutor's patience was almost at an end – I was pestering him too much with my requests for more detail. He gave me a dismissive look in response to one of my more provocative questions about whether klaemet jenj would make everything in life unpredictable and then said:

> Look, for us, there is a time for everything. There is a time to plant the garden and clear a place for it, there is a time for that as well as for the sea. Sometimes you see the sea changing, it swells and brings all the driftwood to the beach. And it's the same with klaemet jenj, everything changes.

Change is something that people in Dixon Reef experience on a daily basis. It is not surprising for them that climate change is happening, because it represents just another change in their lives. Nevertheless, they do not dismiss klaemet jenj but rather consider it as something that has to be addressed, as does every other change in life.

So far, I have explained that women and men of different ages considered klaemet jenj to be part of their 'envaeromen', their surroundings, their gardens and human interaction and behaviour, and to have effects on living together in the community. All aspects are considered with equal importance; however, human agency was always at the centre. People are responsible for changes happening, as well as being responsible for addressing it. Whether or not this was able to be solved remained equally unclear for all those I have asked.

3.4 Conclusion

This chapter has expanded on the ramifications of climate change practices and discussions in Oceania. Heterogeneous climate change knowledges included diverse responses to it. What I was depicting in this chapter from what I have learned from my interlocutors in Vanuatu, was that explanations for changes initially seem contradictory, but their new conceptualisation of climate change did not present anthropogenic influences, environmental impacts and impacts on human life as a causal sequence, but rather side by side as both causes and effects they have met over the past years. Scholars conducting research in Vanuatu described how ni-Vanuatu mentioned problematic issues and changes in their lives which did not fit with a scientific definition of the environmental sphere. According to them, ni-Vanuatu used different categories of 'knowledges' to make sense of climate narratives (Fair 2018; Granderson 2018). Following Rudiak-Gould and expanding his request to think 'beyond the environmental' (Rudiak-Gould 2016), I considered defining climate change and dealing with topics connected to it to lie beyond this environmental sphere. This also means that those 'responses' are not a mere reacting in multifaceted ways, but my interlocutors decided in their practice how to address the changes according to diverse overlapping categories. I looked at what my interlocutors explained to me by not dismissing it as something that does not fit in with explanations of natural science, but as their own specific and novel conception of climate change, which I call, following Pascht, klaemet jenj (Pascht 2019). Urban explanations in Port Vila on climate change concentrated on the destructive forces that will cause environmental problems which result in threats to Vanuatu's agriculture. People in Port Vila and experts from NGOs therefore aimed for country-wide climate awareness and integrated new methods of adaptation to these environmental problems. Those repertoires of climate change in urban areas have been mainly concerned with connecting people in rural areas to new discourses. Through workshops, they have been addressed in order to change their agricultural practices and find methods of adaptation. I showed that people in Dixon Reef talked about the worldwide problem of global warming, as well as expressing their opinion on the shared distribution between Western industrialised countries and their own activities. The responsibility they took in addressing 'respektem envaeromen', expanding their Melanesian communal norms for living together. This anthropocentric approach of my interlocutors brought their 'humanized landscape' (Mondragón 2014) into discussions about degrading environments. Responsibilities lie in human action, both on the islands and abroad.

The garden then builds a bridge and shows that 'envaeromen' and community are part of what people refer to as klaemet jenj. Disregard for gardening also has an impact on community life. Klaemet jenj is the transformation in the 'envaeromen', change in community life and is one of the types of change that people consider themselves to be increasingly aware of. Apparently, while these changes seem to be causing concern among the people of Dixon Reef, it is also animating them to talk about possible responses. When describing how people in Dixon Reef deal with issues of climate change, it may be appropriate to distinguish between two different kinds of knowledge or 'tufala save'. In contrast, they create their climate change world and deliver a novel definition of climate change – namely klaemet jenj – which is holistic and comprises discourses and practices. 'Worlding practices' of climate change led to this klaemet jenj world, influenced by both reception and observation.

4 Projects for Climate Change

"A garden next to the kitchen makes things so much easier. They [the villagers] just go outside and harvest some vegetables. You do not have to go to the bush during a cyclone." For the adaptation programme's advisor, it was especially important that people did not have to walk to their distant gardens during times of adverse weather conditions to supply themselves with vegetables and root crops. Moreover, that every woman, man or child should be able to access fresh vegetables and thus a vitamin-rich diet. Challenges, such as dry times, could be faced by preparing the ground according to principles of permaculture, framed as 'tekem care long graon' (taking care of the soil) – tilling the ground to suit your needs and supporting the growth of your crops, as addressed in the adaptation workshops. The NGO which has worked in the Dixon Reef area (Dixon Reef and Blacksand) regularly since 2012 envisaged challenges of climate change primarily as a matter of livelihood security. Several workshops were held in the village of Dixon Reef, training was undertaken in Santo and Port Vila by a number of community members, and some women and men were trained as multipliers for new agricultural methods. Once the programme had commenced, workshops took place on food security, community management, health services and climate change awareness. The section on food security included training according to the NGO's formulated aims for soil improvement techniques as well as food security through what they called 'innovative and adjusted agricultural practice'. Thus, inhabitants of Dixon Reef established new gardens next to the dwelling houses. Gardening inside the village was uncommon at this time, because the parcels lay behind the coconut and cocoa plantations further inland of the island, but was not totally new to the people of Dixon Reef. They did report how their parents planted cabbage next to the houses. However, the permanent cultivation of vegetables and root crops in tilled soil was a new concept.

As both villagers and NGO representatives reported, when workshops for food security had started, the organisers were enthusiastic that they had many interested people in attendance. When discussing this some years later, it became clear that what motivated villagers at the beginning were the new techniques they expected to learn. In general, every time a workshop or a village get-together had been announced, people were eager to participate. They would gather in the community hall, which had been especially constructed for occasions like gatherings or village courts. Then, even after all those years, many of my interlocutors made time to come to see what was new and the house was filled with attendants. During workshops, people sat on the floor along the walls for instruction, while the narrower end of the building was equipped with a table at which the person in charge of the event took a seat. The second part led people outside, to the specially created community gardens, used as general 'demonstration plots', or to the home gardens. Workshop organisers would first explain the steps of the new approach to cultivation and then put theory into praxis on the plot behind the community hall and directly within the village. Gardening and village life became one and the same in the workshops; however, workshop participants, as I will show on the following pages, saw this as not restricted to the village land itself.

In this chapter, I look at the activities of the food security and climate change adaptation programme in the Dixon Reef area in connection to gardening or mekem garen. As I will show, mekem garen is formed by the processes of climate change and cultivation – both in the eyes of NGO representatives and villagers. However, because workers of the NGO concentrate on climate change as environmental transformation with implications for people's social and cultural life, whereas people in Dixon Reef relate it to life itself, mekem garen becomes a topic of discussions. In the previous chapter, I have described how Dixoners perceive klaemet jenj in connection with the multi-facetted changes in communal life. In this chapter, I show that mekem garen is characterised by change. This will also show how the programme's approach of preparing and tilling soil, taking care of the ground by transforming sandy soil for home gardens into a fertile base for cultivation is juxtaposed with the gardening experience of my interlocutors. However, this does not mean that in practice both approaches do not make sense in their own way – instead people also develop new approaches to cultivation. I thus follow two lines of argument, which both refer to what I will call ontological friction: first, that in the case of discussions with villagers about home gardens, there was no reference to what mekem garen actually is for the people of Dixon

Reef. Second, I argue that diversification in horticulture is the reason why people are always interested in new things, including participating in projects for new agricultural methods. This dissolves the questions as to whether people should continue to cultivate using, what other studies call 'traditional methods', or whether they are open to new ways which allow for constantly creating something new, also seen through frictions in workshops. I argue that a distinction between traditional knowledge and new knowledge does not help in terms of understanding what people do, but that garden praxis is characterised by flexibility, and furthermore that frictions can be moments of creating new ways to move forward.

4.1 The Genealogy of the Abandoned Home Gardens

The food security part of the programme focused on establishing home gardens, inspired by and loosely following the principles of permaculture.[1] Permaculture, in its systemic and holistic approach, tries to think of cultivation from the bottom-up, from soil. It aims to improve and maintain soil quality, considering the work of humans with microbes, water and the soil in general. Permaculture owes its emergence to a counter-movement to industrial monoculture, and the inventors' aim was to promote sustainable soil use, as well as to bring farmers to consider soil quality and more directly into working with the soil (Mollison 2004). Julius Krebs and Sonja Bach explain that the neologism 'permanent' and 'agriculture' puts the focus on sustainability and continuity. Planning and implementation are essential aspects here, and the use and combination of various proven soil management measures of compost with grey water use, mulching, organic fertilisers and polycropping. Permaculture emphasises the sustainability of farming and growing food (Krebs and Bach 2018). Examples from all parts of the world show that new approaches to soil processing are rethinking both agricultural movements and social communities – for an environmentally-friendly mutuality that also restructures communal life (Stodulka

1 Permaculture is an established term for a holistic systemic way of life originating in Australia with a focus on agriculture. "Permaculture's central concept is that humanity can reduce or replace energy and pollution-intensive industrial technologies, especially in agriculture, through intensive use of biological resources and thoughtful, holistic design, patterned after natural ecosystems (eco-mimicry)". (Morel, Léger and Ferguson 2019, 1)

2024). La Puig de la Bellacasa (2017) emphasises the concept of care work in permaculture – and with this, reflects on forms of thinking with the environment and people. In her own involvement in the permaculture movement, she relearned everyday relations to the ground through touching and working with soil and with it 'the earth' and thus 'alternative ecological doings' (ibid., 147). She analyses this transformed approach to the environment as follows: "I take care of Earth, via soil and the worms, because I need them, because they are of use to me." (ibid., 147) This 'working-with-nature' (ibid.) was also reflected in the Dixon Reef area climate change workshops, in which the workshop leaders explained this individualistic permaculture approach as a way of working with the soil in a sustainable manner, not exploiting it through burning, and further giving something back to the soil. The two women from Vanuatu and Papua New Guinea followed 'tekem care long graon' (taking care of the earth), as an all-encompassing change of life through agriculture, and with it preparing everyday practices of soil and human for climate change. Hence the programme was called 'kakai fo laef' (Food for Life) and not only implied food security but also the creation of sustainable lifestyles for changing times. In the adaptation programme, the notion of care became a central notion. Bellacasa finds in her book: "care as the fostering of the endurance of objects through time (maintenance against breakdown), haptic care for the imperceptible politics of the everyday (rather than the irruption of events)" (La Puig de la Bellacasa 2017, 171). For the Dixon Reef area 'tekem care long graon' became the Bislama slogan for transformative methods of giving the ground you chose for your gardening the possibility to be transformed through working with it. These are transforming approaches for times of changing environmental circumstances.

In discussions with the programme coordinator, a woman who had grown up in Vanuatu's urban environment, having her own garden plot next to her town house in Luganville on Espiritu Santo, and experienced in techniques of permaculture, made apparent her support for innovative cultivation methods. Integrating aspects of permaculture into Vanuatu's rural gardening practices would, in her view, be an asset for rural food security and lead the way for a modern way of gardening. Setting fire to the bush in order to make room for new garden plots is considered to further intensify problems of droughts in Vanuatu, and also contribute to emissions. Therefore, the coordinator especially found permaculture methods interesting, on the on hand, because they would fit easily into the way people approach their gardens, having family gardens for self-supply and polycropping, as well as making cultivation in a single place possible, thus providing a new view on cultivation by being equipped to repeatedly grow crops in the same spot. The idea was not to completely leave behind current gardening methods, but to have the home garden as a continuous backup and additional safety net for food security. It was meant to supplement the garden networks people built up – especially in times of prolonged droughts or shifting seasonal weather patterns. The Bislama expression 'tekem care long graon' (caring for the soil and the ground), for the project leader, meant trying to protect it from strong sunlight or flooding. In addition, growth is stimulated by adding nutrients, which participants liked to call 'fidim graon' (feeding the soil). While the gardens in the 'bush', outside of the village, undergo a number of cultivation stages until the plot eventually lies fallow for several years, the home gardens should be continuously cultivated. The programme included a large number of practices of soil preparation with organic fertilisers and nutrients, such as using compost or grey water for soil irrigation, or mixed planting methods that support each other's growth due to nutrient supply and defence against pests, organic fertiliser, accumulation of soil for planting on small mounds, mulching or green manure and intercropping with trees like gliricidia (Gliricidia sepium).

Due to the sandy nature of the soil along the shore where most villagers' houses were located, the NGO intended to teach people to prepare their soil ahead of planting as well as during the whole process of cultivation. The programme therefore included a large amount of soil preparation with organic fertilisers and nutrients, such as using compost or grey water for soil irrigation, or mixed planting methods that support each other's growth due to nutrient supply and defence against pests. Recently-installed showers next to most of the sleeping houses had an additional function – the run-off greywater served as irrigation for the adjacent garden areas. Workshop organisers invited different groups of villagers, among them always one representative of papas, mamas and the youth, to workshops to learn how to make a garden with organic fertilisation. Participants were then encouraged to apply what they had learned within the workshops to their own home gardens close to their dwelling and kitchen houses. And as the work began, they fenced areas next to their house and started to grow all kinds of food, especially aelan kabij (island cabbage; abelmoschus manihot). The permanent cultivation of vegetables and root crops in tilled soil was in fact a new concept. When I was asking among my interlocutors, it became clear that what motivated them to attend the food security programme were the new techniques they were expecting to learn. During one such workshop, we first discussed new approaches and then stepped outside, cleared an area for the community garden, fenced it in and then started to subsoil with manure. The community gardens intended for local people and workshop leaders to try out new methods together.

In 2015, the gardens blossomed. Spring onions and lettuce were planted in the centre and island cabbage, along with manioc, in between, with even a yam or two being planted where space allowed. Retrospectively, workshop participants explained to me that they were very proud of their achievements and Dixon Reef became the NGO's flagship project, with pictures of villagers and their harvest in the reports. One of the women thought back and said: "You could see them everywhere, we all put effort into our garden." One of the chiefs, living only a few metres from the ocean, was proud to tell me that when he managed to grow a banana plant in the sandy soil next to his house, other villagers came by to admire his achievement. My interlocutors told me that they were very proud of their flowering gardens, especially of the fact that they managed to do this despite the sandy, nutrient-poor soil. Subsequently, a few individuals from the village travelled to Espiritu Santo to the Agriculture Training Centre or to Port Vila to the Agriculture Department to learn further innovative approaches to agriculture, returning to share their training with their families.

By the end of 2016, during the continuing El Niño drought, I could count only a few home gardens scattered around the villages, but nothing like the numbers I had been led to believe from stories of the previous years. The NGO supervisor was already complaining that villagers were not maintaining their 'smol garen' (small gardens). In March 2015, Cyclone Pam hit Vanuatu (see Chapter 1). People continued to grow their plots in the 'bush' outside the village, under the aggravating conditions of the drought. Many lost a whole year of the yam harvest and said that the only thing that would grow well in this kind of weather were manioc and mangos. However, most of the home gardens lay fallow and the plants were left to fend for themselves. The representatives of the NGO, especially the programme's coordinator, were irritated by this development. They were surprised that villagers would not follow up on the permaculture approach, since those cultivation methods were especially designed to help in dry weather conditions. When we looked back on this development together, the coordinator would shrug her shoulders and look at me questioningly: "And why would they walk a long time to the bush, when at least vegetables can be cultivated right next to the houses?" The once successful story of transforming the whole village into a garden site had not been continued. Discussion between the NGO representatives and villager heated up when villagers pointed to the more-than-human village residents, like chickens or pigs, who, in times of scarcity ate the last of the fresh leaves of island cabbage. Additionally, they pointed out, the sun heated up the soil and cancelled out all their efforts towards cultivation. In reply to this, the representatives of the NGO insisted that newly-introduced methods like mulching would make sure that ground and plants would be protected from the strong sunlight.

At one of the follow-up workshops, the programme coordinator raised this question again. That time, I looked around the quite full room, just to see people being indifferent to this question. Finally, some of the men reluctantly replied that the extremely dry weather of 2016 simply did not allow them to manage the ground in the way described. According to them, the dry season made it impossible to grow anything in the sandy soil. In fact, over time, Dixoners turned away from these discussions – although the questions of why there were different approaches to gardening remained. Out of professional curiosity, I found this insecurity on all sides interesting and tried to analyse this development with my individual interview partners. One day, during a long conversation, this was put into perspective by the NGO's field officer, Jean. Jean was a man in his 40s, living in the village all his live, always curious to learn different agricultural concepts and to apply them in his current own garden practices. He had been trained as a permaculture expert, then later acted as the link between villagers and the organisation. His own home garden had been one of the more elaborate ones, with a large number of root crops, legumes and vegetables standing side by side. During El Niño he had spent most of his time cultivating his food crops outside the village and over time the garden at the house had become overgrown. Reflecting on these discussions about the abandoned home gardens, he found an expression for the general attitude of the people in Dixon Reef:

> I know, with permaculture they want us to force the ground. With everything, they want us to add and change it. But *we* cannot force the ground. I know that they think with permaculture you can just do the things you planned for, but if the ground soil doesn't want to, there's nothing else you could do.

From Jean's point of view, the anthropogenic influence on the soil had its limits, a limit indicated by the soil itself. Women and men in Dixon Reef could not get the soil to follow human demands. If crops were not supposed to grow, whatever the reason, villagers left it be – for the time being. Here, de la Bellacasa's demand to 'listen to' (2017, 147) more than just the human perspectives in order to know how to work it takes on a new dimension, in which the soil itself determines the possibilities and limits of cultivation. The actors of the NGO grew irritated that villagers enthusiastically followed the 'new approaches' to agriculture for the first couple of years, but then did not keep up the work with continuity in the long run. My interlocutors within the village were not quite as frustrated and still spoke positively about the project because they had learned a lot. A statement from one of the women showed that this was not the end of the process for all: "I tried to do it and it worked – maybe I [will] try it again." Indeed, the story does not end here.

In April and May 2017, while I was still in Dixon Reef, Vanuatu experienced two milder tropical cyclones. Neither caused heavy damage – the bamboo kitchen walls blew away, which people laughed about and immediately set about weaving a replacement from new bamboo plants. However, these storms brought a lot of rain. All of my interlocutors saved some crops they had cultivated along the riverbank in the plain once the winds had calmed down, and replanted them along the hillside. Shortly before I left for Efate, I used these last few days to visit various people on Malekula for a final get-together and attempted to view a few different corners of the village one last time. One day, I walked through Dixon Reef and saw women working behind the last row of houses, which face the hill. They had started to establish new backyard gardens, this time along the hill, where rain had washed soil down to the shore and mixed it with the sand at the beach. They did this using the technique of mulching, putting gliricidia branches (Gliricidia sepium) into the ground. They also dug water channels. At the time of my visit, the women were about to plant banana offshoots and manioc. When I asked them why they were doing this, they replied: "Now is a good time to start a backyard garden." Returning in 2019, I saw a mixed picture. Some villagers had re-established their gardens next to the houses, some had moved them to other locations and some had turned to other garden projects while seeing what they had experienced regarding the home gardens as a test and an interesting learning process. The NGO had, in the meantime, moved onto the next phase of the project which focused on the cultivation and manufacturing of cacao. However, the main representative was still irritated about the fact that people in Dixon Reef had not continuously followed the 'rules of permaculture' which, in her view, made home gardening possible under any weather conditions.

4.2 Ontological Friction in Encounters

The case of the abandoned gardens illuminates two elements: first, prior to the workshops, representatives of the NGO and horticulturalists in the village had failed to explain their respective approaches to the practice of cultivation. Only after village participants had followed another path and ignored the promoted methods, did discussions arise. Second, my interlocutors living in the Dixon Reef area are open to new input and are keen to follow up such ideas, although not necessarily in the way anticipated by the representatives of the NGO. The NGO's approach to gardening was expressed through knowledge about permaculture and 'taking care of the ground' on the one hand and how Dixoners approach it by 'not forcing the ground' on the other. The case of the abandoned home gardens demonstrates the results of what I call 'ontological friction', which is at the same time a re-enactment in praxis (Jensen 2021) of approaches to gardening among my interlocutors.

What happened over the years was that both villagers and representatives of the NGO were gradually more irritated that things did not go the way they expected, or rather, that things were done in a way that seemed incomprehensible to them. Discussions came to a stop when villagers simply stated that they would continue in the way their bubu (ancestors) had told them, and they did not see any alternative. NGO representatives, visiting the village on a regular basis, gave up arguing, saying that people simply did not want to participate with the new methods learnt in the workshop. However, and I will continue to explicate this over the following pages, my understanding is that my interlocutors in and around Dixon Reef were in fact very willing to try out the new methods. However, they did this not in the linear way that was intended, instead using the techniques in other areas, for example, in the garden plots outside the village, and only after some months returning to their home gardens and starting them again. Although this is an example on the micro level, embedded in everyday lives of people living on the western coast of Malekula, these lives are embedded in universalised dialogues through climate change discourses (cf. Tsing 2005).

Climate change as a global topic is based on global interactions while being at the same time the cause of global interactions (Chapter 2). Anna Tsing made us aware that global interactions cause 'friction' between the actors involved, emphasising the unexpected and unstable aspects of global interaction (Tsing 2005). Through these interactions, something new is created, globalised discourses and practices are not localised, but the global is worked out locally (ibid., 2–4). Friction is hereby "the awkward, unequal, unstable, and creative qualities of interconnection across difference" (ibid., 3). The specific is always created by global interactions. I take on Tsing's thoughts, and additionally I follow the approach that "knowledge travels" (ibid., 8) as an idea (de Wit, Pascht and Haug 2018), the notion that through endeavours of different actors, knowledge is produced in different localities and thus is produced as a local topic at the same time as a process of world making (de la Cadena and Blaser 2018; Chapter 2).

Ever since climate change has been high on the list of international organisations' efforts, Vanuatu, as well as other countries in Melanesia, has been at the centre of efforts. Encounters of international, national and local actors in the development discourse show, for example, that different parties approach the matter differently (Sillitoe 2010; West 2006). Paige West explained why the Gimi in the Highland area of Papua New Guinea did not want to follow the conservation-as-development projects' plan to retain the status quo of their forests and livelihoods. What the Gimi expected through building a relationship with the actors of the conservation project was a permanent, future-oriented connection to what they expect to be offered them from the outside, what they refer to as 'development' (West 2006, 217–20). In her case study, West made clear that the various actors involved in the Highlands communicated on the basis of different assumptions. When the development project wanted to proceed in economic and thus material improvement, the Gimi saw development as a way of building relations with people outside their area (West 2006, 221). Taking this discussion into the era of climate change projects, political ecologist Sophie Pascoe considered a case for climate change mitigation of the REDD+ programme in the Milne Province in Papua New Guinea, describing how local people conceptualise the mitigation measure of carbon storage as 'stealing the air' – approaches to preservation were seen here as destruction (Pascoe 2021). Therefore, strategies of saving were perceived as destroying something essential for living in the forest. Pascoe also drew on Tsing's concept for "tracing the relations and frictions" in REDD+ projects (Pascoe 2018, 88) and to show how "ontological assumptions" influence these interactions (Pascoe 2021, 2). Her ethnographic example demonstrated that the actors of the mitigation programme used charts and explanations to define climate change based on climate science, and that their approach described climate change as acting in a linear causality and temporality. People in Suau, where her case study took place, would either say that they have another concept of climate change and its causes or explain that the experts do not explain it well enough for locals to understand. Although operating with specific concepts, a discussion about what people understand by these concepts, e.g. of land, air and conservation, was never given any room (Pascoe 2018; 2021).

I am adding here another perspective and framing from conservation projects in the Americas. Mario Blaser, who is also referred to in the analysis of development projects (cf. Meurer 2021; Pascoe 2021), has provided the impetus for considering such projects on an ontological level. He referred in his ethnographic study of the conflict between members of the Yshiro indigenous group, government representatives and representatives of the NGO in Northern Paraguay, to ontological differences between the actors. He explored the introduction of a new programme for commercial hunting to become more sustainable, by reducing the high amount of animal kills. However, the conflict between the different actors involved, according to Blaser, became obvious when it came to "conservation" (Blaser 2009, 12–13). The "hunting program had been based on a misunderstanding about how to achieve the sustainability of the animal population, albeit a particular kind of misunderstanding" (ibid., 10). The 'Yshiro conservation' in this case was not taken seriously. "But once it became clear that this translation was based on an equivocation, Yshiro conservation was seen either as a clever manipulation of culture or as being based on error" (ibid., 16). Blaser wrote that what really made the difference in these encounters was the existence of different environments, ontologically different worlds that meet, and he criticised the fact that these different environments are never raised for discussion, but are rather seen as a given for the respective parties (ibid., 15–16). The conflicts or misunderstandings which evolve when the different parties encounter each other are ontological ones relating to the meaning of conservation (Blaser 2009; 2013). However, Blaser not only described conflicts and misunderstandings, he also wrote that through these encounters, worlds "are brought into being" (Blaser 2009, 11; 2013), when people meet and interact with each other. Thus, these encounters enact the performance of the practices which again emerge through such performances. Ontological assumptions are not fixed entities, but they are continuously becoming, and are thus part of (or are) the making of worlds (de la Cadena and Blaser 2018, 5–6; see Chapter 2). Through interactions, and this is where I see a connection to Tsing's work, aspects of life come into being. I combine these different but related notions to the concept of ontological friction.[2] Frictions cause irritation but they also have the potential to create something new, and they do this through ontological quarrels. This is why I take the analytical concept of ontological friction as something that causes irritation and raises inequalities in projects, but also as something which brings into being moments of creating what is happening at the moment. The concept under quarrel in the case of the abandoned gardens of the village during the project is the praxis of mekem garen. In a similar way to the examples of encounters just explained, in the case of the abandoned house gardens described above, one important key concept was never discussed: what 'gardening' is for the NGOs and what it is for people in Dixon Reef. In other words, communication between all actors took place, leaving aside an important issue – the actors' approaches to gardening itself.

4.3 Everyday Knowledge and Knowing

Climate change projects are generally future-oriented, concentrating on anticipated challenges and their solutions in the form of adaptation. Studies by geographers for Vanuatu provide examples of how people are facing those anticipated challenges. By this they are referring to local practices as TEK, Traditional Ecological Knowledge (McCarter and Gavin 2014a), indigenous knowledge (Sillitoe 2010; Warrick 2021) or local knowledge systems (McNamara and Prasad 2013). They ask how these practices, knowledge or knowledge systems can be equipped for anticipated changes, or how they can be useful in times of change, though under the threat of being lost. Governmental measures and non-governmental projects in Vanuatu refer to this view and encourage people to use certain agricultural techniques and "standardizing global knowledge" (Tsing 2005, xx), which people can incorporate into their daily lives.

In general, NGOs in Vanuatu working in different villages repeatedly emphasised that many people were interested in and participated in their projects (be it climate change or other areas, e.g. hygiene). People were open to hearing something 'new'. Edward Hviding grounds this curiosity in the practice of the

---

2 The expression 'ontological friction' has been used so far only by a few scholars. Most do not define it at all (e.g. James and Steger 2016; Klenk and Meehan 2015; Miller 2016; Nightingale et al. 2020), while others relate it to Tsing's concept of 'friction' (e.g. Neurath 2018).

dual orientation of people in Oceania, both inward and outward. He describes this as follows:

> The typical approach taken by Pacific Islanders to the islands environment, then, is characterized on the one hand by detailed knowledge of and intense engagement with the land [...], and on the other by a fundamental outwards-looking view of the world as not confined to the home island but connected across the ocean with other natures and cultures. (Hviding 2003, 254–55)

In order to combat climate change, the aim of climate measures in Dixon Reef was both to preserve most of the current practices, including so-called 'traditional knowledge' (because the knowledge to which they refer is a practical knowledge for the cultivation and preservation of crops) and to add new techniques and thus expand people's repertoire. According to their programme goals in working communities like Dixon Reef, the NGO aimed to implement changes, framing these changes as an improvement in the knowledge of communities, which they defined as 'traditional agricultural methods'.

Other scholars theorised what they framed as people moving between the poles of 'traditional ecological knowledge' (McCarter and Gavin, 2014a, 2014b; McNamara and Prasad 2014), indigenous knowledge (Carter 2019; Sillitoe 2010) or local knowledge, encountering new knowledge from external sources.[3] Sillitoe describes development programmes in the highlands of Papua New Guinea as an approach of external actors based on their scientific knowledge, and this is certainly true for programmes in other parts of Melanesia: "[A]gencies assume that they have knowledge relevant to advancing development and that they know what comprises development." (Sillitoe 2010, 16) What people know on the ground is to be assumed to be a valuable asset to be combined with scientific knowledge (ibid., 26). What development discourse calls 'local knowledge' or 'indigenous knowledge', environmental approaches call 'traditional ecological knowledge', adding the ecological connotation. This is also present in measures for climate change adaptation. Ecologist Fikret Berkes defines Traditional Ecological Knowledge (TEK) as "a product of enduring links between humans and the environment" (Berkes 2012, 288).

---

3 Tradition itself is a contested term in the Pacific (Mallon 2010), it is further used in political and academic discourses in Vanuatu (cf. Regenvanu 2010) but now often replaced by the more flexible term kastom, which is used among ni-Vanuatu.

In Vanuatu, according to geographers McCarter and Gavin, this 'traditional ecological knowledge' also includes the 'methods of creating gardens' and 'botanical knowledge'. In their study, they found that ni-Vanuatu (including those in Dixon Reef) see a decline in 'traditional ecological knowledge' and therefore a change in lifestyle, but value such knowledge as necessary to secure their everyday lives (McCarter and Gavin 2014a; 2014b). Other geographical studies assume that the loss of 'traditional ecological knowledge' is seen as something that increasingly challenges ni-Vanuatu when facing climate change (McNamara and Prasad 2013; Warrick 2021). Loss of local knowledge practices are increasingly perceived as critical in political and some scholarly discourses, because they are seen as valuable for dealing with climate change risks. There, scientific knowledge and indigenous knowledge are juxtaposed, but the first is only aiming to influence the latter, giving indigenous communities the opportunity to complement what they 'already' know (Carter 2019; Field et al. 2014; Lebel 2013). All of these studies make a distinction between knowledge which exists at one location and knowledge which comes from outside, describing 'local' knowledge as something requiring preservation or complementation through new knowledge (McDonnell 2020).

Other scholars focus more on the procedural gathering of Oceanic knowledge (Mondragón 2014; Richmond and Sovacool 2012, 843–45; Warrick 2011; 2021). Describing the processes in Vanuatu as corresponding to traditional (ecological) knowledge or new (scientific) knowledge is to risk simplifying the lives of the ni-Vanuatu. Anthropologist Carlos Mondragón explained that to differentiate these two poles is indeed difficult, stating that the lives of people on the Torres Islands, the most northern islands of Vanuatu, are never purely local:

> Local knowledge in the Torres Islands, and indeed in most of Vanuatu today, is neither simply 'traditional' nor purely local, because for at least 150 years it has been defined in dialogue with various extra local actors, frames of reference and agendas. (Mondragón 2014, 4)

Mondragón argued for knowledge in Vanuatu to be understood as processual (ibid.), and therefore undergoing change. As Hviding wrote that knowledge practices are shaped by interacting with different 'environments', this would mean that people are used to encountering new ideas. This is part of their everyday practice.

Anthropologist Verena Keck referred to practice theory approaches in the introduction to 'Common Worlds and Single Lives: Constituting Knowledge in Pacific Societies' (1998), focusing on everyday practice and how such practices "continuously respond to new situations" and that people's knowledge is at the same time situated and performative (Keck 1998, 7). She defined this kind of knowledge as everyday knowledge, thus:

> 'Everyday knowledge' is less a conceptual kind of knowledge than a procedural knowledge connected to specific contexts. It is knowledge that is not only an understanding system but at the same time and in particular an acting system as well. (Keck 1998, 10)

In order to do justice to the procedural, as Mondragón also intended, Keck therefore spoke of "knowing" (ibid.).[4] I will follow this and regard 'knowing' or knowledge practices as performative acts that follow 'scripts' (Keck 1998), but which are produced in the doing. In this chapter, I will point to the processuality and flexibility in garden practice of my interlocutors around Dixon Reef, as part of knowing (Pascht 2019). At the same time, I consider, following Ingold (2000), environmental practices "by watching, listening feeling" (ibid., 99) – and by mekem garen.

Ontological friction is part of these 'knowledge practices' and I will show in the following sections that ontological friction arises here between what is understood by gardening – namely between what the NGO representative calls "caring for the ground" and what one of my interlocutors explained as "not forcing the ground". I will additionally show how Dixoners' approaches to their gardening are processual and are produced and re-produced through ontological frictions in encounters of people from inside and outside. This already starts with their learning how to mekem garen.

4 Keck also refers to Schank and Abelson (1977). Everyday knowledge is also practical knowledge. There is an everyday praxis which forms the 'script' of our everyday lives (Schank and Abelson 1977, 20, in Keck 1998, 9–10). As Hviding describes for people living at the Marovo Lagoon, knowing oneself is processual and must be connected to seeing and hearing (Hviding 1996, 369).

4.4 Learning Gardening

When I lived in Dixon Reef, I learned from my interlocutors how to plant and how to harvest. Although I was not able to do gardening on my own in the same way as the villagers, I was able to gain some insights through glimpses into my learning process and that of others. While I was learning how to handle a knife, how to plant bananas and all the other crops and working in gardens at the house and in the wider area along the coast and inland, I also learned together with children. Saturdays (and of course school holidays) marked moments when families went to 'the bush' together with every family member[5] and they devoted the whole day to gardening. Gardening was also carried out on week-days although adults had only a few working hours, because they had to take care of the school children both ends of the day. When leaving the village to conduct horticulture and visit the garden areas around the village, it meant walking and working in groups. These groups consisted of either nuclear families, individual family members or friends. Young men liked to break away from this habit and roam around alone (for detailed descriptions of a garden day, see Chapter 5). The younger children jumped behind the adults or teenage siblings, spent their days exploring the area or observing the work of others. When I, as an adult who had grown up in town without access to a garden, came to Dixon Reef and asked for a bush knife to carry along with me while I accompanied people to do their work, the reaction of the villagers was understandably sceptical. However, after some time, people expected me to not stand around, but also to work. Since there was little chance of conversation during the working part of the garden day, people rarely bothered to explain things to me.

When I was standing for the first time in the garden plot holding my knife and trying to do some weeding, I realised how challenging it is to hit the branches of the regrowing trees and small shrubs at the right angle so that they are cut down directly. Children are handed a knife at a very early age, accompanying their parents at the weekends and during school holidays.

5 This is true for both of the communities where Arno Pascht and I worked with community members. Since Sunday was the day for church, Saturday was the only day for the whole family (with the children) to achieve gardening work together and work the full day. On other days, couples would go alone or women accompany one other. The school children's holiday period made a welcome exception for all Dixons, young and old. Then they had the full day to take care of their cultivation.

They watch their parents pile up the organic material to make fire, digging out yam or offshoots from banana plants to plant somewhere else. When young Dixoners are about eight years old, they start to work their own gardening plots at the sides, trying out the methods observed. Parents would allow them to continue as they saw fit, judging the results only at the end. When I tried the same, I experienced people coming to see what I was doing and saying, especially my host parents: "Oh, you don't know it, this is wrong." They would then simply let me repeat my actions until I got it 'right'. I therefore tried my best to do what I thought was right. My working group would observe every step, dig and cut, jumping up when they thought something was going wrong. "No, you do not know how to do this, you do it like this" – the person would then take over and show me how to plant, first smaller food crops like manioc, corn and island cabbage, and soon bananas and yam, and then let me do it again. The next time, when I followed another group of women and I wanted to show off my newly acquired skills, my moves would be observed carefully and many comments made about my attempts: "Oh, so that's how you do it. Yes, that is possible." It was obvious that they themselves would do it quite differently, but they let me act in my own way. Kindly-worded indignation spread after some months when most thought that after all this time I must now know how to work the garden. The children were treated in the same way, always teasingly and never in a punitive tone.

There exist only a few detailed descriptions of different ways of planting or working the garden from anthropologists (Calandra 2017; Rio 2007b),[6] which show that gardening techniques differ from one location to the next, and names of planting methods refer to the place of origin. The Malekula style of planting yam tubers is well known on other islands (Calandra 2017), and when I stood in the garden with villagers from Siviri, they told me that what they do differs from what people in Malekula do. In this way, the people of Siviri emphasised that there are different ways of planting manioc, but that it should still be done in the 'right' way. When I planted yam with people around Dixon, they would say "This is how we do it here" and their method indeed resembled what other people would call the Malekula style, but they would also say that in the next village the ground is different, so yam is planted differently.

6 Geographers, biologists and others seem more concerned about plants, cultivation and food security in Vanuatu (cf. Allen 2015; Lebot and Siméoni 2015; Siméoni and Lebot 2012; Walter, Lebot and Sam 2007).

Talking to the few elder people in Dixon Reef about how they learnt their gardening techniques, they referred to the gardening practices up in the hills in the past and thus gave me some insights into gardening before 1950, before people moved down to the coast (see Chapter 1). Unfortunately, only a handful of them still know from first-hand experience how life was up in the mountains at that time. One of them, called 'Tambi with the three legs' because he was walking on a stick, referred to these time as "gardens were plenty, but people were not". However, families spent most of their time in the garden, since they had a lot of time to do so. Living in hamlets with a house for women and the men's house, couples met in their gardens and spent the day there, accompanied by their children.[7] In this way, children slowly learned by imitating their parents and by trying out techniques themselves. Agricultural methods in Melanesia, as everywhere in Oceania, are influenced both by different environments and different plants (Manner and Thaman 2013). However, it is also the case that there are similar plants to be found everywhere. Biologist and ethnographer Jaques Barrau, after visiting different sites in Melanesia at the beginning of the 20th century, wrote down that he learnt that people would undertake their gardening according to their environment, depending on whether they lived in the highlands of Papua New Guinea or the coastline of the Solomons. At the same time, they did their gardening at different spots around their hamlets. Cultivation was not limited to specific localities or plants (Barrau 1958; Weightman 1989). Barrau described for the beginning of the 20th century that agriculture in Melanesia has been under so many influences that neither origins of plants, nor the origins of agricultural methods can be traced back to a certain origin. For the Taro (Xanthosoma) plant he wrote the following:

> In New Caledonia, *Xanthosoma* is known as New Hebrides taro or as *tiwaka* taro after the district where it was introduced from the New Hebrides during the nineteenth century by the Catholic mission. In the New Hebrides, *Xanthosoma* is called Fiji taro […]. In Fiji, however, *Xanthosoma* is called *dalo ni tana*, which apparently means tanna taro, Tanna being a southern island of the New Hebrides. (Barrau 1958, 64)

This document would then refer to gardening in past times, to which interlocutors refer when they talk about their bubu (ancestors). The way in which

7 For past gardening and changing social life see also Chapter 6.

they conduct their horticulture, they say, is according to the ways of the bubu. Although they explain the learning of their gardening techniques by looking back, this learning in fact also includes the practice of always including something new into cultivation, by planting new species or crops or changing planting styles. In the same way, sources for learning for my interlocutors are oriented towards a whole range of sources and are influenced by copying what others do and teach, as well as by their individual practice within their practical learning surroundings.

When I asked the young people, who were accused of being on their mobile phones, where they learnt mekem garen, they mentioned school, where agriculture was part of the curricula, and they explained that they learnt how to grow vegetables and some root crops. Planting yam, on the other hand, all my interlocutors called a family business, because they had learnt it from their parents (or the people they spent most of their time with during their childhood and adolescence). Practices inside the yam garden plot are not often shared amongst larger groups (cf. Rio 2007b). Although today most of the rules are dropped or 'not respected' as some of the men told me, the yam garden marks an exception. How to plant yam stays with the family, or with the community, and people told the representatives of the NGOs that they would never change their methods of undertaking this task. I learnt the whole process of planting a yam garden when I started my own. With the help of our neighbours, some of the nasara chiefs and younger men for the climbing work on the larger trees, we cleared and burnt the vegetation before we planted the yam tubers.

Staff of NGOs as well as from the agriculture department promote and try to implement gardening without slash and burn, because they want the villagers to stop using fire due to its contribution to climate change. However, in conversations with us, these staff members complained because most villagers did not follow the recommendations and new methods of implementation. In most of the villages Arno Pascht and I visited over the course of our fieldwork, we heard people complaining about the implementation of gardening without slash and burn. Dixoners also had this discussion with the staff of the NGO. They assured them and us that preparing the ground for planting with the help of fire is the appropriate way to work. When I asked my garden companions about this, they mostly explained that it was ultimately a matter of preparing the soil. When the soil was good for planting, then the ground could be cleared and dead material left on the ground, similar to what the agriculture department refers to as 'mulching'. The elder people in particular told me that today people did not know the right way of planting yam, or did not show enough respect for the yam garden.

One of the men in Dixon Reef explained that, although he respected the way in which his father and mother taught him, he is discovering his own way of gardening himself.

> Compared to when I was young, at that time I just worked in the garden as it suited me. I didn't follow exactly what my parents taught me. After that, when you grow up and get married, you find out how 'mekem garen' works, you figure it out together.

When I asked him: "But now, do you follow the same style of mekem garen as your father and your mother?", he answered:

> Nowadays, now that we have climate change, ok today we are changing our style a bit, in the garden. For example, how we plant yam has changed. We used to scrape off the top layer of the soil. Then we planted. But nowadays we change that and all the dirt (organic material) just stays. That's what the [the NGO] people said, all the dirt just stays and it feeds the soil where we then plant the yam.

It does not seem to be the aim of the villagers to copy the gardening methods of parents or bubu (ancestors) exactly, or to follow any rules in a precise fashion. Younger people in particular repeatedly emphasised the different sources of learning – parents, school, friends and spouse. However, the decision is ultimately up to the individual, and as pointed out by my informant quoted above, it is through one's own practice, as well as one's own preferences and situational interaction with soil and plants, that mekem garen is a process to be apprehended. At this stage in my fieldwork, I could already discern from people's explanations a certain loss of what they knew before but when I accompanied people to their gardens, they did not focus on what had been 'lost' or 'not done' but rather on the fact that their approaches to gardening were characterised by experimentation, trial and error, of combining methods and by a constant drive for innovation. Moreover, once more it is not clear who introduced a certain technique or method – people from Dixon Reef or people from outside the village. Therefore, on the next pages, I will describe the current approaches and methods of gardening as I have come to know them in Dixon Reef. I explore them from two different perspectives, namely diversification and flexibility.

4.5 Moving Gardens and Plants

Diversification of crops and species was identified by Julie Sardos and colleagues as a strategy in Vanuatu horticulture both in the past and today (Sardos et al. 2016). Anette Reenberg et al. identified for people in the Solomon Islands that alteration in livelihood practices, also in agriculture, is a common practice, and people are used to it (Reenberg et al. 2008, 11). Diversification in agriculture, diversification in life and living conditions before and during difficult situations of disaster are also common in the Pacific (Hetzel and Pascht 2019; Le Dé et al. 2018). Diversification is also identified by geographers Reenberg et al. for securing livelihoods in the Pacific:

> Although the 'room for maneuver' for individual households varies (e.g. access to resources such as land and income opportunities), livelihood strategies components have generally become much more diverse. Hence, people have a wider range of options to rely on if hazards occur. The general conclusion is that people on Bellona have been able to alter their activities and become less vulnerable to external shocks in terms of changes in single components of their livelihood conditions—especially environmental but also economic. (Reenberg et al. 2008, 11)

Diversification in agriculture additionally happened over the last centuries through trade (Barrau 1958), European influences (Sardos et al. 2016) and globalisation (Campbell 2014). Cultivation of diverse crops and species is one way of maintaining food security:

> Numerous species of food crops containing several different varieties (or landraces) are planted in an intricately mixed and multi-layered arrangement. This provides protection against the epidemic spread of crop diseases and pests; a fuller utilization of solar radiation and soil nutrients; a phased harvest of different crops over several months, and the production of a variety of foods thus allowing a better diet. (Sardos et al. 2016, 733)

Without dismissing the importance of cultivating different species in one location (polycropping), what I call diversification also consists of the various other ways in which my interlocutors approach cultivation, especially the practice of planting in many different locations. One such method was to follow the sun to higher areas when water filled their garden plots, or to follow the water when other locations dried up. I will describe this by explaining the two procedures important to the work of my interlocutors: on the one hand, the planting of crops in more than one place, and on the other hand, the cultivation in one place of a variety of crops. I will also elaborate on how new types of plants are part of the approach to agriculture in Dixon Reef, as well as in Oceania.

4.5.1 Gardening in Different Locations

"Many garden plots are always better than one" is what people told me when I asked why they have different small garden plots around the garden area (and not, for example, simply one large garden). The garden area around Dixon Reef, and in many other places around Malekula, starts outside the village. This is the first aspect of diversification – my interlocutors cultivated crops in garden areas around different locations surrounding the village.

The first things I recognised when leaving the village were plantations with their huge coconut trees which were, besides cocoa trees, the only cash crops in the area, processed by hand into copra, and picked up by ships in a bi-monthly routine. In between the coconut trees, a few cattle could be seen grazing around the coconuts on the ground. Reaching the garden, one had to pass roads and thicker bushes. However, suddenly the area opened up into a widespread area where villagers had cut down smaller trees. Only the particularly large ones were left. We were standing in the sun, with no shade in sight. The sun shone on the various plants in their different shades of green; some climbing up, like the yam vines, some crawling on the ground, like pumpkin, and some standing up like manioc, corn or bananas. We reached the garden plots where villagers maintained their mixed gardens; everything was planted in one place, not separating root crops. "This is where we make our gardens", one member of the gardening group of that day, three women and myself, would say the first day I accompanied them, pointing in one direction. I looked and tried to figure out what she meant but only saw a huge area, a sea of different crops. It took me some months to recognise that one planting site merged with that of the neighbour, yet each person knew what each had planted, despite the lack of visible borders. One garden thus joined a whole area of gardens, with permeable boundaries for people to cross, or each community member, or visitors to see what the others were doing, but people took care to always cross with caution so as not to destroy anything.

Horticulturalists in the Dixon Reef area would conduct gardening in areas which formed a route to subsequent gardens, which were planted later. It was usually the case, so I have been told numerous times, that when the first person started their gardening in one area, the next person would follow shortly after. "They all run to the hill and want to make their gardens, after the area was cleared by a big fire", one woman laughed when explaining why a huge area on one of the mountain ranges had been cleared, first by a huge fire and second because people liked the open place and others followed behind. As a result, there were several huge areas where you could see one garden plot next to another. Up on the hill side, next to the river, along the road and in the swamp area, these multiple plots could be found. Not every area was used for cultivation at the same time, but they could rather be cultivated periodically. Since my interlocutors practised their gardening at the time in those areas further away from the village, my interlocutors had to walk long distances. As I will explicate in Chapter 5, it is time-consuming to walk such long distances and so the fact that Dixoners did not concentrate their time and labour in one place (such as home gardens for vegetables) but rather spent a lot of time moving from one garden to the next became a divergent topic of discussion between the NGO and participants in the workshops.

Figure 3: From left to right: Garden on the hill, at the riverside, along the road, in the swamp area

D. Hetzel

While discussions about the home gardens still continued in climate change projects, Dixoners decided against permanently working with the soil next to their houses, using soil preparation methods, as explained above. Instead, they walked long distances in order to decide where to transfer their crop seedlings according to weather and soil conditions. There are different words for what is referred to as graon in Bislama, or etene in Novol and Nasarian (soil), which describe how each piece of earth looks. One of the elder men told me that every soil type is good for something, e.g. emen demende (the Novol and Nasarian for marshland) for vegetables and manioc, while some such as etene meramp/merambe (the Novol and Nasarian for soil of bamboo) was not useful for planting but bamboo provided building material for houses.

The soil that surrounds the village's houses was not categorised as soil, since it is too sandy. For that reason, people call it etene emere suan in Novol, which would be translated as 'beach' in English. This soil was, like that where bamboo or coconut trees grow at the beach, not real soil in the eyes of my interlocuters, and thus not made for cultivation. In addition, the ground around the village, up the hills and along the coast has a different quality, as shown by the following explanation by one of the men in Dixon Reef:

> But only when there is no more water in the river, then you plant there. If you go to Langelip [name of a place], there the soil is good, that's real soil, it works well when there's too much sun. But as soon as it rains again, there is too much water and the crops are not good.

Soil and ground cannot be changed, and elder people in Dixon and in other Novol (or Nasarian) speaking areas on Malekula also refer to good soil/ground when they are looking for a good spot to start planting. Good soil/ground can absorb water and is also identified by its colour, which is why it is called etene rup (the Novol and Nasarian for black soil) or etene miele (the Novoland Nasarian for red soil). The quotation above shows that depending on which soil is appropriate at any given moment, it makes sense to look for the soil for the plants depending on the weather conditions. Mekem garen is thus also a matter of choosing which soil is the best at a particular moment.

Walter, Lebot and Sam differentiate between various kinds of gardens in Vanuatu, such as ones with dry land, where people are burning the vegetation, and others with irrigation, as well as many more. Having different styles of garden is a practice common to ni-Vanuatu on different islands (Walter, Lebot and Sam 2007, 34). Barrau describes Melanesian gardens in the 1950s as huge areas where people had their garden plots, most of them in one area (1958), where they planted food crops in large areas as monoculture, but that they were always interested in supplementing their diet with other vegetables and legumes. These multiple gardens are something which can be found several places in Vanuatu. Maëlle Calandra writes very detailed descriptions of different kinds of gardens and I refer to her research for descriptions of such cultivation gardens, where various plants are grown all year around, so that gardeners are also able to harvest all year round (Calandra 2017, 114). In Siviri, villagers maintained gardens all over the island of Efate, depending on access and where food crops might grow well. The same is true for the gardening praxis of the people around Dixon Reef. All are part of a wider praxis of Melanesian horticulture. In Dixon Reef, people have many garden plots, which they name by associating the cultivated plants with the word garden: the banana garden (Bislama: garen blong banana; Novol/Nasarian: alenge malele), the manioc garden (Bislama: garen blong manioc; Novol/Nasarian: alenge manioc), the yam garden (Bislama: garen blong yam; Novol/Nasarian: alenge etene) and the vegetable garden (Bislama: garen blo ol legume; no equivalent in Novol/Nasarian). People would use these names to identify the first crops planted there, despite the plots ultimately including several species of plants, bananas next to taro and crops like tomato, corn etc. in between – as a result, they are mostly "mixed gardens" (Walter, Lebot and Sam 2007, 34).

Families have several of these gardens, which are located in different areas along the coast, up the hill or in the direction of the next village. These gardening sites are equally distributed throughout the area and bear the names of the sites: Garden on the Mountain, Garden by the River, or more specifically the names of the areas, as named in the Nasarian language, Garden in Langelip (water runs underneath), Garden Wetmur (stones had fallen down), which gives an indication on the soil composition. The number of garden sites one family called their own at the time of my research could be considerable. In my census of the villagers (and all the relatives that were present at this time), I recorded the number of gardens in a household.[8] In the census of January 2017, I let people count their gardens, with each household reporting between 10 and 18 gardens (some also counted the backyard garden). Among these were the yam gardens as the prototype of all gardens, with several divided among the individual family members. Numbers of gardens were not only high because of

8 I define a household as people sharing one kitchen house, which centres around the woman who calls this kitchen hers.

subsequent cultivation over the areas, according to fallow rules of shifting cultivations, but also due to planting in different areas at the same time.

I naïvely asked women and men around Dixon Reef why it was so important to have different gardens, and received a wide variety of answers. One example shows what people mean by having several gardens. Dixoners explained to me that the dry period in 2015 and 2016 meant that they had been forced by circumstances to react and move gardens from one place to another. At that time, banana gardens were located in the higher areas. Bananas supply food all year round, so people expressed their concern when banana trees were not carrying as much fruit as the year before. "The banana shoots had not grown, there were hardly any banana fruits", one villager explained. As a consequence, they moved the gardens to the area next to the river bed, which is usually flooded, and at that time, the soil still stored some moisture. One day, during my daily evening rounds through the kitchen houses, I became caught up in a discussion with one couple about soil and gardening conditions over the past few years. The couple explained how new information became part of their planning for new cultivation areas:

> N: When there is a lot of rain [La Niña], everyone says we should plant on the mountain. Plant your bananas on the mountain, we shouldn't plant on the plain, otherwise the water will destroy everything.
> D: And is that what you did?
> N: Yes, many people did that, and now taro is also being planted on the mountain.
> D: But I have heard that they are mainly cultivated there because there was a fire [which makes the area accessible], or did you do it because a lot of rain was predicted?
> N: We heard about the rain. [His wife intervened:] And then the fire, good for us, that made it easier.

With this they also hinted at the at the ambivalence of further human action, where some fires also exposed more cultivation areas, even though this also meant losing trees and bush areas. Nevertheless, it underlines that strategies of following the water were well known among all villagers. "This is where I plant my vegetables at the moment, because the river is dried up", one of the women explained as she pointed to the dry river bed where she had planted some cabbage and salad. Some weeks during the dry period from May until August, the riverbed had not held any water, the ground broke up, but still underneath the first lighter layer, plants found enough water to grow. "This is because the route of the river still runs underneath the ground", she explained. A few metres further, some other women grew their vegetable gardens right on the shore of the river. At that point, this method still worked, but when the dry time reached its peak, every vegetable garden owner moved into the riverbed.

Women and men would return to their garden plots when they considered it to be the appropriate time to return, either after a fallow time or when the weather conditions were right. They also would refer to the workshops which suggested that this was one strategy to follow. With changing weather conditions, they were told to move up the hill when it was raining too heavily (a period referred to as La Niña) and they were encouraged to return to the plains, closer to the coast, when there had been no rain for a long time. Dixoners insisted that to maintain many gardens was a better strategy than just having one and thus they also used the strategies of the adaptation workshops. What differed was that most of the gardens were grown in several places at the same time, i.e. simultaneously to one another.

Since I wanted to know whether vegetables had been planted in the past, I asked around: "Did your mother have a vegetable garden?". "Yes of course, she planted vegetables." Island cabbage formed an important supplement to the root crops, being part of one of the easy laplap[9] dishes, and over the years other vegetables like cabbage or tomatoes have become very popular. Nowadays vegetables have become even more important in the minds of islanders, largely because of external workshops, which talked about nutrition. Most of the workshops I was aware of combined methods for agriculture with the question of what is best to be cultivated in order to stay healthy. Since the large volume of consumption of imported rice is seen as a growing health problem in Vanuatu, especially in the urban area (Wentworth 2017), NGOs are keen to prevent this in the rural areas. In workshops, the three-kind rule for nutrition was always propagated, which aims to combine nourishment of vitamins with protein sources and starches. Having a vegetable garden was very popular among the women. The more vegetables they had to harvest, the happier they were. They planted various kinds of cabbages, peppers, tomatoes, onions and watermelons alongside island cabbage.

9 A salty, cake-like dish baked in an earth oven, "baked in a fire and transformed into an edible form" (Bolton 2001: 264; cf. Lebot et al. 2015).

4.5.2 Locating Different Plants in one Garden

Monoculture, like other places in the Pacific (Manner and Thaman 2013), is not prevalent around Dixon Reef, except for some areas where people cultivate cash crops like kava (piper methysticum) and peanuts (arachis hypogaea). Many people on the islands have recently become interested in planting kava, since prices across Vanuatu rose during 2018 and 2019 and demand for kava for after-work consumption on the main island of Efate and especially Port Vila continued to rise steadily.

Since on this side of the island of Malekula, access to reliable transport is not easy, people in Dixon mostly follow polycropping methods for their own use. Manner and Thaman point out that horticulture in the Pacific is characterised by constant disintensification, towards the singling out of diversity in order to have less work and only a few crops to care for (Manner and Thaman 2013, 346; Allen 2015). People in the area around Dixon Reef plant different varieties of yam, which they distinguish into the categories of 'yam' and 'round yam'. Round yam is planted by breaking up the soil and pushing the tuber underneath. For all other kinds of yam, which have an elongated shape, a particular sequence of techniques is required to plant it. In the literature, this kind of planting technique is also called the Malekula style of planting (Calandra 2017, 169–71). Dixoners equally complained about losing multiple cultivars of the yam crops. By referring to the bubu (ancestors) and their continuous work of planting yam regularly, they also praised the diversity of yam, some cultivars of which the current residents of Dixon only knew from stories. However, although the number of cultivars of one crop has reduced, the planting of different kinds of plants in their garden plots was still highly valued. In general, the cultivars planted today are those which require less attention. Men and women who still managed to grow different yam in the yam garden, different cultivars of bananas in one place and different types of vegetables in the vegetable garden were admired by their neighbours and other gardeners.

When the yam planting season started, Arno Pascht and I were both in Dixon Reef. We decided to plant our own yam garden after detailed discussions with the villagers. They provided us with an area to work on, surrounded by other new yam gardens. Yam is the first crop to be planted in the new cycle of the garden year, right after klinim (cleaning) and bonem (to burn), there comes the planem of the yam tuber. After we had gone through the first steps of clearing and burning (for detailed description see Calandra 2017, 166), we set about putting the first yam tubers in the ground in one day. Island cabbage[10] had already been planted, accompanied by a 'togai' talk that would protect the yam garden. One of the elder men had given us an old yam tuber as planting material, a yam whose leaves should be red. On the day of planting, all the helpers gathered in our garden and were thrilled that we had such a beautiful yam plant, suggesting that we plant it in the middle of the garden. "Oh, how lucky you are to have got this yam. I hope he will give it to me one day", remarked one participant. More men passed and discussed our planting, also bringing different varieties of yam as planting material, which they were happy to share with us.

Figure 4: Yam garden with polycropping of yam, taro and maize

D. Hetzel

One afternoon, I went with Augustina, her brothers and her brother's wife to plant a yam garden for her mother. She was going away to work in the southeast of Malekula, taking care of another family, and thus missed the start of the planting cycle. Yam tubers had to be planted from October to the beginning of December, and when people were not present to start new parcels, they gave this task to their next of kin. The group sent me straight away

10 Abelmoschus manihot

to sow maize grains between the yam, because maize and yam are supposed to be planted at the same time. The men loosened the soil with the digging stick, dug the holes with the help of their spades and planted the yam. The women helped and, in the meantime, distributed more seeds and seedlings between the heaped-up planting sites. The result was a round area with evenly-distributed yam vines, and in between, maize, taro and island cabbage. All of the gardeners present that day had attended the adaptation workshops and discussed the programme, and then Augustina explained why polycropping is particularly important:

> Now we do it a bit differently, since [the project coordinator] showed us that you should plant mixed. You plant different things, now it's not like before. Because when the sun is strong now, you plant everything together to help, protect and nourish the soil. So that your garden bears well. As soon as I plant all the (yam), I make tanna soup in the garden.

By referring to tanna soup,[11] she emphasised the importance of mixed cultivation. Furthermore, she emphasised that this practice has changed since workshops have been in place, and thus showed a positive reaction to these ideas. This does not mean that mixed cultivation was not a practice before. Like in other places in Vanuatu (Calandra 2017) and Malekula (Walter, Lebot and Sam 2007), diversification of this kind is an important part of any kind of gardening. When passing the different yam gardens, the leaves of the yam vines were clearly visible. At the same time, the maize would be ready to be harvested, and the ripe yellow and reddish maize cobs would tower over the growing leaves of the taro plants, which usually took a little longer to grow than the yam tubers, and therefore received post-yam banana plants as neighbours.

As scientific climate change projections predict longer periods of drought, yam harvesting is also being considered within the programme. A reduced harvest of yam crops because of, for example, a cyclone destroying the yam plants, would lead to less yam being available as planting material for the next planting season. People were advised by the NGO to multiply in this case the planting material for the next period through the Yam Nursery method (called yam

---

11 Tanna Soup is a dish from one of the southern islands of Vanuatu, Tanna. Leftovers from the previous days are processed into a kind of soup, which is characterised by a mix of vegetables, pulses and root crops.

minisett).[12] Agnes, an experienced horticulturalist, tried to multiply her yam tubers by cutting them in her garden. She explained in detail how the yam nursery worked. When I asked Agnes whether she saw this as an option for her gardening in the future, she replied: "Now I have seen that my yam grows so well too. But when I see that I am losing too much yam, I have to apply what we learned in the workshop. That is good." People were able to explain in detail what they had learned from whom, but in the end, they also emphasised repeatedly that they had used this knowledge to work out their own procedure in their own garden. "Mi tan tanem little bit" (I change things a little) was the comment I heard the most. Some of the elder people explained a technique whereby they only planted the yam after clearing the place, burning the vegetation and carefully clearing the ground of any leaves and branches. This method was supposed to make the space clean. Passing the yam garden plots and asking around, people explained that they would not follow this practice at the moment. The slash and burn method was, however, widely practiced and was also a point of discussion between the villagers and staff of the NGO, because the latter wanted to stop the burning of organic material all over Vanuatu. People around Dixon Reef continued, but did not burn everything and some leaves were left on the ground. However, ultimately, it was a very individual practice.

4.6 Gardening in Transformation

Sardos et al. have pointed out that horticultural practices in Vanuatu are flexible and always incorporate change, both through different crops and through different gardens. They have called this "[t]he idea of continuity through change and novelty" (Sardos et al. 2016, 734). This is also expressed through being flexible and diversifying plants and places of cultivation. It is a common praxis in Vanuatu to involve changes in gardening methods. Gardening is a practice whose 'tradition' is to renew itself again and again (ibid.). When looking at mekem garen, I learned that women and men in Dixon Reef use the methods received from their bubu (ancestors) as well as those they allocate to other sources, including the various workshops (not only that of the NGO)

12 For the yam minisett, yam tubers are cut into small pieces and pre-grown in a nursery until they are large enough to be moved to the eventual garden site. This technique is used not only in the Pacific region but also in several African countries in order to make enough planting material at times of scarce harvest.

in their gardens. Change and flexibility were common for my interlocutors, and the reference to the bubu gave this legitimacy to continue. Malekula gardening is characterised by the flexibility of changing locations and cultivation methods. When problems arose, such as a lack of rain and thus a shortage of water, the most important strategy was to change the location of gardens. The women moved their vegetable plants along the riverbed or into the riverbed so that cabbage and tomatoes had access to water. Constant cultivation of the soil is only envisaged in this sense when plants were mixed in the yam garden.

Learning cultivation meant for Dixoners to imitate others, passing various gardens (including yam gardens)[13] and thus seeing the work of others, and developing their own techniques by experimentation. When I asked what to do in the garden, people told me that they had their own style of gardening, based on what their parents had told them, what was agreed in the workshops, what was tried out by imitating others and through experimentation. New gardening techniques were added and integrated into the existing network, and some were temporarily introduced. People were open to trying methods introduced in the workshops. However, they would still refer such learning to its source, and did not call this their own method. There is more than one way to approach the gardener and more than one way to practise mekem garen. It became itself a practice of transformation in itself.

The case of the abandoned home gardens, which I presented at the beginning of this chapter, illustrates quite well that women and men around Dixon Reef never refused any 'new' methods, because of their striving for diversification and retaining many options. I have written elsewhere, together with Arno Pascht, that similar strategies have taken place in Siviri, on the main island of Efate, where people strive to include gardening as just one option for their livelihood. In this article, we showed that all of these livelihood strategies undergo constant diversification (Hetzel and Pascht 2019).

People in Dixon Reef who were involved in the project discussed approaches to gardening and the fact that the work of villagers was not continuous. They started working on their small home gardens, using all available methods of soil preparation through kitchen compost, nitrogen fertilisation, etc. as well as minimal irrigation through grey water from the kitchen house.

---

13 Before, people told me, it would not be possible to visit other people's yam garden plots because they were tabu for members of other lineage groups to enter. Since gardens are now sometimes placed on the road on the way to their own plot, gardening has become visible for everyone.

In stating that they cannot force the soil to do something it does not 'want' to do, they explained one practice of mekem garen, which is characterised by diversification – on the one hand the practice of growing crops in different places and on the other hand cultivating different species and varieties of crops in one place, by finding the appropriate spot at the appropriate time.

Horticulturalists in the Dixon Reef area were happy to learn something new in the climate change workshops, because this means expanding their repertoire of gardening methods and techniques. People were interested in the new aspects of gardening demonstrated in the workshops and applied some of these methods in their individual garden techniques. This is in line with their praxis of learning gardening, because learning mekem garen is about combining all sources available. This is highly valued by people, and furthermore is seen as a necessity to approach good gardening. This praxis of introducing new plants, species and cultivars in Melanesia and Vanuatu is something others have observed as well, today and in the past (Barrau 1958; Lebot and Siméoni 2015, 840; Walter, Lebot and Sam 2007). Lebot and Siméoni have made it clear that communities planting different species are better prepared for environmental change than others, and that it is common praxis in those communities to keep the number of species high (Lebot 1992; Lebot and Siméoni 2015, 839). Diversification has been practised for decades. Calandra describes in her historical sketch how permeable gardening was in Vanuatu over the centuries through various connections to traders, missionaries and seafarers (Calandra 2017, 127–42). However, diversification not only refers to the multiplication of plants, but also to the diversity of methods, the practice of gardening in different places and the constant search for new methods, which also includes flexibility to combine or change methods or to use them only temporarily.

As I have tried to sketch out above, people used new practices but did not follow them in a linear way. Indeed, new techniques, which people are very interested to learn, were applied and reused in their own way. It would be too simple, however, to conclude that people did not feel like doing what they had been 'taught'. People's interest not only shows at the beginning of the encounter with new practices, but also in the fact that aspects are taken up again, for example, when the women started to replant gardens the following year, at other locations and in their own ways. During the drought after the cyclone, villagers were not interested in continuing their work exactly as before, but rather recommenced certain aspects which fitted in with the conditions they found in their gardens. However, the representatives of NGOs had trouble understanding why this would happen, because they were teaching villagers to use mulching, grey water irrigation and other methods for changes in agriculture that they believed would have resulted in a radical change of cultivation in the future.

In addition to gardening and in order to obtain the necessary money to buy supplementary food, Dixoners spent a considerable amount of time in the plantations in order to harvest coconuts, remove the flesh from the shell and dry it in order to obtain copra, which is then sold to regularly-visiting copra buyers. Another important cash activity is the production of cocoa, which is even more labour-intensive. With very few exceptions, inhabitants of Dixon Reef did not plant kava themselves, but imported it mainly from the Southwest Bay region of Malekula. However, during 2019 a group of people set out for a place further inland where they stayed for some days and planted large amounts of kava. This is, we were told, because the price of kava had risen considerably during the previous couple of years (Hetzel and Pascht 2019).

4.7 Conclusion

Over the time of one garden cycle from the first planting of yam to its harvest, I learned the approaches of cultivating a garden and to follow the principle of diversification of plants and locations across a variety of aspects of gardening. When my interlocutors in Dixon Reef are expanding their repertoire of gardening through the adoption of new techniques, they spread their energy rather than concentrating it on one place or one piece of work. This resulted in moving crops and plants, and moving between different locations. At first interpretation, their approaches to the cultivation of crops and to working in changing circumstances differed from the expectations of those leading the NGO programmes. In the case of the abandoned gardens, these different approaches become a matter of caring for the soil in terms of permaculture and caring as a matter of taking crops to letting the soil show what the needs are, rather than forcing it. People involved in the adaptation programmes did not agree with one another when it came to gardening next to the houses. The important aspect was that the involved parties never had a conversation about approaching gardening itself and how villagers actually do what they call 'gardening'. How gardening is conducted only becomes apparent in the current praxis of people around Dixon Reef. Villagers decided on methods according to circumstances, which could be referred to as 'scripts' that are reworked in praxis (Keck 1998).

Gardening is, at the same time, interaction with what is there, as it is permanently confronted with something new, therefore it has to be flexible.

The background of these events and the frictions between my fellow gardeners and the representatives of the NGOs showed the ontological differences about how to undertake gardening. I have described these differences as ontological friction. While villagers stated that they could not continue working at their home gardens because they could not force the ground or the soil, the staff member of the NGO was convinced that home gardens were possible under all circumstances. However, by seeing this as ontological friction, combining Tsing's emphasis on the creative forces of 'friction' with the ontological approach of Blaser that minds encounters in projects as precisely creating these frictions, I have tried to show that these frictions in adaptation projects have in fact also created something new, aside from the original intentions of the parties concerned. Thereby this also initiated reflections on one's own of practices of gardeners and brought up a new practice fit for the challenges of the Anthropocene. The openness of constant striving to transform practices also integrated this into what Dixoners practise as their own way of gardening.

I have shown how diversifying the gardening practice of women and men in the Dixon Reef area does in fact mean that people continue to do what their bubu (ancestors) did, but often in combination with different sources. This is an important aspect of the praxis of mekem garen in the Dixon Reef area and also in Siviri on Efate. Different approaches to gardening had contributed to disagreement, but also to the use diverse knowing of mekem garen. It is not my intention to judge whether the project worked, or whether villagers learned new techniques for dealing with changes in agriculture. What I have demonstrated is that people in Dixon Reef worked out a praxis based on trying out past instructions, experience and new techniques. Mekem garen is a practice of innovation and diversification, which was continued by people, and that the workshop played an integral part in this. With this, I want to move beyond the dichotomous framing of traditional and modern approaches to gardening. These dichotomies do not do justice to the movements and the changes that are being driven forward. The encounters of people in the workshops and the emerging ontological friction created new gardening techniques and, in a way, all the aspects of the mekem garen that took place afterwards. People in Dixon Reef did not continue the practices they 'learnt' in the workshops, but they developed them further in performing their gardening. In the next chapter, this movement of plants and people will be described further and I intend to show how this therefore becomes a practice of making the environment.

5 Gardening in Motion

An important aspect I learnt about mekem garen in Vanuatu was that of people walking to the bush and moving gardens to other locations, due to weather, seasons and individual preferences. When horticulturalists around Dixon Reef decided to restrict the use of their home gardens during El Niño, they followed the water and the sun and relocated their gardens. Until now, I have only mentioned in passing that, the work of cultivation takes place over several years and in several locations.

Only in the bush, my interlocutors explained, does the real gardening take place and that is where you would find the numerous gardens that were continually planted and replanted. During the time of El Niño, villagers left their small home gardens behind and walked several kilometres to plant, weed and harvest a wide variety of food crops. These gardens were located at quite a distance from one another, so that the amount of walking during a day would be considerable. Before the arrival of missionaries on Malekula island, people kept gardens away from the house, and although they were not far away, the gardens were always separated from the gardeners. When I talked to older people, they described gardens as being meeting places for the married couple, because in the village they had stayed in the women's or the men's house. After people came down to Dixon Reef at the western shore of the island and planted coconut and cocoa plantations around the village, gardens had to be moved further away. My interlocuters defined leaving the village as going to 'work'. Even if women stayed around their house, cleaning inside, sweeping outside, washing the dishes, doing the laundry and cooking meals for the children, they would tell me in the afternoon that they had not done any gardening the whole day, and thus would feel that they had not really been productive. Men would be referred to as not manly enough if they hung around the village all day. Ultimately, only church community work, taking care of younger children or an illness would be a valid reason to stay at home. When I stayed close to the house all day to write, people would see it as proof that I needed to rest. People often told me that they felt energetic and strong after a long day in the garden, having walked for hours and would only 'kam bak lo tu dark' (come back when it was already dark) even though it was not always yet dark on their return. After a day working in the gardens, the women especially met in the kitchen and chatted about their day's work. They talked about which gardens they had visited, which routes they took, what they had seen in the gardens of others, how far some crops had grown or whether an area was flooded or dry. Villagers then exchanged information about crops and about the surroundings and how the road, neighbouring gardens, trees and the whole area looked at that point in time. No garden stands alone, because neighbouring gardens are close and so other gardens and important landmarks are passed en route.

By focusing on practice, including walking (Lee and Ingold 2007), I will show in this chapter that gardening or mekem garen in Dixon Reef is a process of movement rather than a single activity taking place in one fixed location. Including literature on the concept of place (Cresswell 2014) and the concept of ples (place) in Vanuatu, which advocates for an understanding of places not as fixed but as dynamic and relational (Bolton 1999; Hess 2009; Rodman 1992), I will then depict how people in Dixon Reef render their gardens and their environment as interaction in motion, seeing them as 'taskscape' (Ingold 1993), since activities drive interaction between people and their surroundings, and 'wayfaring' (Ingold 2007) as an intentional form of navigation through the world.

5.1 On a Garden Day

In the morning, the women started their walk at the house in the middle of the village. Four women, two children, equipped with knives and with long fabric, a calico with flower pattern, wrapped around the hips. Every group member was wearing work clothes, the women a skirt with shorts underneath and a shirt dirty from past work in the garden, some with holes from too much sweat, sun and saltwater. They stood relaxed on the path and waited for me, the houses of my host family being half way out of the village. Martine and Emma, the two 'mamas', smiled, ready and happy to get to work for yet another garden day. I rushed to join the group, because they would probably just head on if they had to wait too long. Then, we slowly started walking on the dirt road which led out of the village. "Where are we going today?" I asked. "We go to our gardens on the side of the hill because we want to harvest some manioc for laplap this afternoon." I knew this area, one hillside that was covered with manioc plants. I also knew the route to get there; I could even find it on rainy days. A short 30-minute walk led across the coconut and cacao plantation and through a creek filled with water taro. With this plan in mind, I joined the walk of the women. It was a hot, sunny day, although it was a little before 8 o'clock, and my body felt sticky and I smelled of sunscreen and mosquito repellent. When we reached the last group of houses at the entrance of the village, Emma entered the yard. She approached the tree and picked some ripe Navel nuts and told us that she wanted to harvest some. After only a few minutes' walk, this was our first stopover of the day. Josephine, who lived in these houses, left her cooking behind when she heard where we were heading and quickly asked my group to bring some manioc for her as well. Some men passed and short questions about the journey were exchanged: "Where are you going?" "Ah, just walking and looking for the gardens." I watched as these men passed and went along the big road, which led to the gardens for bananas. Later, one of the men told me that they had visited five different gardens, went up the hill and to the swamp and took a small detour to look at the cattle. Then, my working group continued the walk following the so-called small road, and we crossed the plantation with its huge coconut trees and walked under the smaller cocoa trees, always walking behind each other in a line because the paths were so narrow. Once we had left the last house behind us, our walk became faster. When we had started, group members had been very chatty, while we had been collecting the nuts, we exchanged some village news, but once outside the village, our steps became faster, and we silently and with concentration walked through the landscape. Now, the members of my working group became focused – we had started the gardening day. Once we came to a fork, leading up to the hill or following the plain, Emma called from the back of the line that she wanted to make a quick detour to one of her gardens, because she had just remembered that she wanted to pick some of her island cabbage and she would meet us later on. She disappeared in the direction of the river and Martine quickly called after her to remind her to look for some spring onions as well. We then reached the bottom of the hill. At this point, we had to cross stagnant water: "Look at my water taros, they look really good." Martine pointed her knife at the heart-shaped leaves of the taro plant. I waded through the water, trying not to get stuck or to lose a shoe from my hands, or my knife, or my clothes. The others checked the tubers as they passed. We were at the foot of the hill and the tree-covered area of the plantation opened up.

The big fire one year before had left a kilometre-wide area without trees and shrubs, and the soil might have been enriched by the ash, making it suitable for planting crops. The next year, families did not hesitate to distribute spots and started planting mostly manioc. We were now standing at one of these sites. I looked up and directly into the sun. Looking uphill, one could see one manioc plant next to another, reaching over my head. It was a hot day, one on which you want to hide in the shade. We climbed up, the others not slowing their pace. The women and children in front of me, light-footed, leapt up the mountain, weaving their way between the plants. At one point, I got lost between the manioc plants. "This is not the path" – I was walking a zigzag course, but apparently took a wrong turn somewhere. "So where is this path?" I looked around me, and down, and up again – everything I saw looked like red soil with manioc plants. "It's here" – a little annoyed, one of the girls pointed at a gap between the plants. I still did not see any path but followed the way she pointed. "How can you tell this is the path?" I asked. With an irritated expression, she explained: "Because they [other people in the village] walked here before, one can see it." It would take me some months before I could see what she meant and actually recognise the different paths.

When we reached the halfway point, we spread out among the plants and without hesitating, the working group went straight to work. In order to remove the manioc tuber, they used their machetes as a digging stick, as a shovel and as an actual cutting instrument. Meanwhile our missing group member Emma returned and brought island cabbage and spring onions, but only stopped for a short progress check and was off again a hundred metres higher to plants she had planted. We took a break from the digging and cutting and walked down again to the shady place underneath the trees to drink our coconut. While we were resting, some women cut several ropes and found sticks to make extra material for transport. It was already foreseeable at this point that we would have a very bountiful harvest. And it was indeed: heaps of manioc! We wrapped them into our patterned fabric calicos, swung the bundles on our backs and tied the ends of the cloth together in front of our chests. On other occasions, I had seen men carrying crops on a stick over their shoulders, but women would take the harvest in the same way they would carry their children.

This was surely not the end of our garden day. When we returned to the junction, a crossing between different roads leading to the village of Blacksand and the gardens further away, which we had passed before, we lowered our spoils back to the ground so that we could take a quick detour. We went in the other direction, further along the coast, and checked on some more gardens for vegetables and bananas. In one, we collected the leaves for the laplap dish in the evening, the women cut the leaves and then split the ends of the stems and rolled up the leaves. The small bundles were evenly distributed among all group members, so that every woman had enough for baking their individual laplaps. In another garden down the road, we checked vegetables for a salad; when wandering through the vegetable gardens at the dried-up river bench, the women bent down, plucking out a creeping grass or taking their knives to clean the pineapples from overgrowing leaves. When we came back to the road, we met another working group: "Where are you coming from?" – they had just returned from the banana garden. Information about the neighbouring plots and the ones they saw on the way were exchanged, some of which also belonged to Emma and Martine. They reached down to cut some bananas and handed a bundle to me. In the end, when we returned to our manioc harvest, it was much too heavy for me to carry, in contrast to my companions, who carried their bundles effortlessly on their backs. The closer we got to the village, the more words were exchanged about the successful working day.

Back in the village, we again passed at Josephine's yard and delivered the 'orders of the day', before stopping at my family's house to distribute the yield. Martine, Emma and the others headed on, with some more stopovers at relatives' houses, finally heading to their own kitchens. Returning in the afternoon, sweaty and dirty from the physical work, the women would immediately start their cooking, before even taking a shower. Men went for kava and to tell the stories of the day: "Where did you go today and what did you do today?" Routes were discussed, among other exchanges of political news. After a 'garden day' the women also met in the kitchen and chatted about their day's work. They talked about which gardens they had visited, which routes they took, what they had seen in the gardens of others, how far some crops had grown or whether an area was flooded or dry. Villagers then exchanged information about crops and about the surroundings and how the road, neighbouring gardens, trees and the whole area looked at that point in time.

5.2 Gardens out of Place

The experiences of a typical garden day described above show several aspects to which I will attend in this chapter. When starting their walk, the women expressed what they wished to do during the day, however, the actual implementation of this plan changed during the activity, as did the plan itself due to either the status of crops, the roads or the weather. Work within the gardens was one part of achieving the garden day, but what happened in between was just as relevant for the wider process of gardening. Plans of where to go changed according to what happened on the road and due to the movements of people through the environment. From an early age, Dixoners learn how to navigate through their environment. The paths, invisible to the untrained eye, are made by traces of human interaction with the ground. Paths lead to the gardens, but, as I will explain on the following pages, neither the paths nor the gardens themselves are static and bound to one location.

There are several detailed descriptions of what happens *in* the gardens of Vanuatu – about what is planted, how it is planted and which rules are to be followed in order to make crops grow (Barrau 1958; Calandra 2017; Gundert-Hock 1984; Rio 2007b; Walter, Lebot and Sam 2007; Weightman 1989). Similarly, in the previous chapter, I have described how diversification of planting and constant innovation is part of the praxis of gardening. However, a large part of the garden day for people in Dixon Reef does not actually happen in the garden, but in the movement between the gardens. This means that, although it is important to see what happens in the garden plot, the process of gardening was achieved both at the location of the garden *and* through the movement to, from and between gardens. Once they arrived in a garden plot, people started planting, weeding and harvesting, working on their own – and communication was reduced to a minimum. Additionally, although the group would stay together for a longer time in one place, one person would often leave the group to have a quick look at another garden plot, or head home earlier. During this time, they picked up planting material or crops, or exchanged some of the yield. Gardening thus comprises largely being on the move through the network of gardens as much as working in one spot. Therefore, in the following paragraphs I want to engage with the garden as place, in order to understand what it means for ni-Vanuatu horticulturalists.

The gardening areas outside of the village consist of several bigger or smaller garden plots that merge into one another. Everyone has implicit permission to access any garden plot as passing through another's plot is often necessary to reach one's own. Borders to neighbours' gardens are thus permeable, but the boundaries of the respective plots are clear-cut. My interlocutors constantly told me about a rule that permits you to even enter another person's garden plot, when feeling hungry, to pass some ripe bananas and cut some of them for eating, without the express permission of the owner. As a result of these arrangements and rules, on my first visit I did not even notice where a garden began and where it ended, or who the owner was. Today, areas where cultivation takes place pass into secondary forest, other cultivated areas or even plantations. All of the areas were at least a 20-minute walk away from the village and most of the garden plots were located at a greater distance, up to one and a half hours' walk.

I was told numerous times that before the arrival of missionaries and the subsequent resettlement of the village, villagers installed their gardens closer to the 'house'[1] and built a fence around it (Rio 2007b). The missionaries and colonial administration placed a focus on plantations for cash crops and animal breeding, so fences were installed around the animal husbandries and the subsistence gardens were located further away from the villages (ibid., 106). Knut Rio points out in his description that in North Ambrym, the yam garden is called lonor, which means 'place inside place'. According to Rio this could mean "a fenced-in space within a larger place" (ibid., 106). I will return to this at the end of this section because, in my opinion, the garden could be described, fenced or not, as a place within a place – not in the sense of a demarcation, but through the connections that are created. Today around the Dixon Reef area, people have tried to fence their gardens in again from time to time, but they explained that this often means too much work for them because the released and now wild cattle destroy most fences without much effort. This is one of the changes they criticised because they took it as an indication that gardening is transforming due to changes to community life (Chapter 6).

The life cycle of a garden plot always started even before the first cultivation. After clearing the bushy surroundings with half-grown Burau trees (Hibiscus tiliaceus) in an oval formation, people would burn down every example of organic material. This is a practice that is now to be refrained from on the request of the government, because it would further increase CO_2 production and thus augment negative processes connected to climate change. The first plant cultivated at that spot would be the yam, which initiated the garden plot as a so-called alenge wowol (a Novol and Nasarian phrase, meaning new garden). The people would put other plants and tubers in between, following the principle of mixed cultivation (see Chapter 3). After the first harvest of yam, the garden has passed from a new garden to an alenge elewir (old garden), in which

1 Only a handful of the older inhabitants of today's Dixon Reef village remember when living together was divided into men's and women's houses, and the nakamal was used as a ceremonial place, or the gardens were a meeting place between women and men.

bananas would be the last crops to be planted. This location must lie fallow before new planting (of yam) can take place after several years. These garden plots are planted with a wide variety of plants in their life cycle that respect crop rotation. The changing positions of gardens was due to the practice of shifting cultivation where the environment is transformed from what people called the 'dark bush', where humans had not yet laid hands, to the 'bush', the old gardens from the previous years with secondary forest, and finally the new gardens, with the crops of this cultivation cycle.

The yam plant is the first crop ni-Vanuatu farmers at many places around the country grow when installing a new garden. Yam is mostly planted with other crops; it hardly ever stands on its own (Chapter 4). The yam garden is always considered to be first and therefore names 'the new garden'. In many places, ni-Vanuatu regarded the yam garden as the most important of all the different kinds of gardens, without which the farmer would have no garden, and even worse, no knowledge of gardening (Calandra 2017; Rio 2007b). Often, when talking about garen in Bislama or alenge in Novol or Nasarian, people in Dixon Reef referred indeed only to the yam garden. Mondragón points out how important the yam garden is to communities in Vanuatu, as it provides the structure for the year. For Torres Strait Islanders, the yearly beginning of yam cultivation marks the beginning of what the Western world would describe as the calendar of the year: it gives structure to community life and agricultural practices (Mondragón 2004, 294). The yam garden as the prototype of the garden also sets the rules for gardening and there are thus many rules regarding the yam garden. For example, women would avoid visiting a yam garden when having their period and people would never make loud noises or wear perfume when going to the yam garden (Calandra 2017; Rio 2007b). Having a strong body smell would prevent the yam for growing well. The yam cultivation was supposed to be a calm and clean process, and this is a further reason why people wanted to burn organic material for the yam garden, since it apparently also kept harmful insects away. The yam garden stands for transformation and movement: every year the new garden can be found at a different location. In the beginning of the garden cycle, Dixoners find a new spot to start their yam gardens.

One of the younger women in the village explained a garden as the following: "The garden is a new place where you brush and clean to plant crops like yam, taro, cabbage, banana, all the new gardens. That means garden. It's a place for mekem garen." (hemi ples blo mekem garen). Looking at her explanation, she calls the garden a ples When asked, the women in particular refer not only to the yam garden as a garden, but to all their different gardens. This is also due to the fact that growing vegetables is mostly women's business and they are very proud of their vegetable gardens. When working at one location, being the yam garden, the taro and banana garden, the mixed garden, Dixoners refer to it as garen (Bislama), or alenge (Novol/Nasarian), and consider it to be a place. In the following sections, I will scrutinise the concept of place in social science and in Vanuatu specifically in order to understand the connection between place and garden.

In social science literature, place[2] is usually conceptualised as the materialisation of social interaction. Place is formed through recursive relationships between human agency and structure (Robin 2002; Snead, Erickson and Darling 2010, 15). Places have a sense of materiality in connection to social interaction – political venues or consumer contexts (Cresswell 2014, 3–4). For Creswell, the material nevertheless has a defining character, also when it comes to gardens. He writes that places are "a collection of buildings and roads and public spaces including the community gardens which are themselves material – made of plants and statues and little sheds and houses with fences around them" (ibid.). I take Creswell's definition as a starting point: he defines places thus, as made by humans and their interaction, and thus as a materialisation of human practices, by referring to Agnew's definition of 'meaningful location' as places with meanings that are made by actors in the environment (ibid., 12).

Gardens as places are also considered to be dynamic. By theorising community gardens, Andrew Cumbers, Deirdre Shaw, John Crossan and Robert McMaster want to see them as active places, and they "view places as more than just the passive backdrop for mediating social relations around the economy and work, but, instead, as containing a more active generative quality in the forging and shaping of these interactions" (Cumbers et al. 2018, 36). They refer to the processual approach of Doreen Massey, that concerns itself with place as "an ever-shifting constellation of trajectories" (Massey 2005, 151). Additionally, Pink writes in her work, which also combines place with garden, that "garden as a place-event that is produced by and engaged with through living bodies" (Pink 2012, 11). In these works, place are products of social action, constituted

2 In this discussion about place, approaches to displacement through migration etc. (e.g. Appadurai 1990; Massey 1997) are not dealt with. Since the 1990s 'place', together with 'landscape' became an important topic, especially in human geography and anthropology (cf. Feld and Basso 2009; Fox 2006; Hirsch 1995). I will further discuss here the specificities of the Melanesian concept of place, or ples in Bislama.

by it, or giving space for social interaction. The conceptualisation of place in Vanuatu adds another thinking point: that human relations and the environment are the key places, through constant movement.

The Melanesian concept of place in general and the concept of ples in Vanuatu has already been discussed in detail (Bolton 1999; Hess 2009; Hirsch 1995; Feld and Basso 2009; Fox 2006; Jolly 1999; Rodman 1992; Weiner 1991, 2002). Similar to results for other regions of the world (Cresswell 2014), these studies conclude that ples is connected to land, identity, belonging, sociality and environment and all of them discuss the difference between a Melanesian and a Western conceptualisation of fixed locations as places in a given landscape.

Place for ni-Vanuatu is at the same time something that everyone has (Rodman 1992), and something that must be produced by people (Hess 2009; Kraemer 2013). Being a 'man ples' (man of the place) means for ni-Vanuatu that you have a connection to people and land and it refers to ni-Vanuatu's sense of belonging (Bolton 1999). Lissant Bolton makes the point for Vanuatu, that the interaction between people and their ples is represented by movement, and she stresses that surroundings are not stable and neither are people (Bolton 1999, 44). Women especially represent ples. Since marriage rules are often exogamous and the virilocal marriage system brings women to live in another village or on another island after marriage, they carry their ples with them wherever they go, and grow like a "branch of the nanggalat – a stingin-nettle tree" in the new location (ibid., 43). Bolton describes that making places for ni-Vanuatu is related to the movement of people, since people and places can only be thought of in connection (ibid.). In Vanuatu, ples also holds the connection to land, which is a part of identity. In the case of women, they could take their place with them and produce new ways of belonging, as do young people in the town of Port Vila, by finding new roots through place-making (Kraemer 2013). Ples also became part of the political discourse when Vanuatu was about to reach independence and it directly refers to kastom, which at that time became part of the "collective identity" (Regenvanu 2005, 38–41). Kastom is defined, in other words, as ni-Vanutu describe it, by their cultural goods and knowledge.

In her book 'Person and Place' (2009), Sabine Hess presents a detailed analysis about the different aspects of ples on Vanua Lava in one of the northern provinces of Vanuatu. She focuses on the relationship between people and environment and places and she also looks at the dialogue of building the relationship of people to their surroundings (Hess 2009). According to Hess, a person in Melanesia has a relationship to a place – not individually, but in a relational way including other places and people as well. Hess refers to what

Marilyn Strathern called the concept of the partible person (Strathern 1992). By drawing on this concept of the partible person, i.e. a person who does not exist for himself but as relations to others, place, according to Hess, is similarly connected to people and person. One does not exist without the other and at the same time neither is a person characterised by individuality nor is a place one-dimensional and original (Hess 2009). "Rather, persons, singular and plural, also have place(s) within, which leads to the conclusion that places are also intrinsically dividual or plural." (ibid., 193) Hess describes in her work the multifaceted Vanuatu concept of ples and how people are connected to landscapes but also to one another through different practices. "Being in place", Hess explains, she learnt by moving through the landscape, following the lead of her interlocutors. During her research on Vanua Lava, she was introduced to places in the same way as she was to people (ibid., 106). Another example is food. Relationships between place and person are built up by the consumption of food, the crops coming out of the garden.

> First, through incorporation of specific foods a person can acquire an individual identity … Second, a person also constitutes a dividual identity by sharing and consuming food with others. (Hess 2009, 75)

In these approaches to the concept of ples in Vanuatu, it becomes clear that practices among people give rise to places. Interactions also take place between people and spirits, or people and bubu (ancestors). In this case too, food plays a special role, when the place of the bubu has not been sufficiently respected by the living, garden crops are used to appease them. Place is thus not stable, but the result of a relationship that needs to be nurtured.

Margaret Rodman describes Melanesian places in a similar way, as less located, and stresses that they are multilocal and multivocal (Rodman 1992). She further defines ples as the multiple everyday interaction between persons and their environment, stressing that there are both multiple places in one place and singular places among multiple persons. Through this formula, she criticises the use of place as a construction or representation of social action and warns us not to fill the notion with Western concepts. Instead, she follows a constructivist approach in which the practices of people and not only narratives make places – not as static, but as relational. We have to look at multivocality and the power relations in places:

> It is time to recognize that places, like voices, are local and multiple. For each inhabitant, a place has unique reality, one in which meaning is shared with other people and places. The links in these chains of experienced places are forged of culture and history. (Rodman 1992, 643)

Rodman sees this multivocality and multilocality in how people move through the environment and relate to it through practices. In Melanesia, and thus also in Vanuatu, place and sociality cannot be seen as separate. As Rodman says, "Places come into being through praxis, not just through narratives." (Rodman 1992, 642) The dialectic of place and praxis is inscribed in the ritual, political and social life of villagers in Vanuatu (ibid., 649–51). In one of her examples, she makes the point that for a ni-Vanuatu boy who runs through the bush and navigates passing places "while regionally zoned, was not locally fragmented, as in our own lives. But it was multilocal in that there were many connected, named places within that territory, places that linked living people and dead ones with the child through landmarks" (ibid., 650–51). Rodman sees place not as materialisation of belonging but as practice and the network of locations that make sense to one person. Included in this network are locations which surround the village but also all the places that have importance in a person's life, like the church (as a building), an area where you can find certain stones, and the network of all those places and the praxis and those places and how it comes together (Hess 2009; Rodman 1992). Not only is ples the interaction between people and the environment (and environment is to be understood here in the broadest sense), but environment itself is also not static and fixed for ni-Vanuatu. Bolton underlines the shifting relational point of relation in the environment:

> [I]n a volcanic zone where islands rise and fall under the ocean, and where hurricanes, earthquakes and even volcanic eruptions frequently modify the landscape in small ways, places are understood to move. (Bolton 1999, 44)

Dixoners use the term ples in everyday conversation only when they want to talk about a specific ples from whence someone originated or where someone went to. However, it is also used as an expression of being in motion. One of the elder women describes it thus:

> When I come to a house and stay there, I only say we are staying here (aundi unde). There is no need to talk about place anymore, because the place (aute) is Dixon and we are already there.[3]

Therefore, once people stay in one location, talking about place becomes pointless – place only exists because people move towards it or from it. People in Dixon Reef distinguished ples from land/ground (graon) that could be owned, worked or cultivated. For this, they do use several descriptions but the common word is 'etene' in Novol (see Chapter 4). In a national context, the word graon is mostly connected to legal disputes about land tenure or ownership. It is something that is there, but under dispute.

For my interlocutors, it was not a question of whether a person made a place or whether the place exists independently: persons and places are similarly a unity – one does not exist without the other. I heard numerous stories about 'sacred' places or places which were tabu for women or people outside the nasara because men held kastom ceremonies there. Other places where ancestors are present today are to be respected and certain activities are to be avoided at this place. Not respecting the place meant that the person who initiated the status of the place, or the ancestors who are present there, would feel insulted and this would have had consequences for the trouble-maker such as disease or destructive weather phenomena such as storms or drought which could harm the whole community. However, this can be remedied by establishing communication between the living and the dead, and places and things.

During the garden day described above, people moved through the area around Dixon Reef, walked up the hills, through valleys and swamps and followed the coastline. The routes themselves changed, because garden plots also moved, to areas where the bush opened up due to fire, to spots where the earth had been kept fallow long enough, to places where watercourses keep the earth moist, or to new spacious spots where people felt they had more freedom to work without neighbours too close by. Locations where Dixoners planted their crops in the wider area around the village were all named. These names were given by people who had lived in the area before or who had started their gardens in that area. The names of the places give clues as to conditions of the places or events that happened there. For example, Lewitetawin means that there is water running underneath the ground. Names show people which areas are best suited for which type of garden, because after all, vegetables

3 For Dixoners, ples in Bislama is translated as aute in Novol and Nasarian.

such as lettuce need more water than root crops. When one of my interlocutors shared that they were heading out and said the name of the area, it was also clear to the listeners which garden crop they would be taking care of that day. The land around Dixon Reef is owned by different chiefs and nasara, who give and deny access to gardening. If a person wants to start a new garden on land that does not belong to her nasara, she has to ask for permission, which, in the case of the area around Dixon Reef, is not to be denied. Gardens themselves, everywhere in Vanuatu, are owned by the people who planted them (Hess 2009, 116) and remain inseparably connected to the farmer as a person. Even if the garden shifts its location, the person to whom it belongs can move and still harvest out of her garden, because it is still connected to her.

If ples in Vanuatu is not static, it makes sense that gardens similarly are not fixed entities and not located at fixed locations. Even though they might move around in a certain area, their particularity is not marked by a location, but by their movement and by interactions. Interactions between people and between people and environment cannot be separated, gardens move because people shift them to other locations, and people move because of shifted gardens and vice versa. Gardens change locations due to weather, season and people's preferences. In the same way, the Melanesian ples is never a fixed entity nor solely the materialisation of social practices. It is more the practice of building up relationships between people and the environment, so gardens as places cannot be fixed. In the same way as ples and people are relational, so are gardens and people. People belong to the garden as gardens belong to them. Furthermore, the garden makes a person part of the place of Dixon Reef and thus the community, a topic I will further discuss in Chapter 6. In a nutshell, a garden in Dixon Reef in itself is not stable but dynamic, not fixed but relational, and above all, it is in motion. My interlocutors referred to the gardens as areas that do not stand for their own, but as places made by the dynamics of mekem garen.

5.3 Gardening on the Way

Movement of people in Dixon Reef is driven by cultivation, a juxtaposition of their different practice during the garden day, which in Ingold's word then becomes a 'taskscape' (Ingold 1993). Ingold takes the perspective that practices come first and the bodily engagement of humans create what can be 'seen' as the surroundings, or what he calls landscape. This landscape is not fixed, unchanging or the fundament on which all further life is built, but is rather processual (ibid., 160–62). He further states: "Landscape is not nature; here I claim that the taskscape is not culture. Landscape and taskscape, then, are not to be opposed as nature to culture." (ibid., 161) Therefore, people's activities are part of what Ingold calls 'landscape' and I call 'environment'.

The purpose of this section is to bring together the topics of movement – and the task that people have that drives their movement – and place, to show how people in Dixon Reef create their environment. I regard environment, like Arno Pascht and Eveline Dürr, as a relational process of making and becoming. Therefore, there is not one definable environment, but many 'environment(s)' (Pascht and Dürr 2017, 9). Pascht and Dürr refer to approaches like Ingold's which seek new ways to conceptualise the environment and refrain from a dichotomous representation. I will show that the movement in mekem garen can be regarded as a way of creating and relating to the environment of people around Dixon Reef. Furthermore, what people experience is contact with the ground and interaction with weather (Ingold 2008; 2011) and in such interaction they make their environment.

5.3.1 The Paths and Roads of Gardening

When I was walking along with others to their gardens, it was important to know beforehand about the conditions of the roads. Constant heavy rain for days transformed the paths into muddy slippery streams, and even a little rain could mean that wet leaves covered the surface. This changed conditions for walking, because it changed the surface and the routes we could take. In dry weather conditions, the surface was solid, sometimes even hard as stone, easy to walk on with flip flops. However, this hard ground sometimes broke up and ridges with sharp edges had to be avoided, also there were dry branches or roots, which were more likely to leave marks or wounds on the body. It was thus essential to exchange information about the conditions of the bush and the paths people walked on, in combination with weather details, before leaving the village. When people were coming back on the main road of Dixon Reef, passing the first houses, others shouted over to them from their kitchen houses: "Was it raining in the bush?" Most of the time the soaked clothes of the returnees were an unquestionable indicator but they answered anyhow: "One big rain in the bush." On some days, we had to hide from the sun in the village, while at the same time, it was raining heavily around the gardens. Walking on rainy days is an experience on its own. The first time I wanted to cross a puddle, I failed to do so straight away, and did an almost elegant balancing act in order to not fall down. The women had to show me how to walk around muddy and slippery places.

Walking towards and between garden-plots did require concentration. People of Dixon Reef normally accelerated their gait, to a quite fast walk with strong legs, gazing straight ahead or concentrating on the ground – at least this is how it looked to me. In one of my first notes into my personal notebook I wrote about my difficulties following the women – I merely had to stumble behind. Especially in the beginning, I did not manage to look at my surroundings and could not remember anything because all my energy and concentration went into not falling down. Sometimes it could happen that one member of the working group misjudged the conditions of the path and stumbled or fell. But most of the time it seemed as though they could walk on the ground, straight, uphill, downhill, through water or through sticky plants. They undertook a straight-legged walk like the city walker aiming for the next train station, knowing where to go, but always able to stop, make a quick detour and walk into a shop or decide to take another route altogether. It was a combination of knowing where to go, how to do it, but at the same time being aware of everything around you. The walk in the bush made a contrast to the strolling, slow walk in the village which required 30 minutes for a distance I would normally walk in 10 minutes. People in Dixon Reef took their time in the village but never outside of it. When someone let you know about the weather conditions and the rain around the garden crops, people replied, "very good for the yam", but also sighed and explained about the exhausting conditions for their next round of walking and working.

When I told my plans about my next trip to one of the garden plots, one of the women looked at me and said: "Watch out, it rained and I only could swim to my garden." This meant that the paths were under water and sometimes could cover your legs up to your hips. Or someone was covered in mud, rolled his eyes and said: "Too much mud!", which was one of the most difficult conditions because every step could mean you were either stuck and your shoes broke or you fell down. Not to mention getting up – especially with a bundle of fresh tubers and other crops on your back. By this, the environment was transformed, people made new paths and others were ignored for the time being. When making daily walks to the bush, people of Dixon Reef avoided the critical points. While they did not slow down their gait, they found new routes, which were better suited for getting around. Following a path meant following the direction or the traces which someone else left behind. That rainy day, if the first person made a small detour and avoided a mud hole, the next group saw traces and slowly, by midday, there was a second path next to the original. Since walkers would only take this route under rainy weather conditions, the ground was transformed again when it had dried up. The next people would find a new detour, thereby creating a pattern of paths in the area.

Over the months, I started to recognise the traces of the different lines of paths and could see where to go when the main path was blocked – just to follow the footsteps of the person who had walked there before me. Only on the main road could more than one person walk next to each other and here people slowed down a little to have a chat, but all of the other paths were narrow and garden groups walked one behind each other. This means that the first person, as head of the group, chose the paths to follow and others followed. If children came, they often ran around in between, but adults followed the line they had formed. However, at crossroads, where the group had to decide which path to take, the group could split again, because for example the father might say: "I will take this path, see you back at the house." There, another trio came through: "Where do you come from?" "We were up the hill and will walk back via the main road now." A new group was formed and stories of the day working around the garden plots discussed. New paths were created again and again through the movement by people – they could meet or move apart again and thus meandered through the surroundings.

The movement of people through their environment occurs through interaction with the environment. Paths were developed through the community work of different groups of people and they are not only based on the goal of the movement. People spent a lot of time wandering through the environment and the paths are traces of their work, showing not only where people went, but also why they went there, because of the weather conditions, or because of practices they undertook. The following explanation from Hess becomes important for these movements and also the question of where one is going when meeting another person in passing: "Unlike in the English context, where people are always very much interested in how one is, in Vanua Lava people are always very much interested in where one is going." (Hess 2009, 108) Walking and movement are not only actions to bring people from one place to the next, a way to move from A to B. Movement and walking are practices of place-making in Vanuatu (Hess 2009; Kraemer 2013). Daniela Kraemer's work is concerned with the processes of place-making of young male ni-Vanuatu in the capital of Vanuatu, Port Vila. For a long time, these young people were referred to by society as the generation without real roots, as they no longer grew up 'on the islands' (Efate is generally referred to as the mainland) but in one of the unplanned and crowded parts of the city. However, Kraemer elaborates on the agency of these young men who made Port Vila their place of belonging through their practice of walking along the streets of the capital (Kraemer 2013). This practice of appropriating the environment reflects not only an urban method of place-making, but one that all ni-Vanuatu have in common. Ni-Vanuatu use walking as a form of engagement with their environment and, by walking paths, make and re-make their environment. In the gardening scene described above, situational decisions led to decisions about where to walk with my friends. Paths changed depending on which gardens we chose to visit, but also according to weather and people's preferences. People did not simply follow the paths but actually made the paths. Ni-Vanuatu move through their environment because moving is a cultural practice for interacting with the environment.

For a better visualisation of the interaction of people, practices and movement during the garden day, I will turn now to the movement maps that people made of their routes after their day's work in the bush. I will explicate and interpret three movement maps and demonstrate the practices of the garden day. As already mentioned, these maps were made in communication with my interlocutors by asking them where they went that day and what they did. People drew their activities and the routes they took over a full gardening day. Routes people sketched out on paper were shaped like circles, even though they might head in the same direction or even take the same road/path back.

Figure 5: Movement map 1

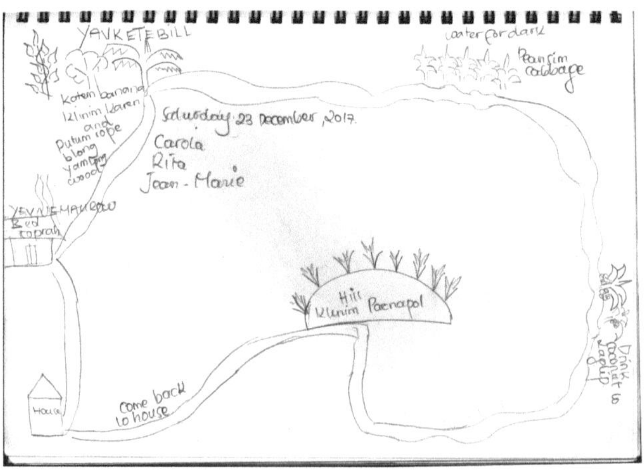

Figure 6: Movement map 2

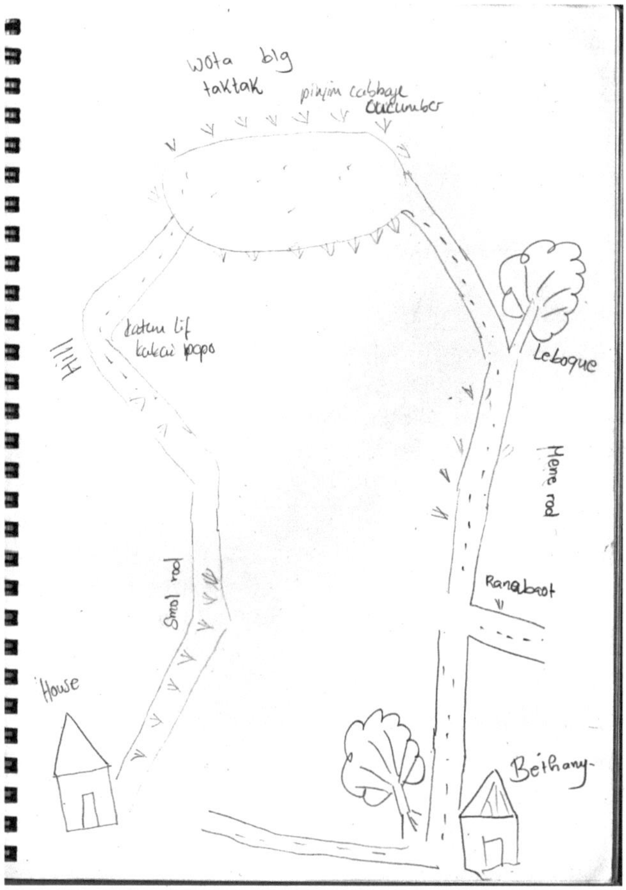

This group consisted of three people, mother, father and daughter. They started their day at the house and then followed the path to Yevnemaurow, which begins the circled road at the top of the map. This path led them to their first stop at their copra oven in the plantation (bed coprah), where they turned the coconut flesh. They then moved on and reached Yavketebill and the first garden, where they harvested some bananas, did some weeding and attached the outgrowths of the yam plant to the climbing aid, which mostly consisted of sticks or small trees that were still in the garden. As they walked on, they passed the swamp area (wota blong dakdak, the water for the ducks), which is an area which is flooded for half of the year, and harvested some leaves of cabbage. After that, they set off in the direction of the hill, stopping for some refreshments en route, harvesting and drinking coconuts. Once on the hill, they cleaned and did some weeding around their group of pineapples. Returning by another path, they completed their journey for this day.

In this map, the group of three women and three girls, including myself, also started in the village and returned in the afternoon, following a different path. The arrangement of the paths as they have been sketched here by the draughtswoman would, do not show the geographical location, but move exactly the other way, the small road (smol rod) leading in the other direction. It shows that we started our walk just on this small road, moving in the direction of the hill, then set off up the hill, and when we reached the top, we made a small stop and cut leaves for the planned laplap and harvested papaya, some of which we ate on the spot. We then moved down to the swamp area (wota blg taktak, water of the ducks) and harvested island cabbage and cucumbers (pinjim, cabbage cucumber). When we returned to the area of Leboque, we took a break at the big tree but followed the main road (mene rod) and met some other groups at the roundabout (Ronabaot), exchanging stories of our day. On our route back to the village we stopped at the houses in Bethany, where we handed over some of our island cabbage.

Figure 7: Movement map 3

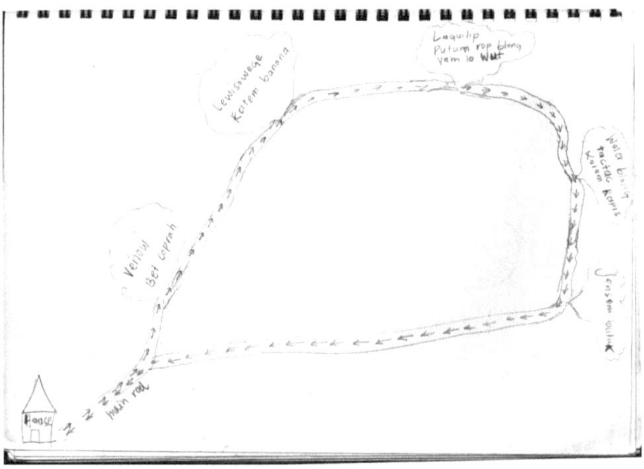

Starting at the village, this couple of husband and wife followed the main road (main rod) before visiting their copra oven (bet coprah), then went to another area and came to Lewisowege, where they harvested banana bundles. Moving on to the next garden, they took care of their yam vines in Lanquilip (putum rop blong yam lo wut, put the rope of the yam on the stick). Crossing the area of the swamp (water blong tactac, water of the ducks), they broke off some leaves of the island cabbage (karem kapis, take cabbage). On their way back to the house they passed their cow and, because it was fastened to a coconut tree, they changed its position so that it had fresh grass to eat (jensem buluk).

By drawing these maps, people in Dixon Reef visualised for me their garden-day and their walking and working practices during one day of work. All the maps describe the round that people walked, visualised by them on the card. Working groups would start their walkabout (wokabaod) in the morning or after lunch and finish it on their return to the village, mostly in the evening, as I have described above. The starting and ending point of their tour was always the place that is called 'house' on the maps. Since there is no word in the languages of Novol and Nasarian that equates to the English word village or the Bislama word vilij, they use the Novol and Nasarian word 'imo' for the big village and their own houses. Therefore, they use the Bislama word 'haos' or the English word 'house' to refer to their journeys' end points. Some of my interlocutors indicated their direction of walking using arrows, which move away from the house and return to it at the end of the day. Most started by sketching out the roads which they took, ignoring all the other paths that were not used by them that day.

When starting their walk, most first put distance behind them, leaving the village, crossing the plantations and then reaching the area where the gardens were located. One can see that paths go to one side or the other, uphill or reach areas where they started to draw little icons, giving insight into what they did in those locations. They included some of the activities they did on the way, such as picking up coconuts to carry home on the way back, cutting leaves to wrap the island cabbage, or leaves for the laplap, or giving water to cattle grazing between the coconut trees. While walking along, some passed the copra oven, taking the opportunity to check process. This could be passing the 'bet coprah' (copra oven) and checking the fire underneath the drying coconut pieces. Their ways led them to different areas, next to which they added names, bubbles and circled areas. Some also drew small pictures of plants, trees or the surroundings, for example bananas which were planted next to a river. In addition, landmarks people had to pass, cross or climb on, like a swamp or a hill, were indicated, or places where villagers had a stopover and cut some leaves, ropes or took refreshment. Upon reaching a garden plot, most wrote the word garen, thus showing that this was a place for working in the garden. All the work that needed to be done in the garden was listed: planting, cutting, taking care of plants and harvesting are written down. All of the maps shown illustrate that the garden group did not just approach one garden on the day in question, but several. In addition, the paths were also lined with practices. People thus did not limit their gardening to one place. The gardening extended both locally over a wide area and temporally throughout the day. Peoples' drawings of the rounds often end with the finishing sentence that the whole group came back to the village (Kam back lo haus/house) and with that they finished their day of work and the full cycle of gardening.

It is rare that one person walked to one place, did work there and directly came back, with the exception of some of the younger boys who were sent by their mothers to bring home something for dinner or who went to 'hang out' and have some quiet time. However, even they checked the cattle on the way or harvested some coconuts, but they hardly enjoyed writing this down or telling me these details. Drawings of their routes had nothing to do with topographies but with their actions of the day. Landmarks were only indicated when needed to tell the story. The important paths to draw were only those on which they definitely set their foot, the ones led by the activity and not a certain place. Other paths, which were not used that day, were left out, because they had nothing to do with what the people had worked on and worked with, not even to indicate the location to which they went.

The maps show that walking is the important factor rather than the routes; paths are there for walking and were made by people walking. For ni-Vanuatu, paths are often an expression of their social relations. John Patrick Taylor explains for the Sia Raga on the island of Pentecost: "The landscape of north Pentecost is deeply inscribed with the tracks and traces that link people to places and thereby to other people" (Taylor 2008, 136). Some paths are accessible to all, literally public. They often connect places of residence. Others connect people with their ancestors and are therefore only accessible to them (Jolly 1999; Taylor 2008, 136–37). Around Dixon Reef some roads were tabu, and especially women had to be careful that they would not cross a road which would lead to or come from a place of kastom. In relation to gardens, Calandra writes that in Tongoa, people have a road to their gardens that is assigned to them (Calandra 2017). That may be partly true for Dixoners as well, although they do not attach that much importance to it, because several people might share paths leading to their garden plots, or cross someone else's garden or path on the way. In the case of the visualisation of their gardening on paper, however, my interlocutors showed only those paths that have been important for the working day. Here, the activities are in the foreground for them, and these paths only appear through such activities.

People chose their direction according to the activities they wanted to do for the day; steps during the working day showed up on the maps not only in the garden, but also in the intermediate space. People walked from one place to another because they wanted to reach their garden plots but nevertheless, small but important work was carried out on the way from one garden to the next. Every person who has ever eaten laplap knows that without leaves, there is no laplap. Gardening is therefore not only a matter of visiting the gardens, working there and returning home, but is an accumulation of different garden practices dispersed over the period and different locations. The work of the garden day is the driving force for movement. After the garden day, people visualised their movement through their environment, which was guided by this practice of gardening. As I described above, paths were made by people's movement and the movement of the gardens, they are the inscription of their activities. Routes changed according to these movements, but people still made detours in order to cut leaves, ropes and coconuts or find certain nuts from trees. Those paths were only visible on the maps because people walked them on the day they drew their maps.

5.3.2 Walking the Environment

Scholars considering the lives of hunters and gatherers above all also scrutinised walking and the use of paths. James Weiner captures in 'The Empty Place: Poetry, Space, and Being Among the Foi of Papua New Guinea' (1991) the relationship of the Foi in the highland of Papua New Guinea with their environment through the seasonal productive movement through place and space:

> Journeying through Hegeso territory on foot is never a matter of merely getting from one point to another. People pause to inspect trees for signs of fruiting, or for the spoor of animals. [...] In these and other casual 'productive' acts, Foi men and women truly turn these paths into conduits of inscribed activity. Motion and movement is always exploitative, productive

> movement in Foi. There is no artificial distinction between 'commuting' and 'work'. (Weiner 1991, 39)

Here, Weiner emphasises that individual locations are not fixed points of work, but that one must see all practices in relation to each other. Similar to the manner in which my interlocutors in Dixon Reef walk their trails, walking among the Foi is driven by their practices, their 'tasks'. Movement through their environment consists of complementary practices and serves again as the impulse for this movement (cf. Robin 2002). Dixoners follow their garden paths, in contrast to the Foi people and their hunting paths, but one can see nonetheless the similarity in their movements. I suggest that it is possible to draw a parallel between horticulturalists, like those in Dixon Reef, and hunter-gatherers, since they have in common daily wanderings through their surroundings. Both draw their life courses by movement through their environment and the way or the route is the goal, rather than the destination itself. Paths are inscriptions of the diverse actions and interactions of the people. The garden itself as a ples is not stable within the environment, but is rather a stopover in the network of paths and activities.

Thomas Widlok writes about the ≠Akhoe Hai//om hunter-gatherers in Namibia and their wayfinding on certain routes that:

> These paths are not deliberately cut but rather emerge as a consequence of regular use. Moreover, at least in some cases, the regular movement also generates the reason for using these paths, through a process that involves the unwitting cooperation of humans, animals and plants. (Widlok 2008, 60)

People in Dixon Reef walk to their garden plots and through plantations, walking between important spots with useful plants. By walking, people in Dixon Reef connect and interact with the ground. In the same vein as Widlok writes that hunters and gatherers in Namibia make their paths through constantly walking them, people in Dixon Reef make theirs, using and not using them, depending on the infrastructure and the weather. Their gardening or mekem garen is a strategy in life for producing enough food. It also means meeting other people, interacting with plants and animals during their movements on their paths and in certain locations. The interaction between human and other-than-human actors creates the environment and constant 'cooperation' and the practice of interaction establishes and re-establishes the environment. Walking through the landscape thus means making the environment. Furthermore, the rhythm of walking takes them from one place and practice to the next, rather than walking in order to reach a certain endpoint. Thus, walking is itself a marker of engagement with the surroundings. Post-structural approaches in archaeology have been working on the relationship between paths, movement and structure for some time. Clarke Erickson, for example, concludes: "Repetitive bodily movement through space and the physical structures that result from and channelize this movement create a tight recursive relationship. Places determine networks of movement and these networks structure new places." (Erickson 2009, 207) In the Dixon Reef area, the daily use of the paths creates them, but they also lead the way for others to continue this way. The network of roads was built up by Dixoners because of their practice of shifting gardens; the location of the gardens was the reason for the paths. Additionally, the gardening practices I have mentioned above do not concentrate on the garden plot alone but also on places and activities en route to or from the garden plot.

As I have described above, what was planned for the day, which work people undertook and where they went was decided according to the needs of the day and what was found en route – the work plan was elaborated in the doing. This plan was interspersed with other decisions that allowed people to take different routes and additionally followed cultural rules of cultivation. The plans of the morning were crossed, diverged or added to. Women and men could structure their day in retrospect on the movement cards, showing the different directions of their working day. I will expand on this with reference to Ingold's concept of 'wayfaring' (Ingold 2007). Ingold distinguishes two types of human movement through the environment: for him there is a difference between wayfaring and transport (ibid., 75–84). Transport is a movement from A to B, unidirectional and with a destination in mind. This would mean that a person had a plan in mind and as long as nothing interfered, this plan could be implemented in a direct 'way'. The practical implementation however differs:

> While the road provides the infrastructural support for transporting persons and their effects from point to point, quotidian life proceeds for the most part along winding paths that infiltrate the ground on either side. (Ingold and Vergunst 2008, 12)

In Dixoners' everyday lives, walking from A to B was intentionally interrupted in order to do something else related to their gardening tasks but not necessarily pre-planned. In this practice, or what Ingold would term 'wayfaring', they depended on taking different paths which were reliant on their needs at that time. Ingold's point is that by 'wayfaring', people inscribe their practices in the ground. Walking here is not solely a practice of making paths, but a method of navigating through the world, and a way of learning about and thus knowing the world (Ingold 2007, 134). Through this method, the wayfarer apprehends what is going on around him/her and can thus act. This he or she has to do by engaging with human and non-human actors, like the ground or the weather (Ingold 2008). Ingold also writes that humans are terrestrial beings who can only move through life in connection with the ground (ibid.). Being terrestrial (cf. Latour 2017) is what makes life as a human – with our bodies, we are always part of what surrounds us (Ingold 1993, 170–72). This may also apply to my ni-Vanuatu interlocutors, as they create a network of paths and gardens in their interactions with the weather, with plants and with their fellow human beings. Here, the driving force for people are their practices on the path which give them something to follow. Paths are inscriptions in the ground which render the network of gardens visible. Looking at the maps of the garden day activities, the person who has crafted the map has usually only depicted those paths that have been travelled. Weiner and Ingold both see paths as traces of human work and life; the physicality of human action made visible. Walking, in combination with what Weiner calls the little 'productive activities', form an interplay.

Activities are not the result of interacting with the environment, but *are* the environment, or as Jeanne Feau de la Croix, writes: "Places are not only performed, they come as rhythms or taskscapes." (Féaux de la Croix 2017, 30) With this statement, she also refers to Ingold's phenomenological approach to place and environment. I consider 'taskscape' to be an appropriate term to capture what I have described as 'making the environment'. With his approach, Ingold once again abolishes the dichotomy of acting people and a passive, pre-existing environment. First, Ingold refers to 'task' as the work of humans, asking:

> How, then, should we describe the practices of work in their concrete particulars? For this purpose I shall adopt the term 'task', defined as any practical operation, carried out by a skilled agent in an environment, as part of his or her normal business. (Ingold 1993, 158)

The taskscape is then represented by mutually complementary and conditional human works, "the ensemble of tasks" (Ingold 1993, 158). Ingold furthermore puts these tasks centre stage and writes that "the landscape is the congealed form of the taskscape" (ibid., 162).

When walking and working in groups, me and my garden working group interacted with plants and people, diverging plans in these interactions. 'Tasks' are only guiding the way. Dixoners walk their paths with a script, but they re-create it continuously on the way. Which paths they follow and what work they do are decided in the situation and therefore the path is only the script that is acted upon, and activities and paths change during their movement. Weiner claims that the Foi create their environment through their seasonal movement from one area to the next along the hunting routes.[4] I argue that people in the Dixon Reef area create their environment through their daily movement. Mekem garen, which to an important part is movement, and which is an important part of the overall taskscape of Dixoners, is thus central for the creation of their environment.

5.4 Conclusion

Each everyday alteration in gardening is woven into this landscape of activities – as mekem garen as well as changes that are attributed to or identified as climate change. I argue that climate change is a part of this process of engagement and interaction. Mekem garen is about the movement of gardens and people in Dixon Reef and thus part of making the environment. The way in which people engage with climate change and see it as contributing to changes in life (Chapter 3) is also characterised by gardening in movement. The movement is necessary to proceed with knowing the landscape, learning where to plant in which season or which year, as well as to connect working spots in the landscape and thus re-work entire surroundings. Spending time and effort on a single location would mean losing connection to this network. Staying at home and not spending time outside the village has been criticised as having a negative influence on communal life and identified as one aspect of klaemet

4 People in the Dixon Reef area also go hunting, although today this is something practised exclusively by the younger men who leave and spend the night in the bush. Longer trips, however, are also combined with a visit to the countryside and the kava gardens in the interior of the island. There is thus, although not as Weiner describes it with the Foi, a hunting season for the Dixoners as well.

jenj (Chapter 3). Thus, including diverse activities in a garden day is one strategy for food security, answering to adverse weather events through caring for people and the environment.

By taking into consideration the concept of ples, I have argued that places are not containers of human actions, nor are they immobile, disconnected locations in the landscape, but rather they are relational and dividual. Gardens around the area of Dixon Reef are not bound to certain locations, as they too move. Every year new locations for new gardens are found and people find and walk on new routes which lead to other garden plots. A garden is primarily a point in the network of gardening, of mekem garen. In this context, it is important to perceive gardens in their context, in their flexibility, and therefore to consider the totality of gardening apart from the garden as simply one (or even several) stable location(s). The connections and practices of gardening in relation to all gardens and what happens on the journey there and back is equally as important as the actions which take place in the garden plot itself. By creating this network of gardens, Dixoners walk through their environment, at the same time interacting with the ground, plants, weather and other people (cf. Ingold 2008; 2011). Moreover, movement in space is led by the location of gardens, but activities that are carried out along the way shape gardening practice in the same way.

People showed on their maps that the practices of gardening set the direction of walking, and thus one important aspect of gardening is walking through the environment. Likewise, talking to people in Siviri on the main island of Efate, I found that they supported this argument through their movement to their gardens, which happens through walking or many times by car, while still making as many stops as possible en route. Mekem garen represents not only work that takes place in the garden but also elsewhere – villagers in both Dixon Reef and Siviri refrain from concentrating on one garden alone. Asking Dixoners why they walked such long distances while learning about home gardens in the climate workshops, some explained that it related to finding a good spot for a garden, but most simply invited me to come along and find out for myself. By using descriptions of garden days and visualisation, I found a way to show what happens while people are mekem garen. This movement is a method of place-making (Bolton 1999; Kraemer 2013), but also a way of making and re-making the environment. I have shown that these practices and interaction with human and non-human actors form the 'taskscape' of actors in the Dixon Reef area (Ingold 1993). In summary, drawing on Ingold's theoretical explications as sketched out above, the environment created through the practices of Dixoners can be interpreted as an interplay of various practices, which, in summary, are constituted by movement. In this chapter, I have concentrated on one important set of activities in terms of mekem garen. This happens to an ever-changing environment (Chapter 3). Correspondingly, therein lies a conceptualisation of climate change as one aspect of this shifting environment, namely an all-encompassing transformation that includes changes in intensity and duration of solar radiation, change of soil richness and changes in community life. As we walked along the paths and passed the gardens, chatting and sometimes stopping for a moment to take a break and hold a longer exchange of thoughts, we talked about things that we had seen or done during the garden day, creating and re-creating social ties anew.

6 Making Relations for the Future

> Climate change is perceived as one of the main future threats to humanity among the vast majority of scientific experts and world leaders. This acknowledgement has spurred the release of international resources allowing scientists to predict the consequences of climate change over a long-term perspective with improved accuracy. [...] And how does this shape people's perceptions and imaginaries of the future among those living in areas prone to flooding whereby climate change threatens the livelihood, housing, health and safety of one's friends, neighbours, relatives and the local population? (Sjöberg 2020, 185)

After having dealt with mekem garen as part of making the environment, I will now look at social aspects of the daily gardening practices of people in Dixon Reef and their way of shaping the future. In the climate change programme implemented in Dixon Reef, horticulture was categorised as a means to secure people's food supply and their future livelihoods – events like Cyclone Pam in 2015 and the El Niño drought afterwards being the first indicators of a challenging future. Therefore, new cultivation approaches of soil preparation and changing planting methods were aimed at providing immediate access to fresh food in front of the village houses and several other new methods were aimed at improving the productivity of gardens outside the village. I have demonstrated that, for my interlocutors, walking distances and moving gardens and plants represented *the* method of flexibility and being able to grow enough crops – and that such movement was in fact a practice of their 'humanized environment' (Mondragón 2015). In everyday gardening, people would interact with each other, through exchange of planting material and information, and through actual and enduring participation in the practice of cultivation itself. Looking at gardening as a way of being in relation with other people extends the view on everyday gardening as a practice of food security and sheds light on gardening as also constituting sociality. The future-oriented topic of climate change now brings new implications not only to gardening as food security, but also as gardening as sociality. Since ni-Vanuatu make their living mainly through horticulture, national political actors in Vanuatu have framed cultivation as an important aspect for economic continuity and for food security. Political actors in town have anticipated future major difficulties for the praxis of horticulture and have requested people to interact with adaptation programmes in order to prepare for what is coming (Chapter 3). In terms of the programme in Dixon Reef, representatives sent the message to workshop participants, that they would face environmental challenges in the future, but that the nature and intensity of such changes remained unclear.

In anthropological literature about Oceania, authors have connected social aspects of gardening mainly with the activities connected to the yield of the garden, which give opportunity for exchange and ceremonies (Bonnemaison 1978; Rio 2009), allow the gardener to earn prestige inside his community (Calandra 2017) or build up special kastom relations to elders or ancestors (Caillon 2012; Rio 2007b). In considering gardening as a fundamental aspect of personhood (Calandra 2017; Malinowski 1935) and for the creation of communal life, I will now focus on the everyday practices of actual cultivation (clearing, burning, planting and harvesting) as they are involved in establishing and maintaining sociality between gardeners. In times of climate change, mekem garen contributes to the establishment and maintenance of spatial and temporal connections between people, also beyond kin relations, and thus helps people to deal with life's changes. Will Rollason's work looks at practices colliding with the future through people's current 'situated projects' of aspiration, what they do in order to live the life they want (Rollason 2014, 2–27). Rollason suggests considering current projects that give people meaning in terms of the future: "[We] need to ask why indigenous people respond to the challenges that they face in the particular ways that they do, inventively and resourcefully to be sure: where is their inventiveness and resourcefulness directed?" (ibid., 2) Anticipating that the future might come with challenges plays a key role in climate change practice in Dixon Reef – gardening becomes such a future project, but not for the sake of securing food alone.

6.1 At the Roundabout

During a garden day around the Dixon Reef area, movement was integral to the praxis of mekem garen, but sometimes this movement came to a halt. People and paths from different directions met at a point and formed a meeting place, giving the opportunity to take a break from the long walk and hide under the shade of a large tree. Moreover, meeting points created a space for people to exchange information, planting material and crops. One of these meeting places was the so-called raonabaot (roundabout). At the raonabaot outside the village of Dixon Reef, various small paths and two larger dirt roads intersected and formed an oval shaped clearing. This clearing was surrounded by fruit and nut trees and some fallen trees, from which someone had carved out benches. It had become aconvenient location with plenty of shady spots for rest and to sit down and connect to others. The location of the site was ideal, as it was here that paths from the village and from the different local areas met with the gardens. It connected the garden areas with the roads to Dixon Reef and the next village. At the raonabaot, one could sit down, drink from water bottles and eat nuts and fruits. This provided the opportunity to pause, take new strength during sunny, humid days and decide where to go next. People sat, cutting ornaments in the trunk of the tree, and had a short conversation. Sometimes the group would split at this point and one of the members would take a detour to the next coconut or cocoa plantation or another garden plot, meeting their companions again at some later point in the day.

Furthermore, this was a space for the exchange of yield, planting material and information. People chatted about the current state of crops in the various garden areas, at the river, in the swamp or on the hill. Maybe a person had passed another gardener's vegetable garden and could relate to the owner whether it would be worth a trip to harvest some island cabbage or capsicum. Sometimes people would send an order with the group going in the direction of their own garden plot, to bring ripe crops back with them. On my way to my own garden, I would meet other villagers and conversation might follow this routine: "Do you want bananas? I have many ripe ones in my garden and I am going to leave some for you at the roundabout under the tree." On their return to the village, I could then take those bananas back to my family's house or pass them on to others. If lucky, one of the two village trucks might pass and take the heavy bundle on its platform, dropping the bananas in front of the owner's kitchen house and leaving them free to carry other items. If a working group did not have the success they had hoped for that day, they could still hope for some relief at the raonabaot. Sharing what was brought back from the day of gardening was highly valued. When a garden group was on its way to see one of the gardening plots and still needed some corn to plant, they might receive some dried corn cob from others who were heading out to do the same work.

As Emma explained to me, the women in particular took this as an opportunity to exchange new material for their gardens. While sitting one day, Emma's kitchen neighbours came by and asked for some seeds, in exchange for food or small coins. These kinds of exchanges happened beyond kin or affinal relations. While men also exchanged planting material, this was mostly delayed exchange among members of the nasara kin group.

Furthermore, this raonabaot was the place where people chatted and therefore discovered what was going on that day, giving an opportunity for interactions in new constellations besides kin relations. On a Saturday, the village was normally deserted, because everyone left early to make their way to their gardens. The children, free from weekly schoolwork, followed their parents to work in the bush, learning valuable life skills themselves. The teachers, busy during the weekdays, would head to the garden, happily strolling around and in their words "getting some things done". Every week, people looked forward to this day on which they concentrated on garden work alone, leaving copra or work for the church behind. The raonabaot then became *the* meeting space for interaction for the villagers. There they enthusiastically shared gardening stories or what was even more important then, what was happening in the village community. Here, also women entered into conversations about current topics discussed in the village community and expressed their opinions to various conversation partners, rather than holding back as they would do when inside the village. In the village, visits were confined to houses, especially for women (although church meetings were an exception). Inside the village, women had to act according to affinal rules, which meant that spontaneous visits only happened between women taowis, the wives of brothers. Men normally met at one of the nakamal, kava bars, to have a drink of kava. This mostly happened according to kinship relations or other loyalties. In contrast to that, the raonabaot brought individuals together by coincidence and therefore in different and sometimes new constellations. While people would not stop for long elsewhere if they met someone or another garden group on the way, they took their time at the raonabaot. Garden days, if possible, included a stopover at one of the key meeting points.

6.2 The Sociality of Gardening

Pauses, such as the one at the raonabaot described above, represented the aspect of gardening that linked it to sociality. Such halts were less of an interruption of the movement of mekem garen than part of the movement that connected people, garden and paths. Brief suspensions of movement on the paths were a part of the movement of one garden day. When people met and came together at the raonabaot or any other meeting point, important interaction and a way of building relations took place – through the exchange of crops and information. It offered not only ways to secure enough food, but also to contact other people. As gardening is characterised by movement, and thus is also about paths making networks of garden locations, the movement of people and gardens is not only part of shaping the environment, but is also constitutive of sociality. People's horticultural practices in Dixon Reef built their relations with the environment and other people, and thus included both into their social relations.

Scholars who scrutinise sociality in Oceania have taken up this point of the connection of movement and sociality (Hviding 1996; Munn 1986; Schneider 2012). The ability to move around and at the same time find routes of trade and exchange, creates space outside of kin relations. Katharina Schneider explains that, for the people in Pororan, living on an offshore island of Papua New Guinea, the 'freedom' of moving around on the water is what they describe as crucial for their lives beyond the terrestrial community days. This is where they could move freely, away from sight and the community rules of kinship. In Schneider's work, this freedom is contrasted to life 'in the bush', meaning on an island's land (Schneider 2012). The freedom of the waterworld stands in contrast to people living on land, since gardens are bound to a certain territory, and thus cultivators have to follow certain paths to reach them (Munn 1986). In the Dixon Reef area, during my daily hourly walks I learnt that although walking is earthbound and certainly has boundaries, gardening is less connected with specific places, but rather encompasses a number of practices, including movements. Paths are an inscription of these movements into the earth rather than forming boundaries of movement. Similar to the sociality of people on water elsewhere, in the Dixon Reef area through movement on land, new constellations of sociality emerge. As a result of this, I see parallels between being on the move on water and on the land in terms of creating relations through movement and its eventual intermittences.

Long and Moore define sociality as processual, and thus as a "dynamic relational matrix within which subjects are constantly interacting in ways that are co-productive, and continually plastic and malleable" (Long and Moore 2012, 4). The conceptualisation of sociality in Oceania, and especially Melanesia, was undertaken by scholars whose work is categorised under the term

'New Melanesian Ethnography'[1] – they identified sociality as 'relational'. This relationalism comes together with the conceptualisation of what makes a person in Melanesia (Scott 2007; Strathern 1988). Although I do recognise the critical discussion around Melanesian relationality (Rollason 2014; Scott 2007),[2] I find this useful because it can give context and insight into what makes a person in Vanuatu. When talking about themselves, ni-Vanuatu refer only in relation to their kinship ties (cf. Hess 2006). Dixoners define who they are primarily in reference to their own position in these kin relations. For example, for a woman this means that she sees and talks about herself as a mother *of* a child, a sister *of* a sibling or in affinal relations with a taowi (sister-in-law) *to* her husband's brothers and sisters. When they talked about themselves, villagers would always use terms in those categorisations, in reference to their own. Children would always refer to adults as papa blong [name], or mama blong [name] (father and mother *of*). For knowing your way around in the village community, it is always important to know who to address with which kin term (cf. Hess 2009). Saying Christian names out loud is often taboo, so talking about others can only happen in the context of the relationship network. Furthermore, as relational persons, people are entangled not as individuals but as people with relations to place (ples), which again evolve solely in correspondence to people's relations with each other (see Chapter 5). This is what Marilyn Strathern calls 'dividual' (Strathern 1988; see Chapter 5). Strathern writes that this relationalism is the core of being a person:

> Far from being regarded as unique entities, Melanesian persons are as dividually as they are individually conceived. They contain a generalized sociality within. Indeed, persons are frequently constructed as the plural and composite site of the relationships that produce them. (Strathern 1988, 13)

Building and keeping relations are an important part of the everyday lives of ni-Vanuatu. However, this does not mean that relations cannot change or be

1 The best-known representatives are Marilyn Strathern and Roy Wagner (Scott 2007).

2 Especially when dealing with the topic of Christian diversion, the theoretical assumption of the New Melanesian Ethnography has been criticised as having limits. Christian conversion is marked as a rupture of social relations (Robbins 2004; 2007). This opens up the discussion of whether a person sees themself as 'relational' or individual. Others have, however, argued that relations are extended and the concept of relational could therefore be transformed (Holbraad and Pedersen 2017).

extended. What this relationality contains is processual and when dealing with relation-building in Vanuatu, I consider it to be possible to change and be extended to new areas of life (cf. Holbraad and Pedersen 2017, 247–77). In order to capture the extension of these relations, Holbraad and Pedersen developed the term "self-relational individual" (ibid., 263), which continues relationality beyond kin relations. In Vanuatu, village organisations in particular develop new positions for a person which brings up new constellations moving beyond nasara relations. In talking about a certain male villager, therefore, the father of a certain child (papa blong) can also be referred to as the Chairman blong skul (Chairman of the school). In daily conversation, this position in the village organisation is used instead of using the name. I want to emphasise two aspects here, firstly the sociality that creates the community and secondly the person themselves. In my argument, these aspects also apply when it comes to daily horticultural practices.

The first account of the importance of gardening as sociality in Melanesia in an anthropological publication goes back to Malinowski's 'Coral Gardens' (1935). Malinowski emphasised the importance of gardening for Trobriand Islanders not solely for consumption but also for enabling entrance into circles of exchange. Being a gardener on the Trobriand Islands was a fundamental part of social life because it enabled a person to be part of the exchange system of kula (Malinowski 1935). Building relations through kula practices is a common practice of reaching beyond the island community as well as bringing prestige and material gain. Kula values can furthermore be accessed through garden yield, as well as giving a person access to garden land (Kuehling 2017, 198). Malinowski further wrote that if the harvest of the garden plots in one year was insufficient, the entire exchange system of the kula was postponed for one year. Gardening for Trobriand Islanders formed the base of sociality and working in gardens was driven by interests and ambitions to gain status (Malinowski 1922; 1935).

For Vanuatu, Joel Bonnemaison stresses the importance of gardening for sociality: "If the Melanesians spend long hours each day in their gardens it is not because they are driven by a problem of subsistence. They could in fact ensure their subsistence with less expense and with much less work." (Bonnemaison 1978, 29) Bonnemaison describes for the north of Vanuatu in the 1970s that the gardener used the surplus of his harvest as gifts in ceremonies and thus became a respected person (big man); the more he could give, the better was his standing (ibid., 30). Today, by contributing what they have gained from the garden, the male gardeners build relations in ceremonies inside the nasara group as well as ties in the extended nasara. The yam root is of particular importance on many islands and is the most important ceremonial crop (Jolly 1999). Birch-Thomsen et al. have emphasised "the importance of yam gardens for cultural identity, in helping maintain the social institutions that still provide an important social safety net" (Birch-Thomsen et al. 2010, 38). The yam tuber takes on the purpose of a gift or payment in ceremonies of marriage, circumcision, death or grade-taking ceremonies (Rio 2007b, 112–16). Furthermore, cultivation itself also influences other aspects of the sociality of people in Vanuatu. Sophie Caillon describes how taro cultivation on Vanua Lava is a way of relating to the next generation and maintaining ties to elders and ancestors. Garden plots are passed on from generation to generation, and thus provide entrance into clan relations (Caillon 2012). Preparing plots for cultivation is, according to Knut Rio, an approach for male gardeners on Ambrym (an island in the Malampa Province) to create special ties between father and son. Through yam cultivation, the genitor becomes the father (Rio 2007b, 103–31). Gardening in Vanuatu is often interpreted as a performance and a creative interplay of social relations during cultivation and after harvest (Conan 1999; Rio 2007b). Furthermore, being a horticulturalist can be considered a part of one's personality as well as forming the nature of a person itself. Calandra stresses that a person on Tongoa is made through practices of gardening: through cultivation, the person enters into competition with others in terms of growing the biggest crops, also in a circle of exchange (Calandra 2017, 358). The author further writes:

> The work undertaken by the individual, his skill and involvement in his gardens are the corollary of his social recognition. It is because he devotes his life to his crops that he is a good worker, a Man-Tongoa par excellence. (ibid., 192, translation from French by D. Hetzel)

If the emphasis here is on the result of the work, which then measures the gardener, Malinowski again indicated that furthermore, cultivation makes it clear what a person stands for. He describes this status of horticulture for a person as follows:

> [T]he Trobriander is above all a gardener, who digs with pleasure and collects with pride, to whom accumulated food gives the sense of safety and pleasure in achievement, to whom the rich foliage of yam-vines or taro leaves is a direct expression of beauty. (Malinowski 1935, 9)

I gain two insights from this. One is that a person is made of their relationships and is therefore relational and thus these relationships also find expression in the events that revolve around gardening. Second, the work of gardening itself can be fundamental for a Melanesian person. In the following section, I will extend this approach and show that relations are made and maintained through the everyday practice of cultivation itself, from the first clearing of the bush until the harvest. Furthermore, I will address the practices of women and men.

6.3 Relational Gardening in Dixon Reef

Learning the process of how to cultivate starts at an early age. While children first accompany their parents and observe them in their work from infancy, they begin to work the soil themselves at the age of about eight (Chapter 4). In this way, they not only gain access to the ability to feed themselves, but also become a person connected to other gardeners. In contrast to people on Vanua Lava, reference to the ancestors is not given through the ritualisation of cultivation in Dixon Reef (Caillon 2012). Nevertheless, my interlocutors could exactly point out who has already planted a garden in which place, and thus weave these locations of former gardens and owners into their own garden network. They stress the importance of learning how to cultivate a garden and this gardening as sociality binds them to communal life. Next to ceremonial exchange, here everyday practices of gardening build up and maintain social relations, first through entering into gardening and then through its continuance, through the work of others.

6.3.1 Being a Communal Person in Mekem Garen

"No-one has to go on hungry when passing a garden", Marie-France explained to me, pointing around her. I was on my way back from the gardens and had only a meagre harvest of a few maize cobs in my bundle. I had already been introduced to gardening practices and could follow the rules of cultivation, but was still waiting for my garden plot to reap rewards. This was one of the few times I went alone to the garden areas, because most of the time this would worry the family with whom I was staying. However, after months of me walking around in the area, they sometimes let me leave on my own. This day I visited my own garden and chatted with some people on the way. On my way back to the village, being exhausted from the walk but without obvious success in gardening, I met my friends walking back from their work. Marie-France and Claudine were on their way to what they called 'go kam back' (let's go fast and come back), a short round of gardening in the afternoon, putting a few crops into their cloths on their backs. We took a rest to exchange stories from the day. They looked pitifully at my corn and asked me if I could not have taken the ripe bananas at the road which belonged to one of them. "There are nice bananas next to the road, we cannot eat them all." Not saying that I was not even sure which road and which banana plants she meant, I expressed my hesitation that I was not sure whether I could just go into another person's area and gather crops. I thought that those were their bananas and therefore were only for them to harvest. The women were amazed at my hesitation, which in turn irritated me. Of course, I could just take off ripe bananas, they insisted. When someone passed a garden and felt like he or she needed something to eat, they could just take it. Normally people would pass the kitchen house of the owner in the evening or send a child to let them know of their bounty, but sharing was an unspoken rule in the community of Dixon Reef.

A story of an incident in which this access to garden crops was denied illustrates this. The story, some of my interlocutors told me individually, goes as follows. Some of the boys were strolling in 'the bush', having been on their journey for several days, hunting, taking care of the more distant gardens and spending time on the road, being on the move. On their way towards the village, they passed by the garden of a relative of one of the young men. They cut a bunch of bananas, prepared them on the spot in the fire and ate them. After returning to the village, this group of young men did not consider this meal to be an incident of any importance and neglected to tell the owner of the garden. They thus also did not immediately tell their mothers and fathers about their meal. When the wife of the garden owner heard this, she was not pleased at all. She accused the young men of stealing her bananas and of unauthorised entry into her garden area. The woman's accusation provoked members of the family and the nasara of each of the boys to feel aggrieved. They, in turn, did not agree with the woman at all. They first started a discussion that in their view the young men had behaved according to the rules and had only taken what they could consume. Since the woman who started the accusation would not refrain from her accusations, the members of the different nasara took a course of action the next day. They all left for their garden areas in order to look for fresh harvest. Each couple gathered as many ripe crops as they could find. They then carried these heavy loads back to the village and stacked them in front of the accuser's kitchen house. Thus, in front of the woman's house, a considerable number of crops were accumulated, including a wide variety such as cassava, banana, taro, various vegetables and island cabbage, all of it in such quantities that it was hopeless for one person (or even one family) to consume it all without refrigeration. The accuser then had to endure the whole village seeing this abundance of crops in front of her kitchen for some days, and inevitably, some of the crops rotted.

My interlocutors considered this to be a sign that someone had not kept to the unspoken agreement to share the yields of the gardens. The punishment was to humiliate the accuser by showing that she had received more than she could eat. The woman had broken the rule of allowing a person, a fellow gardener who was hungry, to enter her garden and take what they needed. The reaction of the members of different nasara was a common practice to embarrass the person who did not show respect for the unspoken social rules of gardening. Following this background story, I will return to my unplanned meeting with the women on the road to or from the garden areas. For the women, the behaviour of the accuser would have been criticised as being 'selfish', for they, and by extension also their husbands, would gladly share the harvest from their gardens. This was not only true for kin relations but also for other people with no direct kin relations. I concluded from this episode that although gardens have an owner who also owns the yield of this area, gardening is a praxis of sociality.

Around Dixon Reef, garden plots were always assigned to one person or one couple by the landowners, who themselves always had the first pick of the best spots. Non-landowners had to obtain the permission of landowners to use a particular garden plot. In general, this was not a problem, and everyone could have as many garden plots as they liked. Once people started gardening next to the village of Dixon Reef, they became part of the social relations, which, as I will demonstrate in the next paragraph, reached far beyond the community's land borders. Moreover, when it then came to the yields, there was no longer any great sense of exclusivity. People would give and receive harvest out of their gardens on a daily basis. This does not mean that everyone could just take what he or she wanted. As we learned from the story above, the rule which allows everyone to take part in another's crops allows everyone to have enough to eat and be part of the exchange system. In other words, as soon as any person started to share, they became part of the social relations in the village community on the assumption that they, too, would share when the times called for it. When the women with who I was speaking at the beginning of this section said "No one would go hungry", they implicitly referred to the rule that you cannot deny someone food but also that you are part of the social community and thus are allowed to take when you have given.

These activities can be read as principles in terms of food security. Everyone receives enough food to get by, also in times of bigger and smaller crises, for example if one's own garden did not show the yield expected. This means that the practice of laying out gardens in different locations and planting different crops (see Chapter 4) is extended beyond the nuclear family circle or the lineage structure of the nasara. An example of an extension of this kind on another island in Vanuatu is Cyclone Pam. This storm had milder effects on the crops in Malekula, mostly affecting those on the eastern and southern parts of the island nations and Port Vila, where I was staying at that time. People there experienced immense solidarity with the islands to which they felt connected by common origin and could share some of their harvest.[3] As soon as people on Efate and Port Vila had any shortage, they turned to people on other 'home islands' where relatives lived and had something sent to them, so that crops were exchanged across the islands. In the immediate aftermath of Cyclone Pam, the local airport in Port Vila was overflowing with parcels containing local produce from another island. Residents of the town would hold up their end when it came to sending products out of the town, such as rice. Some women in Dixon Reef had found friends in town with whom they had conversations over the phone, posting orders to fulfil their needs and exchanging parcels, sending garden crops and receiving manufactured foodstuffs in return.

This part of the exchange of the harvest among gardeners can also be read as a process of establishing and maintaining social relations and thus a person can be considered to be a communal person. Assuming you participate in gardening, you can be part of (immediate or delayed) exchanges. This is different to the display of the success of one person's cultivation in ceremonies which shows their skill (Calandra 2017, 103–05)[4] or participation in ceremonial interactions which render them a woman, a wife or a man and thus grant them a certain position in the village (Rio 2007b). My point is that through gardening you enter into relationships with people – you are giving something and

3 In Port Vila, people originate from different islands, and thus, although they might never have lived on one of the other islands of Vanuatu, they would refer to themselves as 'man Malekula' or 'man Tanna' (see Kraemer 2013; Lindstrom 2011).

4 Something that I never experienced in Dixon Reef although I was told about it a number of times.

you are expected to give something in return. Through gardening, my interlocutors are part of the making of relations. Malinowski formulated this in a drastic way for the Trobriand Islanders:

> A man who had no gardens would be an outcast, whereas a man who for one reason or another is no good at gardening is an object for contempt. Everybody has to make gardens, and the more garden plots a man is capable of tilling, the greater is his renown. (Malinowski 1935, 60)[5]

In Siviri, an interlocutor even explained in Bislama that gardening "hemi laef" (it's life), and an essential part of being human. If younger people spend too much time in boarding schools, their parents or grandparents make sure that they visit the garden sites during their holidays in order to learn the basic skills. At the time of Arno Pascht's and my stay in Siviri, we identified only one community member who did not follow up his gardening practices. The only reason, and this was an exception, that this person was still part of the community, was because he was praised for his pig breeding. People underlined the connection between agricultural methods and a person's contribution to the community of Siviri. Being in a relationship with others is what makes one a (social) person, and gardening is an important part, if not the most important part, of being related to people. If a person was not present in the community, their relatives would still make sure that they were represented in the garden networks and had their own garden plot. Once children started gardening, they not only showed their skills by being able to actually do it and become a skilful gardener which Calandra describes as the highest reward for a ni-Vanuatu person (Calandra 2017, 103). They also become a person through the relational practice of gardening themselves, since without gardening you do 'nothing'.

Thus, gardening is sociality in the making through entering the praxis of cultivation itself. Through this, ni-Vanuatu become part of the exchange systems among kins and over islands (nation-wide). If, on the other hand, one person does not participate in cultivation, people become sceptical. This person has not built up relations, and not being part of the community, through gardening, they cannot offer anything that is valued to the community. Furthermore, they do not even follow the basic practice of being human. Once a per-

5 Women and men in Vanuatu both have their gardens and are considered owners of their garden plots. Even though the landowners are mostly male, there are also some elder women who hold rights to land.

son has started gardening, they enter social relationships which are also maintained when the person cannot be physically present (Jolly 1999; Rodman 1992) and continue this practice of gardening. Other people make sure to continue mekem garen on behalf of absent members of the community. Arno Pascht and I had once been developing my own garden and were becoming part of the garden cycle through the planting of a new yam garden. People from Dixon Reef passed by, explaining the most important techniques and bringing us especially valuable planting material. Immediately, once we started gardening, people proudly announced to visitors that we were really learning how to live there, the women happily telling outsiders that it's good to spend time in the bush and get gardening. Those of my interlocutors who had given some of their yam tubers at planting time took some back at harvest. Gardening not only brought us together with people while working, but also some conversations in the village revolved around our actions in the garden areas. Commencing our own gardening made it possible to be included into their relations and to become part of the community. Interestingly, when Arno Pascht and I were not present, our host family continued to work our garden, following a principle I further describe as gardening for others (by also securing cultivation land).

6.3.2 Mekem Garen for Others

Mary, one of the girls from Dixon Reef in her 20s, did not live in the village in 2019. She had moved to town in order to work in a shop and take care of the children of some of her family members. It was not uncommon for younger women to spend time in another region of Vanuatu, either going to school, earning money as 'house girls' or holding several jobs in town. During their adolescence, before marriage, they would visit their parents and home village, a stay which normally extended up to a few months. Some young men who were also trying their luck in town resumed their gardening activities when they happened to be in the area.[6] Some married men who had left Dixon Reef and followed their wives to their own villages also tried to continue their cultivation in Dixon Reef, securing their rights to land and keeping up gardening there. This is how things were handled by Mary – during her time in the village, Mary, like every other adolescent, participated in every family and village activity, including gardening. However, people such as Mary might miss the

6 Boys had stronger ties with the village and therefore returned regularly. Girls, however, were prepared to move away because of exogamous marriage rules (Bolton 1999).

season for planting or sometimes an absence could last for several years. At one point, at which Mary had already been working in town for many months, I was sitting in her mother's kitchen, while she prepared the meal for the rest of the family: "I have to go and take care of Mary's garden today", she said. It was the time of the calendar year to prepare new gardens by planting yam, marking the start of a new cultivation cycle. This was also the time when the villagers spent more time gardening than making copra (to which they usually dedicated equal amounts of time), simply because people always needed money for their children and school. On our way to the garden sites, we passed another couple busy preparing the ground, digging holes for yam tubers. We stopped for a quick exchange of words and I heard them say that this new garden was for their daughter. I had never met their daughter and was told that she lived with one of her sisters on another island in the north. Apparently, she had not visited her parents for some years. I asked again whether this garden was not actually assigned to them, the parents, as the daughter in question was not present and was probably not going to return any time soon. They laughed because of my naïve question and confirmed that they definitely had planted this garden plot for their daughter. It was certainly her garden – she had asked her parents to continue her cultivation in the Dixon Reef area.

When Mary's mother and I reached the garden in question, I noticed that some of the yam tubers had already sprouted and the shoots snaked across the ground. I then realised that this too was no garden from last year, but a newly-planted garden plot. Mary had never worked on this garden herself. Her brothers had planted the yam in her absence and started the new garden.[7] That afternoon, it was our turn to make what Mary's mother referred to as 'tanna soup' within the design of her garden. "I am surprised that we make a garden for the daughter. She is not even here and will not eat any of this yam" I said. Her mother looked at me and I saw that she was astonished by my statement: "But we will eat it, we all need a garden." Mary's garden was for everyone. Her mother told me that she was very happy that I was working with her that day, because it was Mary's garden and for me to work in it would make her very happy and feel connected to me. It was clear that her daughter would need a garden in the Dixon Reef area, even though she herself would not prepare it, and likely not see or use anything of the harvest. We then started our work, transplanted corn and carried heavy banana shoots (banana suckers) for

7 See description of alenge wowol, the new garden and alenge elewir, the old garden in Chapter 5.

placement between the growing yam tubers. In the afternoon, back in the village, Mary's mother called her on the mobile phone to tell her about the work we had accomplished, and I overheard her happy voice. We had worked in her garden and now her garden would grow very well.

This method created a family garden, despite the owner of the garden being a person who was not present in the community at that particular moment or any time within the foreseeable future. This is distinguished from someone who merely had to leave the village for a day or two, or even a month, for hunting or visiting relatives. Despite prolonged absence, this garden and the resulting yield stood in connection to this person. I learnt during my time with the people in Dixon Reef that families did not like to lose the area in which they had once gained the right to start a new garden, and therefore they continued to cultivate that space. If they moved on, or left the area fallow for more than a couple of years, others could come and see that it was an area where no one was working and start their new gardens on the spot. However, this was only one way to look at it. The other reason for the shared maintenance of family gardens is that people had already started their gardening and now others wanted to continue this work, in order to keep up relations with family and the wider community. Mary's mother, as well as the couple we met on the way, explicitly told me that they had continued to cultivate crops *for* a family member. They could have continued working on their own garden or start cultivating a different spot for themselves. It was not unusual for the number of garden areas of a family, or a couple, or even an individual, to increase within a year. Having many gardens was also considered a sign of being a hard worker or having exceptional skills in cultivation. Thus, people's emphasis on the fact that this work was explicitly done for someone else pointed to the social relationships that this person had built up and which were maintained by the continuation of 'their' gardening.

In terms of my own yam garden, since one tuber apparently was very long and heavy, an exceptionally beautiful one, when I was back in Germany my host family decided to carry it with them to church when the first harvest of that season was blessed. Following that ceremony, they made laplap of it and invited several families to partake in it. This harvest was shared among everyone, and people shared their thoughts on the taste of our yam, which had apparently been very tasty. When we returned to the village at the beginning of 2019, the season for planting the new yam tubers had already passed. We would have missed our chance to continue what we had started the year before, moving our yam garden to the next spot, transforming the yam garden of last year into an old garden, and planting more bananas, manioc and taro. Villagers always choose a larger area and start in one corner, in order to shift the garden to the side the following year. When we returned to the garden areas, we therefore expected to find our plot overgrown with Burau trees (Hibiscus tiliaceus). The first time we returned to the bush, however, we found that our host family had started a new yam garden next to the one from the previous year and had transformed the garden we had prepared into an old one, planting mainly taro and banana plants. They still referred to it as our garden and this was also common knowledge among the rest of the villagers. They thereby extended our social interaction in the form of gardening to the following year. At harvest time, the yield was then distributed among community members (not by us but by our host family who represented us). Participating in walking through the garden areas and collecting planting material for a new garden makes up one part of the relations extending the community via cultivation. As I have exemplified through activities of parents continuing cultivating for their children (which also occurred the other way around, when parents were absent for a longer time period), relations were continued by family members remaining within the village. As a result, the relations once built up through gardening, which is a central human activity for ni-Vanuatu, are continued through periods of absence. Relationships are also maintained, even if a contribution to the community is no longer made through physical presence and one's own work. It was important that this person remained a part of the relations she had built through gardening. Since gardening made a person, this then leads to her being part of a community and island, or a kin group. Through this method, relationships are extended over time and place.

6.4 Future Projects in Uncertain Times

According to Rollason, it is worth turning to the small everyday activities of Pacific Islanders to find out about their aspirations[8] as projects for the future. Those projects can take any form and can include both personal and communal wishes (Rollason 2014, 2). Craig Lind argues that ni-Vanuatu thereby do not strive to change current situations; by taking on future projects, they are placing wishes in the present that refer to what they experienced in the past, and

8 In a similar vein, Appadurai uses aspirations to grasp the future in terms of possibilities (Appadurai 2013; Haug 2021, 75).

now lead the present to what lies ahead. He writes, that "[the] future does not appear to be a conservative reproduction of the past or a simple break from it; rather, it emerges as a range of potentials that must be responded to creatively, with an aim in mind" (Lind 2014, 72). Furthermore, in Vanuatu, the projects of a person are seen in relation to the totality of their relationships with others. For ni-Vanuatu this also directly influences their social relations of today and the future accordingly. Lind explains in his ethnographic example for people from the island of Paama, that if ni-Vanuatu women do not bear children, this concurrently influences the people she stands in relation to. Through migration to town and leading a life as an 'individual', this kind of self-determination breaks with the kin-making of their islands of origin. This influences how 'man Paama' (the people from Paama) as a community in town can secure their status in evolving urban social space. Children are a driving force keeping this community alive, as well as a perspective on the future (Lind 2014).

Annelin Eriksen also poses the question whether different intergenerational approaches of ni-Vanuatu from Ambrym to Christian beliefs might form a radical break within their community (Eriksen 2014). She states that this might sometimes mean that there are several visons for the future which can lead to generational conflicts. In Eriksen's example, the question of how to build up church communities is on different levels a negotiation between individual and community ideas (Eriksen 2014, 147–49). These projects move in the field of tension between the interests of the community and individual choices. In addition, this can lead to a new constellation of a person per se, which defines itself through its relations and thus in turn has an effect on the group itself (cf. Eriksen 2007; Hess 2006). Future projects, in these examples, always stand in connection not only to the immediate kin group, but also larger social groups like the group from the island of origin or church groups. What is at stake in the future might be social relations. Climate change discourses bring people to consider matters of future changes by analysing the current circumstances and also referring to the past.

Taking into consideration the aspect of uncertainty when approaching the topic of the future (Bryant and Knight 2019), practices around climate change can be traced back to the idea that the future is expected to change conditions, but how this change is shaped is still a projection, how changes might look and how challenging this will be remaining imprecise. Scientific projection for the future depends on modelling what might come, using scenarios. With regard to climate change, this would mean that the expectation (that something will happen) of the changes also anticipate how it will affect peoples' lives, and this in a negative way (Bryant and Knight 2019, 28). Even if peoples' lives are not turned upside down by a "radical" rupture or change (Robbins 2007, 293) like that projected by climate scientists, such changes might still raise uncertainties for people's lived realities. According to Bryant and Knight, one has to look at "future oriented actions: ones that projected the present into the future and attempted to shape the future in the present" (2019, 22). They have distinguished expectations from anticipation when writing about the future. Whereas 'expectations' means to know that something is happening, 'anticipation' shows how it is happening and means 'imagining the future in the present' (ibid.). Anticipation is thus a human drive towards an end in terms of something that is wanted (ibid.). However, anticipation is also linked to an evolving uncertainty, as the authors further explain:

> We find that anticipation is linked to particular moments of uncertain or threatening futures. Anticipation, in these instances, is a collective way of addressing the anxiety of uncertainty, and of forestalling or altering something that threatens a radical revision of the present. (Bryant and Knight 2019, 48)

Climate change brings up the topic of uncertainty for the future, alongside anticipated problems, which moves hand in hand with the worries of Pacific Islanders. These fears are also directed towards the future generation, anticipating that losing their land (should the land become uninhabitable) could not only pose risks for food supply but also for their entire way of living (Hereniko 2014). The challenges of the Anthropocene could change the way we live together in certain localities, but also the way in which we interact as a global community. For the island states of Oceania, these challenges include migration and international trade relations or dependencies as well as climate change itself (Jolly 2018). Environmental transformation and social transformation cannot be separated from each other, and responding to one means addressing the other (Hau'ofa 2008). Climate change threatens people in terms of food security but it also leads to a far greater threat – existential in the broadest sense (Schorch and Pascht 2017, 117). Although adaptation is in Vanuatu a declared aim of national policy, and thus draws a picture that shows people how to 'adapt', discourses and practices still transport negative connotations of uncertainty with the subject. In the climate change workshops, the topic of changes that can be met by transforming cultivation practices was meant to prepare for all probabilities. Mekem garen became a future project in itself, stimulated by urban political discussions of challenges through weather and seasonal changes, which were then met by Cyclone Pam and the subsequent El Niño drought, proving that changes can happen but nevertheless it remains unclear when they will happen and what effects they will have on people's lives. Over the last chapters, I have described how these uncertainties through climate change might affect not only food supply but also the creation of sociality. Dixoners underlined that what they consider as klaemet jenj (Chapter 3) also initiated new ways of living together in the community, taking more time for individual pleasures, staying in the village on their phone or increasingly following village administration. Since gardening is also a way of being relational and being part of a community, this brings another aspect to this project, not only in the sense of livelihood but also in the sense of being a person within a community. Before I go into further detail about mekem garen as a future 'project', I will now discuss the role of mekem garen in reference to perception of time and the future of Pacific Islanders.

6.5 Perception of Time through Gardening Cycles

For women, men and children in the Dixon Reef area, horticulture provides a reference point to organise their daily lives:[9] when they wanted to explain the time of year at a particular moment, they referred to one of the two major seasons of gardening and thus the year. The first season is Lewudau (in Novol or Nasarian) which means 'everything grows'. This indicates the start of a new round of mekem garen with the steps of klinim (clearing), bonem (burning) and planem (planting) the alengen wowol (the new garden), putting the yam tubers into the ground (see Chapter 4). At the same time, the old yam gardens of the last garden year are transformed by planting bananas and manioc. This also means that at this point in the cultivation cycle, crops would be about to grow but people would still have to wait for the yield to ripen before they could consume it. Due to this, Dixoners also referred to Lewudau as the season where they would have to go hungry because the stored yam tubers were

9 I describe how time is expressed in relation to horticulture, or how horticultural practices give insights into temporalities of Dixoners. This is not intended to give a general definition of time in Dixon Reef, but rather expressions of time practices (cf. Mondragón 2006). For examples of seasonal calendars which also show that start and end of yam cultivation are markers of the year, see Lindstrom 2011 and Mondragón 2004.

already consumed and only manioc was available. During that period, people would eat manioc with island cabbage every day for every meal. The start of this season of Lewudau is marked by the beginning of heavy rains within the month of November. However, since the rain does not come at fixed times, the beginning of the season of Lewudau is variable, can vary by weeks and can be pushed back as far as mid-December. Mondragón describes this as the typical "overlapping of time-related spheres" of the Gregorian calendar and the actual time when cultivation takes place (Mondragón 2006, 6), which gives a hint to the characteristic that time for ni-Vanuatu is flexible, albeit constituted by repetitions.

The other season, of Renbunde (in Novol or Nasarian), refers to the time when there would be an abundance of food crops – the yam and banana harvest would be in full swing, while fruit trees would bear fruits. People referred to Renbunde as the time of the year when they had plenty to eat and everybody's stomachs were always full. This sequence of gardening remained the same, even during rainy seasons and scarcity of rain such as at the time of El Niño, and people explained that they would keep the routine and start planting by December at the latest. These two seasons, marked by the beginning of the yam cultivation and its eventual harvest, structured the year; once the yam is harvested, six months have gone by and after another six months the rain starts again. Indeed, the vernacular word for year in both Novol and Nasarian, 'etam', is equivalent to the English term 'yam'. For Tanna in the south of Vanuatu, Lindstrom explains that people "pay attention to specific time marks as spurs to practical activity" (Lindstrom 2011, 145) and similarly to Dixoners they mark the beginning of the year when they start a new garden cycle and end the year at the end of the cycle. Time is measured according to time spans; time spans are experienced in a circular way, in which activities are constantly repeated. The Gregorian calendar's years, months or days are mainly important in connection with Christian holidays. Otherwise, people orient themselves within the planting cycle. Everyone can name the Latin calendar months' names, but in everyday lives they are not significant. Duration and measurement of time are of less concern (Lindstrom 2011; Mondragón 2004). Lindstrom also refers to this conception of time as 'static time', because the past falls together with the future.[10] In this static time, there is a centre, while future as well as past are arranged circularly around it (Lindstrom 2011, 144–47).

10 He does not imply, however, that everything always remains the same. Lindstrom refers to changes as "sudden temporal disjunctions" (Lindstrom 2011, 147).

In addition, weather events in Vanuatu are recurring, e.g. storms, and environmental fluctuations caused by weather events are well known and help plants to regrow (Mondragón 2015). Horticulturalists live their lives according to these phenomena and cultivate their food accordingly (Bonnemaison 1978). They do this in relation to what surrounds them, which is at the same time part of the spiritual world and a connection to the ancestors, inscribing past relations in their current practices (Mondragón 2015, 19). In the Dixon Reef area, relationships with 'spirits' are not established or maintained in the form of gardening, yet the environment is dotted with tabu places where certain rules of behaviour apply. For gardening, people concentrate on relations between living community members. Circular approaches to time through gardening become apparent in the context of the Climate Change and Food Security Programme. The case of the abandoned home gardens illustrated that horticulturalist in the Dixon Reef area left them behind at one point but eventually turned their attention back to these small gardens: techniques of mulching, composting and gardening next to the houses were recommenced when people considered it appropriate. This adds to the picture of never leaving something behind but building up on aspects learnt over time.

These relationships to a circular time through gardening are also related to the larger context of dealing with time, past and future in Oceania. Emde, Dürr and Schorch have stated, by referring to Hau'ofa (2008), that "in Oceania time is both circular and linear" (Emde, Dürr and Schorch 2020, 8). Hau'ofa noted that in Oceania, the environment, environmental changes and the histories inscribed in them dictate time. Explaining the circular character of time, Hau'ofa wrote that things in the past are not behind – they lead the way: "The past then is going ahead of us, leading into the future, which is behind us. Is this, then, the case of the dog chasing its tail? I believe so." (Hau'ofa 2008, 67) He differentiated between "traditional notions" of linearity (ibid., 66), which he characterised as "sequential" rather than evolutionary and teleological, and a "notion of linear progression that takes little or no consideration of natural cycles" (ibid., 66). Both can be found in Oceania today, whereby Pacific Islanders encounter the latter notion together with new technologies into the region. Hau'ofa stressed that the notion of linear progression "is the necessity and hence the moral imperative of the transfer of technology" (ibid., 68). Although he considered that people living in rural areas engage in coping "with invasive technologies and adapt them to their familiar cycles" (ibid., 69), he stated that linear developments connected to the introduction of technology have to be considered when working with Oceanic people today.

Global climate change discussions can be seen in line with a teleological view of slow but steady changes leading to a degrading planet, a narrative which Pacific Islanders have encountered over the centuries and perceive as such. When talking about klaemet jenj, Dixoners recognised changes that might lead to problematic futures in a teleological way, such as the intensification of solar radiation. However, they also perceived alterations as recurring, such as El Niño in 2016. I will go into this in more detail shortly. So far, Hau'ofa proposes to capture this simultaneous view ahead and backwards with "the notion of the spiral, which connotes both cyclic and lineal movements" (Hau'ofa 2008, 69). This happens in order to maintain connection to the "natural surrounding" in which time is inscribed (ibid., 67). Or, to rephrase Hau'ofa and look at connotations of time in Dixon Reef, how the past practice of mekem garen is moving ahead of Dixoners, leading them into the future, which lies behind them. Through their explanations, they differentiated between events and changes that have short-term effects and may recur (such as the weather phenomenon El Niño) and long-term changes (such as certain gardening practices) that have changed their lives over the course of time. Referring to Hau'ofa's statements of 'time' in Oceania, these processes as circular and linear aspects of changes both influence the perception of the future of people in the Dixon Reef area.

6.5.1 Gardening over Time

All over Vanuatu, historic interactions have led to alterations in gardening practice and to the introduction of new plants and species (Pollock 2017) as well as other fundamental changes. One important discussion along the west coast of Malekula was that with klaemet jenj, challenges could make gardening harder. This led to discussions about the present status of their garden work. "We already see that things are changing, our lives are changing", the men would say in the evening while enjoying their kava and the news of the day, referring to things that started in the past in order to say that this might or might not affect their future. People not only perceived the introduction of technology such as the mobile phone as a linear process, but also, for example, the irreversible changes through loss of language and kastom knowledge for ceremonial purposes or their responsibilities for church work which affected the structure of everyday life (Regenvanu 2005).

Such changes have also influenced horticultural practices. Both elderly people, talking about their own experiences in their youth, and younger people, referring to what they heard from their parents, stressed that substantial changes had occurred when people moved down from the hills in the interior of the island to the coast to join the Catholic mission, which founded the compound village of Dixon Reef. Since that time, people explained, gardening practices have steadily changed, which has affected the quantity and diversity of yield. This in turn has influenced how residents scheduled their daily lives according to gardening days. Many community members criticised those changes because in their view a reduction of gardening could have far-reaching consequences for their communal living. During our discussion, when my interlocutors talked about this status and the changes in their gardens and crops, and the concomitant changes of community life, they often referred to changes they had already seen in comparison with how their parents approached cultivation. Such argumentation mainly revolved around assertions that villagers now cared less about their gardening because they were forced to focus more on monetary income. Ni-Vanuatu are in constant negotiation between following monetary work and having time for gardening. Although this is widely discussed as a problem of urban dwellers (James n.d.), there are aspects of these challenges all over Vanuatu (and the Pacific):

> A secure future has become problematic in the face of globalisation, where householders must choose between a range of moral concerns every time they provide for their families. Cash does not necessarily increase the range of foods accessible to those households, or simplify moral concerns. (Pollock 2017, 283)

Jean Mitchell and her two local research partners, Lesbeth Niefau and Joan Niras, noticed the same for inhabitants of villages on Tanna, an island in the southern province of Vanuatu. People had not spent the same amount of time in their gardens because monetary pressure did not allow it (Mitchell, Niras and Niefeu 2020). What my interlocutors explained gives more context to this new lifestyle and working in the gardens part time.

In Dixon Reef, plantations of coconuts and cacao had spread and now occupied a large part of the area around the village and along the coast. Cash crops were introduced by the missionaries around 1950 and have continued to gain importance. People expressed their ambivalence about the coconut plantations: working there shifted attention away from gardening, but they also depended on the plantations as a steady source of income. Because plantations were expanding, Dixoners had to move their garden areas further away from their homes, thus increasing the distance for daily work. The space for plantations continuously expanded, because people would replant coconut trees once they had harvested their gardens. The space was thus transformed and villagers had to look for other locations to make new gardens which increasingly led them further away from the village. Although, on the one hand, they were not convinced that they wanted to invest so much of their time into working on the coconut and cocoa plantations, they also felt pressured to earn money from copra to support their families (especially their children). "We are also responsible, there was a time when my father replaced every harvested yam with a coconut", one of the women explained. Old gardens were then slowly replaced with coconut plants, meaning more time spent on the cultivation of copra.

During certain times of the year, Dixoners would dedicate themselves to copra production in work groups several times a week. This work includes a number of tasks, separating the pulp from the coconuts that had been split in half, drying the coconut flesh in drying stoves and then packaging it. A similar approach applies to the production of cocoa beans, except that harvesting is much rarer. This work and church services, people continuously complained, took too much time from their gardening processes. Tambi Alfred explained to me: "In those days, while people were living separated in women's houses and men's houses, couples would meet during the day and spend it gardening. The couple with their children are together in gardens, the women doing their work, and the men theirs." Since gardening was the main occupation, days were structured by it (as was social life).

The changes this elder man saw in modern life mirrored what people around the village had noticed: that they had other responsibilities and thus spent less time gardening. The time they spend in the garden today needs to be used more effectively. They justified this by saying that nowadays more time is spent on work within the village. The school and kindergarten needed attention and the entire village community was responsible for repairing the buildings. A number of villagers said that community work took up most of their time, meaning that their time in the garden was reduced. Time dedicated to gardening practices in Vanuatu had generally decreased over the generations, something that was reflected in a reduction in variety of the subsistence practices of gardening (Mitchell, Niras and Niefeu 2020). Other villagers mention that spending less time in the gardens had led to a decrease in the variety of species and cultivars. When discussing this among my interlocutors, they explained that the yield of gardening in the past was plenty. People referred to their own memories or to the tales of their parents of the numerous and bountiful harvests of yam. The fathers and mothers of today's village inhabitants planted many yam tubers and thus had numerous stories to tell about their successful work. The yield of the yam plants was stored in so-called 'yam houses', houses directly in the gardens, of considerable size, which were stuffed with yam tubers up to the roof. The surplus produce had reduced over the years, as people adjusted to new life in the village.

Mama Agriculture, as one of the oldest women in the community, remembered that she and her father, many years before, would walk towards their yam gardens to fill the beds and follow the principle of auraur mambele (in Novol or Nasarian), which meant that they would make a house for the yam. She further mentioned that if surplus was not forthcoming in a particular year, and people were not able to rely on their own gardens' yields, they would turn away from the new gardens and walk along the paths they had walked before. Along those paths, several wild yams would have been planted in previous years. Wild yam can stay underground for years and remain fresh. Thus, people could harvest them when needed. In those days, not only did people plant more inside their new garden plots, but they also spent more time securing crops for difficult times. "I remember my parents still planting wild yam everywhere when I was younger, today not that much." "Do people today still know how to plant wild yam?" I asked. "Yes, of course they do [know], but they're not doing it anymore." Additionally, people not only consider this a downfall for keeping up aelan kakae (island food) but they also see that it is keeping community members away from building up relations, because they spend less time in 'the bush'. Thus, people interpret this on the one hand as a linear change, but on the other hand they do not preclude the possibility that they could restart planting wild yam in the future, because specific gardening practices might always recur. In the past, according to the stories, there were several tabu, which accompanied cultivation, mostly concerning yam cultivation and taro gardens. These tabu mainly restricted interactions between humans and plants, with the idea being that this would lead to the growth of the plants not being disturbed. It was seen as detrimental to the growth of the yam plants to go to the garden, for example, when just returning from a journey, or having just said goodbye to people, just having had intercourse with a spouse or having been at a funeral over the past few days. Today, complaints are aimed towards the people who do not follow these tabu, but ultimately, everyone had to admit that hardly anyone would follow those rules anymore, with some key exceptions, for example during the mourning period after a member of the village community had passed away. The strict rules of the past were losing considerable weight. Another change is related to laying out the gardens. People told me that they do not fence their gardens anymore, which makes it easy for wild pigs and cattle to walk in and eat the harvest. Although losing harvest was frustrating to many, when I asked them, most of the women and men were reluctant to invest their time to resume this practice.

My interlocutors explained that those changes today in relation to the past pave the way to the future, and that they consider it a necessity to spend as much time mekem garen as possible. Here, past, present and future coincide (cf. Hau'ofa 2008); life may change but mekem garen remains constant. However, mekem garen can be transformed in itself. New responsibilities aside from gardening have reduced the working hours of my interlocutors, who then placed less focus on cultivation rules or storage. Gardening had to be adjusted to the multiplication of further responsibilities in their lives. Furthermore, diversification of plants was reduced and people said that they had fewer varieties – the food for dinner after a successful garden day accordingly differed to before. Through those developments in the gardens, however, people came to value their praxis of mekem garen increasingly and the importance of knowing gardening formed the basis of many conversations with me, but also those I overheard when parents were talking to their children. Despite regarding some knowledge as having been lost, Dixoners also perceived a general change in gardening. The model of a spiral, which Hau'ofa refers to in his deliberations about time in Oceania (Hau'ofa 2008, 69) may be apt to grasp these linear and cyclic movements. Some changes were permanent, but other practices could be picked up again under different circumstances. Some of these changes were criticised and people expressed their wish that more time could be spend on gardening in the future. However, they anticipated that other aspects of klaemet jenj might make mekem garen harder for them and bring about new aspects in the future. Dixoners recognise linear as well as cyclical processes regarding changes in their lives. Those influenced mekem garen as well as alternations in mekem garen influencing them in return.

6.5.2 "We will always make our gardens"

When we discussed changes, klaemet jenj was one of the topics of most concern, especially for those who had attended many of the adaptation workshops. Practices in the adaptation programme in Dixon Reef on the one hand highlighted problems for future agriculture, and on the other hand pointed to 'solutions'. This included the notion that current cultivation techniques seemed lacking for the future and therefore people had to 'adapt' them. Thus, people were aware of changes in gardening style and community life during the last decades and the ideas about future changes and effects such as El Niño introduced problems in the gardens. Having encountered climate change practices, for example, people recognised the El Niño drought as something exceptional, but also as something that had happened in another place in the past, which opened the possibility for it to recur in the future. Particularly the women of Dixon Reef, who came into the community by marriage and grew up in another part of Malekula or another island of Vanuatu, referred to their experiences on other islands of Vanuatu when they were younger and reported that similar events had occurred there. Asking them their opinion about whether an event like El Niño could happen again, they agreed. They anticipate that it could happen again. Everything that had happened in the past might occur again today or in the future. When I asked about the destructive force of climate change, they expressed their concerns for the future, because problems might occur which are worse than those today. Changes they mentioned regarding klaemet jenj are part of a changing world that progresses and always returns or recurs in a cyclical movement. When talking about klaemet jenj and the question whether something could be done to keep it from worsening, there was unanimity among all the people I talked to: my interlocutors regarded it as a matter of permanent renewal that must be accepted. The way forward is to pursue community cohesion and for many that meant to focus on gardening to the extent that it was possible, alongside the changes that their gardening practices had already been through.

During one of our conversations, I asked Mama Agriculture what she thought about the lifestyle of her children and grandchildren and whether she thought that they would still be interested in gardening in the future. I asked this because children of today were more often absent from the village due to school or work opportunities, and the fathers and mothers in the village had to supply for their children's lives as well as their own. I asked her what might happen if younger people spent more time in school surroundings, or working in Port Vila or Luganville. Moreover, I asked whether they would still be interested in spending time tilling the ground and cultivating their own food, and what would happen if they simply bought it instead. She shook her head and assured me: "Children come back for their holidays, they come back and they go with us and work." She was convinced that they would continue to know this kind of work. "Everyone has to learn how to make their garden." She pointed at her daughter and said: "Yesterday she [the daughter] went and worked around her new garden, and she took the little one with her [the girl living with them], this one did her own work." Her daughter nodded and said: "I was working in that way [pointing in one direction], and she did her work over there [pointing in the opposite direction]. She is still small, but she has a garden."

One of the younger men, Yannick, stated that although he was sometimes lazy, he had to listen to what his parents told him and work in their garden. However, their actions drew a contrary picture, in fact implying that young men happily strolled through the garden area, not working. Next to hunting, horticulture in one of the areas far from the village (and of course watching movies on their mobile phones) was one of the favourite activities of younger men. They walked for several days towards their land in the interior of Malekula and cultivated the land there, for example by raising kava crops in order to sell them for cash. Their hunting activity would additionally supply their families with meat. Around the garden areas closer to the village, younger boys were the ones helping their parents to clear the bush for new areas of gardening and they were the ones who helped carry the large bundles of bananas. When I asked them about the future, these boys would become very serious and said that one day they wanted to provide for their families, and that meant that they needed to know how to do the work. One day, the brother of my host father came to visit. At that time, he spent most of his time in the town working for hotels and other service providers. After the first night in the village, he grabbed his knife early in the morning and set off to the garden area, as it had been so long since he had been out to look around. He also wanted to plant a few yam tubers. After a long garden day, he returned, very tired but very happy. At dinner he laughed with his brother, my host father, who in turn explained that the reason for this good atmosphere was because for our guest it was important to have done some 'real work' again, and make a new garden, 'mekem wan garen'. Our guest's children, on the other hand, had only seen urban life, and both brothers regrettably recognised that they would probably miss out on knowledge of horticulture. All my other interlocutors who grew up in rural areas were sure that they had and would continue to follow practices of gardening. For them, gardening was a 'project' they wanted to continue.

A mother of four children, however, described her worries for the future: "Of course I'm a bit scared. Things are happening because of the [climate change] things. I think in the future our life will become much more difficult. I think that will also affect our aelan kakae (island food)." In March 2019, we experienced a prolonged low-pressure area in Dixon Reef, with high swells and recurring gusts of wind. The principal chief of the village simply shook his head and said "Another long depression, how is this going to continue in the future?", referring to the unsettled weather predicted by climate experts for the coming period. People made short trips to their gardens. I stayed at home as the people around me were too worried that a coconut would fall on my head en route. When a tropical cyclone actually came over this stretch of coast, it destroyed the banana gardens already in bloom. Shortly afterwards, a group formed to assess the extent of damage in the gardens. Group members were male representatives of the different nasara, as well as myself. We went around the garden areas and documented what had been damaged and what was to be given to the regional government for possible reception of compensation (in the form of emergency relief). As we walked around, we saw some areas badly damaged and some only mildly, but everywhere the men threw their hands up in the air and said that they had never seen anything like this before and that this was another sign that the times were changing. "We may see more of this now." "And what can you do about it?", I tried to ask in passing. "Nothing, you have to accept it", I received in response. Another of the younger women agreed with this statement in a different conversation and confirmed that those changes are in fact permanent. Additionally, people see that klaemet jenj might affect their gardening. "I think it will be harder for us to do our gardening in the future" one of the women explained. I asked her what that would mean for the future of their garden practices: "Will you still make your gardens?" She replied, and this mirrors opinions of others, "Yes, I think so. We will have to find solutions. For example, move our gardens to other spots like the riverbed." Thus, she expressed what I described in Chapter 3 in terms of 'humanized landscape' (Mondragón 2004), namely that people refer to their own agency in terms of changing gardens and gardening practices. Both women and men firmly confirmed that they see themselves as responsible for gardening and that they are able to change their gardening practices themselves. They would refer to the changes that they experienced in the community in reference to gardening.

Returning to the conversation at the beginning of this subchapter, Mama Agriculture, whose family included even the smallest children in their horticultural activities, put this into one phrase: "Yumi stap mekem garen blo yumi" (we will always make our garden). "This is just what we do", she added. With this statement, she emphasised that the villagers wanted to keep on gardening. The mother of the four children cited above also emphasised that one way of doing this is to concentrate on educating children: "We just have to talk to our children a lot now. Our children are the future now. Now is the time to teach them the right things and to correct them in what they are doing. Only in this way can we not lose our kastom." With this expression that gardening will be what they want and anticipate doing in the future, gardening becomes one of the key projects for the future, if not the primary one. Although it undergoes changes over time, gardening itself remains a constant in ni-Vanuatu lives.

6.6 Conclusion

People around Dixon Reef regarded gardening as a practice which they wanted to continue, but by discussing the future, they first looked at changes to their past. This looking forward and backward I frame with Epeli Hau'ofa's concept of time in Oceania as being both linear and circular (Hau'ofa 2008). My interlocutors were aware that life may be more difficult in the future. Nevertheless, they were not in despair because they relied on their gardening. When I asked them about future gardening, they first discussed long-term transformations in gardening and described a line of changes that led to how they live and work today. They referred to what has happened to their parents and bubu (ancestors) and then connected this to future generations. What they want to do in the future is articulated according to terms of gardening today and in the past. Referring to Hau'ofa's perspective, who saw the need to deal with Pacific lineal as well as circular perceptions of pasts in order to "present to the future" (Hau'ofa 2008, 69), I learnt that Dixoners' pasts are important to them to explain what they want to do in the future, however neither by a delimitation nor by a linear continuation of the past, but in an articulation between returning aspects and a processual present. Mekem garen has been a constant from the time when people lived up in the mountains to when they moved down to the sea and founded Dixon Reef, but it had to be altered to fit new circumstances and it changed because people purposefully reformed it. Now, with climate change looming and with the adaptation programme becoming part of a future directed discourse, mekem garen becomes once more a future project, representing what my interlocutors aspire to and simultaneously expressed in reference to the past by weaving in aspects of anticipation. They dealt with the anticipation of an uncertain garden future in relation to gardening in and as sociality as a reocurring pattern, rather than focusing on climate change-related food insecurity as a possible destructive future. Gardening as the constant in their lives has changing connotations and influences but recurring practices within. It returns in different phases, different times and different styles, but is never lost. Mekem garen is a praxis of making relations and thus remains a constant in people's lives, with its inherent changes. Thus, the future projects incorporate this dynamic.

In this chapter, I have illustrated how mekem garen is part of sociality among ni-Vanuatu horticulturalists. Once introduced to the praxis of gardening, a person is embedded in various social relations as well as part of the community, which means making relations beyond kin relations. Mekem garen is social because it contributes to making a relational person (Strathern 1988). Knowing what to do in the gardens means to enter a network that is an essential part of being a human, a person in relations. Gardening provides access to the community, information, trails and areas in the land that are meant for gardening. At the same time, people are involved in a network that keeps everyone 'alive' – not only through access to food, but also through the constant building of relationships. Mekem garen is only a basis of social relations if people work on it constantly. When it is no longer possible for some villagers to be on site, others continue to run their gardens and thus secure the original gardener's status in the community. People continued to cultivate gardens for others who had at one time entered the social relations. This was extended by the circle of exchange in which my interlocutors were included because they had been able to give harvest and therefore could receive the fruits of others' planting. Without a garden, people would fall out of the web of relationships and lose an important quality that makes them a socially-constituted person.

At the same time, changes in gardening praxis were considered as problematic, precisely because of this importance for sociality. My interlocutors expressed this by underlining that when they gardened, everything in the community worked too. This is why, for the future, they see no other way than to continue to mekem garen. In this sense, mekem garen becomes a future project, including social life, food, urban political climate change narratives and the changes ni-Vanuatu in rural areas envisage. From what I learnt from my interlocutors in the Dixon Reef area, they do not question that this practice must be continued. They communicated that klaemet jenj as a new phenomenon could also bring changes that people did not know about before. However, people had to make sure to continue gardening. One of the travelling men, who often spent his time in the city, waved off objections and my doubts as to whether less gardening will be done in future years, saying: "Oh, we here, we concentrate on our lives. Yes, the white people have to develop new techniques. But that is for them, not for us." People living on the islands, however, clearly see the advantage that they are closer to learning cultivation practices from an early stage. Even there, however, villagers dispersed over islands and communities loose from the common praxis of horticulture bear the biggest risk for radical ruptures, as many have explained to me over the years. At that point, keeping up with gardening becomes a project for all to see that klaemet jenj will not be allowed to take over.

The uncertainty that comes with the anticipated challenges of climate change discourses did not make people doubt the importance and persistence of their own gardening. My interlocutors live in a time in which they experience a lot of change, including klaemet jenj (which touches many parts of their lives). They accept and sometimes even embrace these changes but this does not prevent them from taking care of their gardens. On the contrary, continuing gardening is part of these changes. Thus, the future is connected with the past and provides new options for the future. Fundamentally, things will not change, and climate change does not represent a break here either. This is because the process of gardening is under continuous change, regardless of climate or any other transformations.

7 Cultivating with Climate Change

Over the centuries, gardening and cultivation in Vanuatu have been characterised by constant change. When people had moved to the shores through missionaries' ambitions, founded new villages, installed coconut and cocoa plantations, started keeping cattle around the village and pigs in the village, their gardening also changed. These changes brought new cultivars, new planting material, but also diseases for plants, animals and humans, and shifts in nutrition habits and reduced working time for cultivation. When reflecting on these past transformations, people point to the ambivalences and aspects of violent inflictions through outsiders. However, my interlocutors in both Dixon Reef and Siviri took on these pasts not with total resentment, because they wanted to draw productive lessons from them. Since the early 2010s, through involvement in the adaptation programme, gardens and people entered the process of worlding climate change including changes within the community as well as in relation to their more-than-human surroundings – in a flexible and self-reflexive way. Underlining their own ability to act in terms of shaping their daily lives, my interlocutors embraced their responsibilities in terms of their futures on the islands. In this book, I have focused on mekem garen as a praxis connected to the idea of the Anthropocene and to worlding climate change through mekem garen. The latter became entangled in ni-Vanuatu national discourse about political, environmental, economic and social changes. It brings together village communities with urban narratives about issues connected to weather hazards and food security, and makes them part of a globalised narrative of climate change. Through these narratives, ni-Vanuatu horticulturalists engage both in changes in their gardens and with climate politics in the country as a whole. This they do out of concern for climate change meanings for gardens and communal life, mutually changing both. However, this concern has not turned into a desperate mood.

This corresponds to political approaches in the whole Pacific region, where islanders are inclined to take climate change issues seriously, but reject the idea that they might be disruptive or paralysing inconveniences (Crook and Rudiak-Gould 2018, 8). These ways of thinking and acting are also reflected in public appearances on international platforms. Pacific people have caught world-wide attention not least when the former Prime Minister of Kiribati, Anote Tong, addressed the international community with the words: "[T]he issue of climate change remains the most single pressing challenge for us in Kiribati [...] The global community cannot afford to NOT listen to our stories and the plight of our people." (Tong 2014) Tong referred in his speech to poet Kathy Jetnil-Kijiner who addressed the international politicians of the United Nations with her poem expressing the goals of Pacific people in the face of climate change, writing it for her daughter: "[W]e are drawing the line here, because baby we are going to fight" (Jetnil-Kijiner 2014). These two representatives are both from low-lying island states in Micronesia, which bring with them their own specific issues and framings. Nevertheless, these two contributions to the UN Climate Summit in 2014 make us aware of important aspects when dealing with the topic of climate change in Oceania. Pacific Islanders will not passively stand back, but will fight, making the international community aware of the entanglement that climate change entails. They underlined, on the one hand, the fact that global action is needed, and on the other hand that Pacific people are already experiencing the consequences of global warming and will continue to do so to an even greater degree in the future, but that they will not passively endure its challenges.

7.1 Challenges and Changes

In Vanuatu, political policies focus on enabling citizens to continue living 'on the islands' in the wake of challenging weather and climatic conditions. The pair of events of Cyclone Pam and the drought of El Niño brought climate change projections into the present and initiated a whole discussion about agriculture and climate change. After several years of dealing with heat and dryness, in April 2019, my interlocutors in the Dixon Reef area and Siviri announced that their gardens and lives were finally 'back to normal' – rain and sun again made their usual interplay and gardening practices could be undertaken according to the seasons once again. With the harvest of 2019, it became clear that the cultivation of root crops had been highly successful and the men proudly talked about the yam harvest, looking forward to giving it as gifts or for exchange.

In terms of their daily routines, my interlocutors in Dixon Reef were happy to keep their rice diet to a minimum and invited me for meals into their kitchen houses to taste their freshly harvested taro and yam, praising the excellent taste. In Siviri, people had turned more to wage labour over the years, but were able to take advantage of their reinvigorated supply on the markets. Many used their free time to continue cultivation. Nevertheless, young people continue to be drawn to the urban lifestyle, where growing their own crops plays a lesser role. Their abilities are heavily dependent on how much they co-operate with their parents. Still many of my interlocutors in both locations were in a positive mood – cultivation was not restricted by bigger weather events. Although there were several warnings from the meteorological department about possible El Niño or La Niña threats, they were lifted again soon afterwards. Additionally, the cyclone seasons in March and April 2019 brought, according to the villagers, the usual wind and rain, which then supported their cultivation cycle. Officials of the government and NGOs also confirmed that the whole country had recovered, and that ni-Vanuatu could work their gardens again. Nevertheless, they added, this optimism had to be treated with caution, as conditions could change again quickly (which it did a few years later). People in the villages were equally aware that the events they had experienced could occur again at any time. According to them, they did not know what the future would bring, and since klaemet jenj was part of their daily routines now, they were aware of the uncertainties of this time. As I described in Chapters 3 and 4, Dixoners also identified those transformations as part of a wider development beyond their cultivation practices. However, they rooted their lives in practices of gardening and viewed this as a way to move forward.

By 2019, families in Dixon Reef again broke new ground, deciding to walk even further up into the mountains, preparing gardens there. They did this despite the fact that apparently conditions for cultivation at the coast were good. They went inland into the higher regions, in groups of extended family members, to their nasara land, where their ancestors had lived before the arrival of the missionaries. This meant that they had to accept a walk of, at times, more than a day and had to stay away from the coastal village for a couple of days or even weeks. At this time, they also built sleeping houses, formed small hamlets on their own land and started new garden plots, this time directly in front of their kitchen doors. They told me that there they could find excellent conditions for gardening practices: fertile and, as they put it, cold, moist soil and mild temperatures all year round. The advantage for them was that temperatures 'antap lo bus' (up there in the bush) are cooler, rainfall comes at a higher frequency, and thus crops grow much better so that the gardens produce a greater yield. Due to this, horticulturalists did not have to burn the ground before starting a new plot, but could simply cut the higher plants to make room for the new crops. This would certainly have made representatives of the NGOs happy, because they constantly promoted approaches with lower emissions. However, when I asked my gardening group why they would refrain from slash and burn, they said that in some locations it is not needed, and the whole endeavour once again became a matter of working with the ground rather than forcing it (Chapter 4).

Many women and men continued to ignore the notion of working in only one location, investing their time for cultivation intensively at one garden plot. Instead of staying in one place to secure the main supply for difficult times, and further make sure that they spent less time on cultivation, people added even more garden plots in the mountains and extended their garden network further. In this manner, gardening time and gardening space was extended. At that time, I increasingly asked myself whether the members of the village would disperse and thus live again up in the mountains, leaving Dixon Reef at the shore behind. However, they started new home gardens in the village and started planting extra crops. In 2019, some of the households had small home gardens and some were keeping these skills for another time, some had abandoned the idea, because they lacked a water supply, but would pick it up when they considered it appropriate. In the village of Siviri, interaction with the idea of the home gardens presented itself a little differently. There, women expanded their own home gardens, with fruits, vegetables and yam, while their families drove to other parts of the islands, because they created new plots for planting banana and manioc there. Both strategies, installing new gardens and moving them, was followed in both communities. Moving plants and gardens meant for them also going forward and remaining prepared for any changes, while following their own paths of cultivation and expanding their repertoires.

I asked my interlocutors in the Dixon Reef area about their reasons for starting more gardens on their ancestors' land in the mountains and whether they wanted to move back to their land and their own nasara where they would find better conditions for gardening. Most waved this idea off and were not interested in moving permanently 'antap' (up there). What they wanted was to take advantage of the opportunity to live in the mountains temporarily and follow their cultivation seasonally. Reasons they referred to circled around responsibilities of their life in the village, possibilities for earning money, better access to health services and that the children had to go to school. In any case, cultivation around the Dixon Reef area had to be continued and was simply complemented by new garden plots. Their seasonal movement to other areas was another step of orienting their gardening towards the future and dealing with klaemet jenj. Instead of investing additional time in adapting one place, they added more locations to their garden plots. This also included more time spent with their children gardening along paths of the bubu (ancestors) who had previously lived in the mountains. This was their way of dealing with the uncertainties of changing climate and weather and extending garden networks, ensuring the continuation of gardening.

In 2020, another kind of crisis entered the political agenda. With the onset of the Covid-19 pandemic, the government of Vanuatu soon closed its borders, not only for tourism but also for cargo. Cash income through work that concentrated on tourism, other services or selling cash crops came to a standstill. As a result, even on the main island of Efate, many ni-Vanuatu were thrown back into growing their own food. When I caught my host family in Siviri on the phone, those at the other end of the line were more concerned because of the news in Europe. They told me that they were not affected by the pandemic and that life for them was much quieter. Since they all had access to land and had been involved in cultivation their whole lives, even if the children and other professionals had only had time for it on holidays or weekends, they could easily just turn to (only) being horticulturalists. They even saw this (temporary) change in their daily lives rather as a liberation than a burden, and happily spent their days preparing new garden plots. In Dixon Reef, everyday economic and social life is strongly shaped by gardening in any case; the general isolation of Vanuatu only impacted their lives in terms of income from cash crops being lost due to the lack of transport. In terms of continuing their daily lives, this crisis had affected them the least. Again, their focus on mekem garen could be interpreted as a strength, their method of securing gardening as preparation for crisis. These crises were never any less concerning for people on the islands, but were rather their progressive way of dealing with (new) challenges. As these challenges grew and changed, ni-Vanuatu were moving forward, incorporating and creating new knowledge, discerning what was best for them and including their own actions while remaining critical of them.

7.2 Moving Lives through Mekem Garen

In the course of this book, I have drawn connections between mekem garen and politics of climate change from national narratives to daily practices of ni-Vanuatu in rural areas. Like politicians and representatives of local and international organisations, horticulturalists on both Malekula island and Efate island trust that horticulture is important to secure future lives. In this way, gardening has been connected to a broader worlding process which must be considered when approaching climate change. Activities in Vanuatu not only present an example of what actors make of climate change effects, or how they localise the discourses, narratives, prognosis etc. of international forums. As Crook and Rudiak-Gould point out, Pacific Islanders are "living climate change" (Crook and Rudiak-Gould 2018, 1). From a focus on agency in local adaptation measures, I consider climate change to be conceptually worked out not only in international panels, with a radiating effect into individual places, but rather, as created by actors in different localities synchronically. In my ethnographic context of village communities in Vanuatu, people become part of a dialogue of both reception and observation. They also explained, discussed and acted on their experiences on a daily basis. In addition to the political engagement described above, in this actor's perspective, encounters and practices further become defining moments of climate change (see Chapter 3).

People in Vanuatu do this creatively, with possibly surprising results in encounters with other people and practices. When dealing with encounters, I have drawn parallels to Tsing's concept of 'friction' (2005). Tsing scrutinises universalities in environmental discourses through ideas, concepts and practices coming together. Exemplified through the case of the abandoned home gardens and the adaptation workshops (Chapter 4), I have argued that frictions occurring in the context of encounters regarding climate change adaptation can be interpreted as ontological frictions. This means that I decided to approach these moments of irritation in encounters ontologically, by 'thinking through' the topic of climate change (Henare, Holbraad and Wastell 2006). Concepts might be re-defined in the process of working with them, a process which is happening in daily practices (Holbraad and Pedersen 2017; Salmond 2017). Thus, 'worlding practices' bring different worlds into being through the interaction of people and ontological assumptions. Those climate change worlding practices are responsible for creating many 'climate change worlds'; this also happened in Vanuatu, where the people I worked with created their klaemet jenj world. There are several climate change worldings happening and people are involved in one or more of them to try to make sense of changes. In so doing, they create their own concepts and raise notions that highlight the demand for rethinking mainstream definitions of anthropogenic influences with their effects on living conditions which then need adaptation. I will now revisit my learning from horticulturalists in rural Vanuatu, especially people living in the Dixon Reef area, on how mekem garen shows connective points of thinking with climate change.

The starting point of my research were the policy measures on climate change adaptation in Vanuatu. Those measures were developed in the context of scientific climate projections which show that current adverse weather phenomena will intensify all over the Pacific, including Vanuatu. This depicted a future in which islanders in Vanuatu experience more forceful and frequent cyclones, more dry periods as well as heavy rainfall events and shifting seasons due to intensification of the ENSO weather phenomenon (such as El Niño and La Niña). Representatives of the Vanuatu Agriculture Department, the Ministry for Climate Change and NGOs stated that the consequences of global warming and effects for weather events in Vanuatu could be especially harmful for rural communities, because there ni-Vanuatu mostly live off what they grow in their gardens. Cultivation of food crops remains the strongest economic branch in Vanuatu. Stemming from the discourse in urban areas, I have shown that town residents' concerns were related to family members in rural areas, 'on the islands'. Their connection to information hubs has brought them into new roles as experts. They perceived their role because of being, on the one hand, 'aware' of climate change-induced environmental threats and, on the other hand, given the tools for dealing with such threats (Chapter 3). With this they supported programmes for information dissemination and adaptative measures. In the village of Dixon Reef, one of those programmes called 'kakai fo laef' (Food for Life), conducted in the form of workshops and several visits per year over a period of almost 10 years, aimed to introduce alternative methods for cultivation based on permaculture principles. This mainly included climate friendly methods of preparing the soil with mulching, organic fertiliser, nitrogen fertilisation with trees and intercropping of different plants as well as irrigation with grey water. The use of these methods was intended to benefit the installation of home gardens, next to the family's kitchen houses. At the same time, people encountered topics that included natural scientific explanations like greenhouse effects as a cause and change in weather patterns as an effect. The sense of this approach of awareness and first-hand strategies for adaptation by national officials was considered to be confirmed by the two events: first, the category 5 Cyclone Pam, which had devastating results for that year's harvest, and second, what disturbed lives of ni-Vanuatu even more, the subsequent El Niño drought. Consequently, the political atmosphere that emerged with those two events was concerned, although not desperate. This progressive and pragmatic attitude was also reflected in the adaptation programmes. The representatives of the organisations expected climate change measures, especially soil preparation and home gardens, to be useful tools in order to face problematic times for horticulture, such as dry periods. So-called environmental problems were supposed to be countered with methods to work with this shifting environment.

Urban discussions drew a more dramatic picture when they addressed the possibilities of losing grounds for food production, framing this as nature 'will die'. Especially for younger ni-Vanuatu in Port Vila, climate change is considered to be an environmental problem and a way of life which relies on the weather; the environment renders people less prepared to address these new problems. Furthermore, they took the view that problems must be solved by incorporating new practices, especially by those parts of the population living in rural areas (Chapter 3). I have shown that by taking the conceptualisation they called 'klaemet jenj' as a new phenomenon, originating elsewhere but re-created in encounters and thereby influencing their lives, connecting them to places beyond their village, Dixoners have ultimately became part of global practice. Instead of seeing themselves as affected by but not responsible for global issues, my interlocutors in Siviri and Dixon Reef addressed the activities of both industrial countries and their own and thus formulated argumentations of universal self-blame. They included scientific explanations into their klaemet jenj practices, as well as observations of changing weather and experiences of changing human behaviour (Chapter 3). Responses to their own contribution to reducing damage and avoiding further fuelling of klaemet jenj is characterised in what they call 'respektem envaeromen'. This is their newly-named principle of taking care of everything around them, human or more-than-human, and equally taking care of the community in which they live. They act in their "humanized landscapes" (Mondragón 2018, 25), crafting everything around them, which includes building houses, relations to others – and gardening. Mekem garen bridges climate change worlds and shows that 'envaeromen' and community are part of what people call klaemet jenj.

After initial successful implementation, the food security part of the adaptation project in Dixon Reef temporarily concluded in the case of the 'abandoned home gardens' and discussion about it began (Chapter 4). Debates between villagers and representatives of the NGO were initiated through this heated discussion over those home gardens, because of the different approaches to it. The NGO's approach considered 'taking care of the ground' with methods of soil preparation and a constant build-up of a humus layer in one location. In the view of the NGOs, this gives gardeners permanent access to fresh food, especially when they are prevented from taking on the long and time-consuming walks into 'the bush' every day. People in the Dixon Reef area did at first embrace new techniques of mulching, composting etc. outside, but especially inside, their home gardens according to the NGO's intention, and the project accordingly became an early success story. However, during the El Niño event, they did not follow these methods up. During that time, people in Dixon Reef did not focus on the home gardens. Discussions were characterised by friction and did not reach the point of talking about what gardening actually is for people in Dixon Reef. Reflecting on these events, I interpreted their approach as the frequent statement of 'we cannot force the ground' in their relational approach to the ground. Villagers continued to prepare gardens according to shifting plots and following the principle of cultivating in different locations and different gardens with a diversity of plants. Instead of seeing these moments as a problem or possible failure of the whole programme and workshops, I argue that these frictions opened up discussion and moments to reflect about practices among my interlocutors and between me and my interlocutors, to further make sense of these ontological differences. In their own discussions during the programme, villagers tried to reflect on their own approaches to cultivation, opening up discussion about their climate change worlding. They approached mekem garen as constant innovation, in time of crises but also through circular approaches to starting and re-starting their cultivation parcels, both inside and outside the village.

Gardening practices in the past have been inspired by and alternated through contact with people, crops and plants from elsewhere and people have created what other scholars considered as 'traditional ecological knowledge' (McCarter and Gavin 2015). In contrast to the methods of the food security programme seeking to complement 'traditional' with new 'outside knowledge', I argue that this approach is part of a constant worlding praxis that needs encounters. The way people acted was different from what the NGO representatives wanted, but the new methods certainly did not fall on barren ground. Instead, some ideas and practices were taken up in the Dixoners' gardening practice. For my interlocutors, learning how to garden always means embracing the new and adapting it according to individual preferences and experiences. Learning mekem garen is characterised by doing and by adding observations and reception of new practices. Every workshop participant was able to repeat the content of the workshop or at least to refer to someone who seemingly knew. The application, however, was tied into flexibility and seasonality. Here, horticulturalists followed the NGO's linear practices only temporally – and this temporality itself brought up discussions. Interactions preliminarily resulted in the villagers' gardening practices taking the form of the elaborated new ways. People's actions are the product of their engagement with ontological assumptions and thus diversification and flexibility marked additional aspects of mekem garen. Planting many kinds of plants in one location and relocating them to other locations in the next season according to weather conditions was commonly practised, including new ways of mulching or composting. Through shifting and relocation, gardens, plants and people were constantly in motion. Although adaptation programmes did not aim for this, it brought in new ideas and also sparked discussions about how to deal with challenges.

Moving crops to better spots in order to gain higher yields is only one reason why people decided to walk longer distances between gardens (Chapter 5). The second reason is that they practise what I frame by referring to 'wayfaring' (Ingold 2007), following paths, with the aim of connecting the various locations along the way. When I followed my fellow Dixon Reef gardeners throughout their garden day, they led me from the coast up the hill, through swamp sites and through plantations. Every step of the way was one essential part of their gardening practice. Gardens and people around the area of Dixon Reef move. If people decide to move their gardens to other locations, they follow weather conditions and conditions of the soil. Then they follow new routes and thus create new paths. This process goes far beyond food production but is also a way to create the location and environment in which they live. I tried to capture this through discussions about mobile gardening and questioned the image of the garden as the sole place where activities happen. I first drew on the conceptualisation of place (Cresswell 2014; Massey 2005), which argues that place is shaped by human practices, and that although it contains and is made by practices, it remains within a certain locality. I complemented this with an approach to the concept of ples in Vanuatu. Here in this relational form, locations themselves are not fixed, but are rather made by relations between people and their surroundings (Hess 2009; Rodman 1992). The paths and garden locations are the visualisation of practices that have been carried out during the garden day. Accordingly, gardening is first and foremost to be seen as a practice that keeps people in motion and is created in motion. Thus, gardening is not place-bound but praxis-bound and, I argue, therefore the environment also comes into being through sequential activities that Ingold (1993) calls 'taskscape'. Thus, this taskscape is being constantly evolved and reshaped. What horticulturalists in Dixon Reef emphasised was that this environment in the context of klaemet jenj is one worth preserving. They are making this happen through following up on their gardening work. Cultivation in different places is also an extended practice to produce the environment, transforming dark bush into bush and then gardens.

Siviri presents a different picture due to its proximity to Port Vila, but one can also draw some parallels. Women have moved their gardens closer to the house so that they can grow their own crops at shorter distances. Supplies are diversified in families by the fact that additional products can be purchased through wage labour. This has intensified since the experience of El Niño. Nevertheless, gardens are still highly valued, forming a connection of land and family ties as well as backup in times of crisis. By acquiring new land and moving around with their own vehicles, residents are even expanding their network of weekend gardening. Either they distribute growing areas among family members in different villages around the island, or, if financially possible, new growing areas are developed through new joint land purchases or leases. In both cases, opportunities for cultivation are pushed further and gardeners are not stationary but move through the environment in their cultivation practices.

In these movements, interactions with plants and people become equally important, for food production but also for aspects of villager's sociality. Meeting points, like the 'raonabaot', in Dixoners' garden areas are characterised by practices of exchange – both information and plants or harvest change hands (Chapter 6) – and I have shown that everyday gardening practices are embedded in the production of social relations. The garden as a space of sociality has so far been connected by several scholars to exchange of crops in ceremonies, the cultivation of the ceremonial plant yam and on prestige through the special skill of the individual man through high crop yield. The sociality of gardening practices in Melanesia relates back to Malinowski's descriptions in his work on the Trobriand Coral Gardens (1935) in which he considered gardens in Melanesia as both social and personal. I referred to sociality as processual in the making (Long and Moore 2012) and then combined it with Melanesian sociality in a person itself as being a part of their social relation-making (Strathern 1988).

The sociality of mekem garen is expressed in how ni-Vanuatu enter and maintain their position in a network of social relations (even through gardening for others) and consider it as a daily activity which is fundamental for being a (relational) person. Everyone should learn and participate in this practice. Now, when political climate change practices present trends for the future as increasingly difficult for rural life, this is also an aspect that needs to be considered. People in Vanuatu very much see gardening as a "situated project" for the future (Rollason 2014), which integrates a perspective from the past and considers past changes and, in the eyes of my interlocutors, continues to change, considering what is ahead by looking back (Hau'ofa 2008). The uncertainties of anticipation (Bryant and Knight 2019) in relation to climate change did not make people want to leave their gardens behind but rather made them value them even more. Also, because gardens secure relations, i.e. something fundamental for a person in Vanuatu itself, the fact remained: "we will always make our garden".

In all of this, mekem garen as climate change praxis moves and is in motion, shaping surroundings, lives and futures. While it moves people, plants and gardens, at the same time people move mekem garen into new contexts, through challenging times and into the future. It is a praxis that guides people to act flexibly and is itself characterised by change. Mekem garen creates and preserves social life and the environment. Moreover, this environment is again made up of social lives – people's relations to each other – in the same way that activities are also related to making the environment. It has become evident that the focus on everyday gardening in relation to climate change solely as the basis for food security is one-sided. Like klaemet jenj, people consider their gardening to touch upon every aspect of their lives, and stamp it as being both influenced by their doing and an influence on themselves. Changes in behaviour and actions are at the same time explained as causes of and methods of dealing with all aspects of klaemet jenj.

Following encounters in climate change programmes, people in the Dixon Reef area actively demanded implementation of novel techniques in their village community. They welcomed the interaction with measures of adaptation, because encounters also raise new ideas. Their lives, and this is also apparent in their gardening practices, is characterised by a dualistic view, facing both outward and inward (Hviding 2003). Knowing about climate change discourse was felt to be a necessity to deal with changes around them. People do not wait for help, but rather take up the opportunities offered. However, while they encounter new practices, they continue to follow their own gardening practices.

Mekem garen is self-determined and thus, according to my interlocutors, also brings self-responsibility. If one aspect of life changes, e.g. communal life, so does gardening, as does the environment. However, the praxis itself, people want to remain a constant.

I started with a depiction of worlding practice and then showed how gardening fits into it and how the two influence each other. I have argued that apprehending mekem garen as a worlding praxis within the context of encounters in food security programmes also helps us to understand the climate change worlding of people living in Dixon Reef. My interlocutors' klaemet jenj world is characterised by both temporal and permanent changes, which both affect their community life and vice versa. Workshops, in their linear approaches, projected that climate issues are increasing in severity and explicate this phenomenon as a rupture that might be disruptive to ni-Vanuatu lives. The located adaptation methods are received with interest by the many ni-Vanuatu horticulturalists I have worked with over the years. However, rather than being taken on board wholly, such methods are woven into the flexible praxis of mekem garen and thus into their klaemet jenj worlds. Practices such as fishing or gathering shellfish are, like mekem garen, part of both everyday life and food supply. The way in which those practices of the sea, or water in the broadest sense, constitute 'worlding practices' could thus itself be a topic of further research. In other places in Vanuatu, small-scale fishing and the creation of marine spaces play a greater role than in Dixon Reef (cf. Calandra 2017). In the context of climate change, the national government emphasises 'conservation', i.e. preserving what is available (Westoby et al. 2020). In Dixon Reef and Siviri, people formulate their view of the sea as something that is "always there" and gives them what they need, although only seasonally. However, fish and shellfish constitute variety rather than staples in the diet of the villagers and in their view, their work evolves around their horticulturalist practices.

During my time walking and working with people in the Dixon Reef area and Siviri, I met my interlocutors as climate change actors. Although they move in a context of being conceptualised as the victims of circumstances who can no longer rely on what they currently 'know', they continue to move confidently in this context. They do not let themselves be told what to do or how to act according to climate change implementation. Risk and new developments are taken seriously but they do not see climate change as a radical rupture that cuts through their lives, preferring to continue their praxis in mekem garen, worlding new ontological assumptions. When they formulate that everything is different than before, pointing out permanent changes, they then look to mekem garen as a project for the future. The former foreign minister of Vanuatu, Ralph Regenvanu, argued against the vulnerable status of his country, because ni-Vanuatu are determined to do everything possible to address issues of climate change today. I see something similar at another level in Dixon Reef. People want to be informed, but do not allow themselves to become irritated or divert from their paths. However, what has to be borne in mind is that their klaemet jenj world is not yet included into political discussion.

7.3 Climate Change Revisited

In October 2023, we gathered around the kitchen table in Makin's kitchens right at the shoreline in the village in Dixon Reef. I was invited to join the family for lunch after attending church. Since my previous visit to Vanuatu, the country had experienced a series of cyclones. Two consecutive storms occurred at the beginning of 2023. The twin tropical Cyclones Judy and Kevin were the subject of discussion when I was seated at the table with my hosts. Dixon Reef was situated within the cyclone's eye this time, and thus experienced the consequences of the storm to a particularly acute degree. During the course of the meal, Makin and her husband informed me that they had once again lost all of their banana plants (referring to Cyclone Pam in 2015) as a result of the storm and that they were still engaged in the process of rebuilding the destroyed kitchen structures. "Of course we are tired of storms, but we have to go on", they explained to me when I asked how they put this into context after experiencing several such storms. Furthermore, they stated that the clean-up work and planting of root crops would be at risk of being impeded without the involvement of younger villagers. In recent years, there has been a notable decline in the number of young people in the area of Dixon Reef, because they have chosen to reside in the city for extended periods of time. Those still residing in the village have become increasingly concerned about the impact of these developments on the community. It was emphasised that gardens sometimes had to be visited by their actual gardeners, but that family tasks could be shared out. These events were challenging for community life and were of significant concern to my hosts, meaning that they required concerted action. The mention of these two events and developments simultaneously aligns with the explanations of climate change provided by ni-Vanuatu, in which the causes and effects of climate change come together, as well as the social and environmental aspects (Chapter 3). The media raised the narrative that Vanuatu is particularly vulnerable to new and intensified weather phenomena (e.g. The Guardian 2023). This gets explained from a new angle by the ni-Vanuatu population on the islands.

This short sequence again illustrates what I have explicated over the course of this climate ethnography. When Hulme asks why we disagree about climate change (2009), this is because we are supposed to strive for a universal definition, but he does not recognise that there are several climate change worldings which come with their own explanations. Having diverse explanations does not mean, however, that they cannot be placed in dialogue with each other, or that one is taking the situation less seriously than the other. I have provided a climate ethnography which gives further insight into the topic of man-made climate change and human activities. In so doing, I not only follow 'worlding practices' but have also included 'islanding' the phenomenon (Teaiwa 2007) in the context of climate change practices in other island societies in Oceania. The aim has been to show how a specific group of people in Oceania lives in an unsettling yet also transformative era called the Anthropocene. This example from Vanuatu shows important aspects of the volcanic islands of Melanesia. People in Dixon Reef and Siviri once more show themselves as people of the land and emphasise their role as gardeners. The option of migration, as considered by Pacific Islanders living on low lying atolls, is not discussed at the moment. Rather ni-Vanuatu think about and practise possibilities for creative handling of anticipated challenges for living conditions on their islands.

In the context of anthropological climate change research, this book is on the one hand ethnographically informed but on the other hand an 'experiment' of thinking further about the concept of climate change (Salmond 2017). In order to consider this, we have to look not only at how we use concepts, but further how we visit and re-visit political concepts within our research spaces. One important question must be how we can see and engage with the experiences and conceptualisations of climate change for different people in different localities. Further theoretical insights can be taken from Arno Pascht's contribution on knowledge practices and climate change in Vanuatu (Pascht 2019). I have concentrated on practices in Dixon Reef and therefore employed myself with the 'what is' and 'how' people see and live the concept of climate change. This book has not followed an approach in which I asked about how people act upon climate change or how they have interpreted it in their local context, because I approached this topic through exploring climate change encounters and climate change worlding practices. Inequalities and hierarchies in the politically-informed conceptualisation of climate change inform many academic and political discussions. The question of interpretive sovereignty of current status quo in climate change debates and actions was raised at the beginning of the book and I have shown in the course of my research that people in Vanuatu perceive themselves as agents in the dialogue on climate change. At the same time, of course, there is also a political issue: when Blaser and de la Cadena (2018) demand a view of the world as being many worlds, they call for a change in political thinking, which can equally be applied to the issue of climate change. The demand stands thus: the need to acknowledge a world of many climate change worlds that encounter and re-encounter each other in order to learn together how we approach the challenges of our time.

Bibliography

Adams, R. and Foster, S. (2024). Vanuatu. Encyclopedia Britannica, (2024, June 13). https://www.britannica.com/place/Vanuatu.

Ahlgren, I., Yamada, S. & A. Wong (2014). Rising Oceans, Climate Change, Food Aid, and Human Rights in the Marshall Islands. *Health and Human Rights Journal,* 16(1). Retrieved from https://www.hhrjournal.org/2014/07/rising-oceans-climate-change-food-aid-and-human-rights-in-the-marshall-islands/ [accessed 13/05/2020].

Allen, M. G. (2015). Framing food security in the Pacific Islands: empirical evidence from an island in the Western Pacific. *Regional Environmental Change,* 15(7), 1341–1353. https://doi.org/10.1007/s10113-014-0734-5.

Appadurai, A. (1990). Disjuncture and Difference in the Global Cultural Economy. *Theory, Culture & Society,* 7(2-3), 295–310. https://doi.org/10.1177/026327690007002017.

Appadurai, A. (1996). *Modernity at Large.* London [u.a.]: Univ. of Minnesota Press

Appadurai, A. (2013). *The Future as Cultural Fact: Essays on the Global Condition* (1. publ). London u.a.: Verso.

Arnall, A., Kothari, U.; & Kelman, I. (2014). Introduction to politics of climate change: discourses of policy and practice in developing countries. *The Geographical Journal,* 180(2), 98–101. Retrieved from http://www.jstor.org/stable/43868594 [accessed 08/10/2021].

Babon, A., McIntyre, D., Gowae, G. Y., Gallemore, C., Carmenta, R., Di Gregorio, M., & Brockhaus, M. (2014). Advocacy coalitions, REDD+, and forest governance in Papua New Guinea: how likely is transformational change? *Ecology and Society,* 19(3). https://doi.org/10.5751/ES-06486-190316.

Baer, H. A., & Singer, M. (2018). The Anthropology of Climate Change: An Integrated Critical Perspective (2nd ed.). *Routledge Advances in Climate Change Research* Ser. Milton. London: Routledge.

Ballard, C., McDonnell, S., & Calandra, M. (2020). Confronting the Naturalness of Disaster in the Pacific. *Anthropological Forum*, 30(1-2), 1–14. https://doi.org/10.1080/00664677.2020.1729698.

Barnes, J., Dove, M., Lahsen, M., Mathews, A., McElwee, P., McIntosh, R., ..., & Yager, K. (2013). Contribution of anthropology to the study of climate change. *Nature Climate Change*, 3(6), 541–544. https://doi.org/10.1038/nclimate1775.

Barnett, J., & Campbell, J. (2010). *Climate Change and Small Island States: Power, Knowledge, and the South Pacific*. London, Washington DC: Earthscan.

Barrau, J. (1958). *Subsistence Agriculture in Melanesia. Bernice P. Bishop Museum Bulletin: Vol. 219*. Bernice P. Bishop Museum.

Beck, U. (2008). *The cosmopolitan vision* (Reprinted.). Polity Press.

Berkes, F. (2012). *Sacred ecology* (3. ed.). New York u.a.: Routledge Taylor & Francis Group.

Birch-Thomsen, T., Reenberg, A., Mertz, O., & Fog, B. (2010). Continuity and change: Spatiotemporal land use dynamics on Bellona Island, Solomon Islands. *Singapore Journal of Tropical Geography*, 31(1), 27–40. https://doi.org/10.1111/j.1467-9493.2010.00383.x.

Blaser, M. (2009). The Threat of the Yrmo: The Political Ontology of a Sustainable Hunting Program. *American Anthropologist*, 111(1), 10–20. https://doi.org/10.1111/j.1548-1433.2009.01073.x.

Blaser, M. (2013). Ontological Conflicts and the Stories of Peoples in Spite of Europe. *Current Anthropology*, 54(5), 547–568. https://doi.org/10.1086/672270.

Blaser, M. (2014). Ontology and indigeneity: on the political ontology of heterogeneous assemblages. *Cultural Geographies*, 21(1), 49–58. https://doi.org/10.1177/1474474012462534.

Blaser, M., & de la Cadena, M. (2018). Pluriverse: Proposals for a World of Many Worlds. In M. de la Cadena & M. Blaser (Eds.), *A World of Many Worlds* (pp. 1–22). Durham: Duke University Press.

Boege, V. (2016). Climate Change and Planned Relocation in Oceania. *Sicherheit Und Frieden (S+F) / Security and Peace*, 34(1), 60–65.

Boliko, M. C. (2019). FAO and the Situation of Food Security and Nutrition in the World. *Journal of Nutritional Science and Vitaminology*, 65(Supplement), S4-S8. https://doi.org/10.3177/jnsv.65.S4.

Bollig, M. (2018). Afterword: Anthropology, Climate Change and Social-Ecological Transformations in the Anthropocene. *Sociologus*, 68(1), 85–94.

Bolton, L. (1999). Women, Place and Practice in Vanuatu: A View from Ambae. *Oceania*, 70(1), 43–55.

Bolton, L. (2001). Classifying the Material. *Journal of Material Culture*, 6(3), 251–268. https://doi.org/10.1177/135918350100600301.

Bolton, L. and J. Mitchell. (2021). "The Art of Gardens: An Introduction." *Anthropological Forum* 31 (4): 339–51. doi:10.1080/00664677.2021.2006603.

Bønnelykke Robertson, M. L. (2018). Crafting Certainty in Liquid Worlds: Encountering Climate Change in Kiribati. In T. Crook & P. Rudiak-Gould (Eds.), *Pacific Climate Cultures: Living Climate Change in Oceania* (pp. 45–59). Warsaw: De Gruyter.

Bonnemaison, J. (1974). Espaces et paysages agraires dans le nord des Nouvelles-Hébrides. L'exemple des îles d'Aoba et de Maewo (étude de géographie agraire) (1ère partie). *Journal De La Société Des Océanistes*, 30(44), 163–232. https://doi.org/10.3406/jso.1974.2676.

Bonnemaison, J. (1978). Custom and Money: Integration or Breakdown in Melanesian Systems of Food Production. In E. K. Fisk (Ed.), *The Adaptation of Traditional Agriculture: Socioeconomic Problems of Urbanization* (pp. 25–45). Canberra: Australian National University.

Bratrud, T. (2011): *Finding ways. Community and its challenges on Ahamb, Vanuatu.* Oslo, University of Oslo. (Unpublished Master of Arts thesis).

Bravo, M. T. (2009). Voices from the Sea Ice: The Reception of Climate Impact Narratives. *Journal of Historical Geography*, 35(2), 256–278. https://doi.org/10.1016/j.jhg.2008.09.007.

Bryant, R., & Knight, D. M. (2019). *The anthropology of the future.* Cambridge, New York, Melbourne, New Delhi, Singapore: Cambridge University Press.

Buggy, L., & McNamara, K. E. (2016). The need to reinterpret "community" for climate change adaptation: a case study of Pele Island, Vanuatu. *Climate and Development*, 8(3), 270–280. https://doi.org/10.1080/17565529.2015.1041445.

Burman, A. (2017). The Political Ontology of Climate Change: Moral Meteorology, Climate Justice, and the Colonial of Reality in the Bolivian Andes. *Journal of Political Ecology*, 24(1), 921–938.

Caillon, S. (2012). Produce to Exchange: The Taro Water-Gardens on Vanua Lava (Vanuatu), a Social and Sustainable Place. *Senri Ethnological Studies*, 78, 189–208.

Calandra, M. (2017). *Jardins de Terre, Jardins de Mer à Tongoa (Vanuatu): Une Anthropologie de la Nature Domestique dans un Milieu Affecté par la Catastrophe.* Volume

1. Marseille: École des Hautes Études en Sciences Sociales. (unpublished Doctorat en Anthropologie Sociale et en Ethnologie).

Calandra, M. (2020). Disasta: Rethinking the Notion of Disaster in the Wake of Cyclone Pam. *Anthropological Forum*, *30*(1–2), 42–54. https://doi.org/10.1080/00664677.2019.1647826.

Callon, M. (1986). Some Elements of a Sociology of Translation: Domestication of the Scallops and the Fishermen of St Brieuc. In J. Law J (Ed.) *Power, action and belief: a new sociology of knowledge?* (pp. 196–233). London: Routledge & Kegan Paul.

Campbell, J. R. (2014). Climate-Change Migration in the Pacific. *The Contemporary Pacific*, 26(1), 1–28. https://doi.org/10.1353/cp.2014.0023.

Campbell, J. R. (2015). Development, global change and traditional food security in Pacific Island countries. *Regional Environmental Change*, 15(7), 1313–1324. https://doi.org/10.1007/s10113-014-0697-6.

Carreon, B. & Doherty, B. (2021). *Pacific Islands Forum in crisis as one-third of member nations quit.* Retrieved from https://www.theguardian.com/world/2021/feb/09/pacific-islands-forum-in-crisis-as-one-third-of-member-nations-quit [accessed 11.10.2021].

Carter, L. (2019). *Indigenous Pacific Approaches to Climate Change: Aotearoa/New Zealand*. Cham, Switzerland: Springer International Publishing. https://doi.org/10.1007/978-3-319-96439-3.

Chao, S., & Enari, D. (2021). Decolonising Climate Change: A Call for Beyond-Human Imaginaries and Knowledge Generation. *ETropic: Electronic Journal of Studies in the Tropics*, 20(2), 32–54. https://doi.org/10.25120/etropic.20.2.2021.3796.

Cheesman, L. E. (1933). The Island of Malekula, New Hebrides. *The Geographical Journal*, 81(3), 193–207.

Chowdhury, M. R., Chu, P.-S., & Schroeder, T. (2007). ENSO and seasonal sea-level variability – A diagnostic discussion for the U.S.-Affiliated Pacific Islands. *Theoretical and Applied Climatology*, 88(3-4), 213–224. https://doi.org/10.1007/s00704-006-0245-5.

Chua, L. and H. Fair. ((2019) 2023). "Anthropocene". In F. Stein (Ed.), *The Open Encyclopedia of Anthropology*. Facsimile of the first edition in *The Cambridge Encyclopedia of Anthropology*. Online: http://doi.org/10.29164/19anthro.

Clark, A. (2011). Multimodal map making with young children: exploring ethnographic and participatory methods. *Qualitative Research*, 11(3), 311–330. https://doi.org/10.1177/1468794111400532.

Clarke, M., Leach, M. & Scambary, J. (2013). Reconciling Custom, Citizenship and Colonial Legacies: Ni-Vanuatu Tertiary Student Attitudes to National Identity. *Nations and Nationalism*, 19(4), 715–738.

Clarke, T., McNamara, K. E., Clissold, R., & Nunn, P. D. (2019). Community-based adaptation to climate change: lessons from Tanna Island, Vanuatu. *Island Studies Journal*, 14(1). https://doi.org/10.24043/isj.80.

Clissold, R., & McNamara, K. E. (2020). Exploring local perspectives on the performance of a community-based adaptation project on Aniwa, Vanuatu. *Climate and Development*, 12(5), 457–468. https://doi.org/10.1080/17565529.2019.1640656.

Conan, M. (Ed.). (1999). *Perspectives on garden histories*. Washington, DC: Dumbarton Oaks Research Library and Collection.

Connell, J. (2015). Food security in the island Pacific: Is Micronesia as far away as ever? *Regional Environmental Change*, 15(7), 1299–1311. https://doi.org/10.1007/s10113-014-0696-7.

Constable, A. L. (2017). Climate change and migration in the Pacific: options for Tuvalu and the Marshall Islands. *Regional Environmental Change*, 17(4), 1029–1038. https://doi.org/10.1007/s10113-016-1004-5.

Crate, S. A. (2008). Gone the Bull of Winter? *Current Anthropology*, 49(4), 569–595. https://doi.org/10.1086/529543.

Crate, S. A. (2011). Climate and Culture: Anthropology in the Era of Contemporary Climate Change. *Annual Review of Anthropology*, 40, 175–194.

Crate, S. A., & Nuttall, M. (2009). Introduction: Anthropology and Climate Change. In S. A. Crate & M. Nuttall (Eds.), *Anthropology and Climate Change: From Encounters to Actions* (pp. 9–38). Walnut Creek, Calif.: Left Coast Press.

Crate, S. A., & Nuttall, M. (Eds.). (2009). *Anthropology and Climate Change: From Encounters to Actions*. Walnut Creek, Calif.: Left Coast Press.

Craven, L. K. (2015). Migration-affected change and vulnerability in rural Vanuatu. *Asia Pacific Viewpoint*, 56(2), 223–236.

Cresswell, T. (2014). *Place: An Introduction* (2. Auflage). New York, NY: John Wiley & Sons.

Crook, T., & Rudiak-Gould, P. (2018). Introduction: Pacific Climate Cultures. In T. Crook & P. Rudiak-Gould (Eds.), *Pacific Climate Cultures: Living Climate Change in Oceania* (pp. 1–20). Warsaw: De Gruyter.

Crowley, T. (1995). *A New Bislama Dictionary*. Suva, Fiji: Institute of Pacific Studies, The University of the South Pacific.

CSIRO – Australian Bureau of Meteorology. (2014). *Climate Variability, Extremes and Change in the Western Tropical Pacific: New Science and Updated Country Re-*

ports. Pacific-Australia Climate Change Science and Adaptation Planning Program Technical Report, Australian Bureau of Meteorology and Commonwealth Scientific and Industrial Research Organisation, Melbourne, Australia.

Cumbers, A., Shaw, D., Crossan, J., & McMaster, R. (2018). The Work of Community Gardens: Reclaiming Place for Community in the City. *Work, Employment and Society*, 32(1), 133–149. https://doi.org/10.1177/0950017017695042.

Czarniawska, B., & Sevón, G. (2005). Translation Is a Vehicle, Imitation its Motor, and Fashion Sits at the Wheel. In B. Czarniawska-Joerges & G. Sevón (Eds.), *Global Ideas: How Ideas, Objects and Practices Travel in the Global Economy* (pp. 7–14). Malmö, Sweden, Herndon, VA: Liber & Copenhagen Business School Press.

Daswani, G. (2021). The (Im)Possibility of Decolonizing Anthropology. *Everyday Orientalism*, 11/18/2021. https://everydayorientalism.wordpress.com/2021/11/18/the-impossibility-of-decolonizing-anthropology/.

Davies, C. A. (2008). *Reflexive ethnography: A guide to researching selves and others*. London: Routledge.

Declercq, J., & Ayaka, R. A. (2017). Examining "Elite" Power Dynamics in Informant–Research Relations and Its Impact on Ethnographic Data Construction: A Case Study From Pharmaceutical Health Communication. *The International Journal of Qualitative Methods*, 16(1), 1–12.

Deo, A., Chand, S. S., Ramsay, H., Holbrook, N. J., McGree, S., Magee, A., Bell, S., Titimaea, M., Haruhiru, A., Malsale, P., Mulitalo, S., Daphne, A., Prakash, B., Vainikolo, V., & Koshiba, S. (2021). Tropical cyclone contribution to extreme rainfall over southwest Pacific Island nations. *Climate Dynamics*, 56(11-12), 3967–3993. https://doi.org/10.1007/s00382-021-05680-5.

Descola, P. (2013). *Beyond Nature and Culture*. Translated by Janet Lloyd. Chicago, London: The University of Chicago Press. https://ebookcentral.proquest.com/lib/kxp/detail.action?docID=3038515.

Diogo, M. P., Simões, A., Rodrigues, A.D., &Scarso, D. (2019). Introduction. In M.P. Diogo, A. Simões, A.D. Rodrigues, and D. Scarso (Eds.), *Gardens and Human Agency in the Anthropocene* (pp.1-16). Abingdon, Oxon, New York, NY: Routledge, 2019. Series: Routledge environmental humanities: Routledge.

Downey, G. (2007). Seeing with a 'sideways glance': visuomotor 'knowing' and the plasticity of perception. In M. Harris (Ed.), *Methodology and history in anthropology: Vol. 18. Ways of knowing: Anthropological approaches to crafting experience and knowledge*. New York, NY: Berghahn Books.

Emde, S., Dürr, E., & Schorch, P. (2020). Experiencing Pacific Environments: Pasts, Presents, Futures. *The Contemporary Pacific*, 32(1), 1–20. https://doi.org/10.1353/cp.2020.0001.

Erickson, C. L. (2009). Agency, Causeways, Canals, and the Landscapes of Everyday Life in the Bolivian Amazon. In J. E. Snead, C. L. Erickson, & J. A. (H.) Darling (Eds.), *Landscapes of Movement: trails, paths, and roads in anthropological perspective* (pp. 204–231). Philadelphia: University of Pennsylvania Press.

Erickson, K., & Stull, D. (2011(1998)). *Doing Team Ethnography*. 2455 Teller Road, Thousand Oaks California 91320 United States of America: SAGE Publications, Inc. https://doi.org/10.4135/9781412983976.

Eriksen, A. (2007). Understanding Cultural Change: The Return of Core Anthropological Concepts. *Reviews in Anthropology*, 36(2), 131–154. https://doi.org/10.1080/00938150701344673.

Eriksen, A. (2014). A Cursed Past and a Prosperous Future in Vanuatu. A Comparison of Different Conceptions of Self and Healing. In W. Rollason (Ed.), *Pacific perspectives: Vol. 2. Pacific futures: Projects, politics and interests* (1. ed., pp. 133–151). Berghahn Books.

Eriksen, T. H. (2020). A Better Impact Factor: Anthropology and Climate Change. *Anthropology Today*, 36(1), 1–3.

Fache, E., Dumas, P., & Ramon N'Yeurt, A. de (2019). Introduction: Synthèse interdisciplinaire de quelques Discours at Réponses liés au climate dans le Pacific. *Journal De La Société Des Océanistes – Le Pacific En Première Ligne Face Au Changement Climatique*, 149(2), 199–210.

Fair, H. (2018). Three stories of Noah: Navigating religious climate change narratives in the Pacific Island region. *Geo: Geography and Environment*, 5(2), 1–15. https://doi.org/10.1002/geo2.68.

Fair, H. (2020). Their Sea of Islands? Pacific Climate Warriors, Oceanic Identities, and World Enlargement. *The Contemporary Pacific*, 32(2), 341–369.

FAO. (2008). *Climate Change and Food Security in Pacific Island Countries*. Food and Agriculture Organization of the United Nations (FAO). Rome, Italy.

FAO. (2013). *Food wastage footprint: Impacts on natural resource*. Summary Report. Food and Agriculture Organization of the United Nations (FAO). Rome, Italy.

FAO. (2016). *AQUASTAT Country Profile –Vanuatu*. Food and Agriculture Organization of the United Nations (FAO). Rome, Italy.

FAO. (2020). *Country Gender Assessment of Agriculture and the Rural Sector in Vanuatu*. Port Vila.

Farbotko, C. (2010). Wishful Sinking: Disappearing Islands, Climate Refugees and Cosmopolitan Experimentation. *Asia Pacific Viewpoint*, 51(1), 47–60. https://doi.org/10.1111/j.1467-8373.2010.001413.x.

Farran, S. (2002). Land in Vanuatu: Moving Forward, Looking Backward. Hors Series Volume II, *Contemporary Challenges in the Pacific: Towards a New Consensus*, 213–223.

Farran, S. (2010). Law, Land, Development and Narrative: A Case-Study From the South Pacific. *International Journal of Law in Context*, 6(1), col. 1–21.

Féaux de La Croix, J. (2017). Iconic Places in Central Asia: The Moral Geography of Dams, Pastures and Holy Sites (1st ed.). *Kultur und soziale Praxis*. Transcipt Verlag.

Feld, S., & Basso, K. H. (2009). Introduction. In S. Feld & K. H. Basso (Eds.), *School of American Research Advanced Seminar Series. Senses of Place* (pp. 3–11). Santa Fe, NM: School of American Research Press.

Feld, S., & Basso, K. H. (Eds.). (2009). *School of American Research Advanced Seminar Series. Senses of Place* (pp. 3–11). Santa Fe, NM: School of American Research Press.

Field, C. B., Barros, V. R., Dokken, D. J., Mach, K. J., & Mastrandrea, M. D. (2014). *Climate Change 2014 – Impacts, Adaptation, and Vulnerability.* Cambridge University Press. https://doi.org/10.1017/CBO9781107415379.

Fox, J. J. (2006). Place and Landscape in Comparative Austronesian Perspective. In J. J. Fox (Ed.), *The Poetic Power of Place: Comparative Perspectives on Austronesian Ideas of Locality* (pp. 1–21). Canberra: ANU E Press.

Gesing, F. (2019). The Politics of Artificial Dunes: Sustainable Coastal Protection Measures and Contested Socio-natural Objects. *DIE ERDE*, 150(3), 145–157.

Goldman, M. J., Turner, M. D., & Daly, M. (2018). A critical political ecology of human dimensions of climate change: Epistemology, ontology, and ethics. *Wiley Interdisciplinary Reviews: Climate Change*, 9(4), 228. https://doi.org/10.1002/wcc.526.

Golub, A. (2014). *Ontology and wonder: an interview with Michael W. Scott.* Retrieved from https://savageminds.org/2014/03/19/ontology-and-wonder-an-interview-with-michael-w-scott/ [accessed 20/05/2020].

Goodenough, W., & Ivens (1933). The Island of Malekula, New Hebrides: Discussion. *The Geographical Journal*, 81(3), 208–210.

Goodman, J. (2018). Researching climate crisis and energy transitions: Some issues for ethnography. *Energy Research & Social Science*, 45(2–3), 340–347. https://doi.org/10.1016/j.erss.2018.07.032.

Government of Vanuatu, Department of Climate Change (2021). *The new DoCC in Vanuatu*. Retrieved from https://docc.gov.vu/index.php/about-us/the-new-docc-in-vanuatu [accessed 20/10/2021].

Granderson, A. A. (2018). Value conflicts and the politics of risk: challenges in assessing climate change impacts and risk priorities in rural Vanuatu. *Climate and Development*, 10(6), 481–494. https://doi.org/10.1080/17565529.2017.1318743.

Gundert-Hock, S. (1984). *Der historische Rahmen der wirtschaftlichen und politischen Entwicklung von Vanuatu*. Münchner ethnologische Abhandlungen: Bd. 4. München: Minerva.

Gutro, R. (2015). *Pam (Southern Pacific Ocean)*. NASA's Goddard Space Flight Center. Retrieved from https://www.nasa.gov/content/goddard/pam-southern-pacific-ocean/ [accessed 07/10/2021].

Haraway, D. (1988). Situated Knowledges: The Science Question in Feminism and the Privilege of Partial Perspective. *Feminist Studies*, 14(3), 575–599. https://doi.org/10.2307/3178066.

Hastrup, F. (2011). *Weathering the world: Recovery in the wake of the tsunami in a Tamil fishing village. Studies in environmental anthropology and ethnobiology: v. 16*. New York: Berghahn Books.

Hastrup, K. (2016). Climate Knowledge: Assemblage, Anticipation, Action. In S. A. Crate & M. Nuttall (Eds.), *Anthropology and Climate Change: From Actions to Transformations* (pp. 35–57). New York, London: Routledge.

Hastrup, K. (2018). Auf dem Weg zu einem globalen sozialen Imaginären? Der Klimawandel und das Ende einer Ära in den Sozialwissenschaften. In F. Gesing, M. Knecht, M. Flitner, & K. Amelang (Eds.), *Edition Kulturwissenschaft: Band 146. NaturenKulturen: Denkräume und Werkzeuge für neue politische Ökologien* (pp. 315–338). Bielefeld: transcript.

Hau'ofa, E. (2008). Pasts to Remember. In E. Hau'ofa (Ed.), *We Are the Ocean* (pp. 60–79). University of Hawaii Press. https://doi.org/10.1515/9780824865542-007.

Hau'ofa, E. (1994). Our Sea of Islands. *The Contemporary Pacific*, 6(1), 147–161.

Haug, M. (2021). Framing the Future through the Lens of Hope: Environmental Change, Diverse Hopes and The Challenges of Engagement. *ZfE/JSCA (Zeitschrift Für Ethnologie)*, 145(2020), 71–92.

Henare, Amiria J. M., Holbraad, M., & Wastell, S. (2006). Introduction: Thinking Through Things. In Henare, Amiria J. M., M. Holbraad, & S. Wastell (Eds.), *Thinking Through Things: Theorising Artefacts in Ethnographic Perspective* (pp. 1–31). Milton Park, Abingdon, Oxon, New York: Routledge.

Hereniko, V. (2014). The Human Climate Change. In W. Rollason (Ed.), *Pacific perspectives: Vol. 2. Pacific futures: Projects, politics and interests* (1st ed., pp. 226–235). New York NY u.a.: Berghahn Books.

Hermann, E. (2018). *Social capital in the face of climate change*. Göttingen: GISCA, Göttingen Institute for Social and Cultural Anthropology, Georg-August-Universität Göttingen. https://doi.org/10.3249/2363-894X-gisca-18.

Hermann, E., & Kempf, W. (2019). Adaptation and the question of migration: directions in dealing with climate change in Kiribati. In C. Klöck & M. Fink (Eds.), *Dealing with climate change on small islands: Towards effective and sustainable adaptation* (pp. 293–313). Göttingen: Göttingen University Press. https://doi.org/10.17875/gup2019-1221.

Hermann, E., Kempf, W., & van Meijl, T. (Eds.). (2014). *Pacific perspectives: volume 3. Belonging in Oceania: Movement, Place-making and Multiple Identifications* (First edition). Berghahn.

Hess, S. (2006). Strathern's Melanesian ⨯Dividual' and the Christian ⨯Individual': A Perspective from Vanua Lava, Vanuatu. *Oceania*, 76(3), 285–296.

Hess, S. C. (2009). *Person and Place: Ideas, Ideals and Practice of Sociality on Vanua Lava, Vanuatu. Person, space and memory in the contemporary Pacific: Vol. 2*. New York, NY u.a.: Berghahn Books.

Hetzel, D. (2016). *Über Klimawandel reden. Verbreitung neuer Diskurse und Gestaltung sozialer Rollen unter jungen ni-Vanuatu*. Köln: Universität zu Köln. (Unpublished Master Thesis).

Hetzel, D., & Pascht, A. (2017). Young ni-Vanuatu Encounter Climate Change: Reception of Knowledge and New Discourses. In E. Dürr & A. Pascht (Eds.), *Environmental Transformations and Cultural Responses: Ontologies, Discourses, and Practices in Oceania* (pp. 103–124). New York, s.l.: Palgrave Macmillan US.

Hetzel, D., & Pascht, A. (2019). Climate change and livelihood practices in Vanuatu. In C. Klöck & M. Fink (Eds.), *Dealing with climate change on small islands: Towards effective and sustainable adaptation* (pp. 195–216). Göttingen: Göttingen University Press. https://doi.org/10.17875/gup2019-1217.

Hirsch, E. (Ed.). (1995). *Oxford studies in social and cultural anthropology Cultural forms. The Anthropology of Landscape: Perspectives on Place and Space.* Oxford: Oxford Univ. Press.

Hofmann, R. (2014). Culturecide in Changing Micronesian Climates? About the Unintenionality of Climate Change. *International Journal of Human Rights*, 18(3), 336–349.

Hofmann, R. (2016). *Situating climate change in Chuuk: navigating "belonging" through environmental and social transformations in Micronesia*. Dissertationsschrift LMU München. München.

Holbraad, M. (2009). Ontography and Alterity: Defining Anthropological Truth. *Social Analysis*, 53(2), 80–93.

Holbraad, M., & Pedersen, M. A. (2017). *The ontological turn: An anthropological exposition. New departures in anthropology*. Cambridge: Cambridge University Press. https://doi.org/10.1017/9781316218907.

Holbraad, M., Pedersen, M. A. and Viveiros de Castro, E. (2014). *The Politics of Ontology: Anthropological Positions*. Theorizing the Contemporary. *Fieldsights*, January 13. Retrieved from https://culanth.org/fieldsights/the-politics-of-ontology-anthropological-positions [accessed 10/10/2021].

Hughes, D. M. (2013). Climate change and the victim slot: From oil to innocence. *American Anthropologist: Journal of the American Anthropological Association*, 115(4), 570–581.

Hulme, M. (2009). *Why We Disagree about Climate Change: Understanding Controversy, Inaction and Opportunity*. Cambridge, UK, New York: Cambridge University Press.

Hulme, M. (2010). Problems with Making and Governing Global Kinds of Knowledge. *Global Environmental Change*, 20(4), 558–564. https://doi.org/10.1016/j.gloenvcha.2010.07.005.

Hulme, M. (2015). Afterword: The Many Uses of Climate Change. In J. Barnes & M. Dove (Eds.), *Climate cultures: Anthropological perspectives on climate change. Yale Agrarian Studies Series* (pp. 289–299). New Haven: Yale University Press.

Hviding, E. (1996). *Guardians of Marovo Lagoon: Practice, Place, and Politics in Maritime Melanesia. Pacific islands monograph series: no. 14*. Honolulu, [Manoa]: University of Hawai'i Press; Center for Pacific Islands Studies, School of Hawaiian, Asian, and Pacific Studies, University of Hawai'i.

Hviding, E. (2003). Both Sides of the Beach: Knowledges of Nature in Oceania. In H. Selin (Ed.), *Science across cultures. The history of non-western science: Vol. 4. Nature across cultures: Views of nature and the environment in non-western cultures* (pp. 245–276). Dordrecht, London: Springer.

Hyslop, C. (2006). Bislama. In E.K. Brown *Encyclopedia of Language & Linguistics* (pp. 53–54). London: Elsevier. https://doi.org/10.1016/B0-08-044854-2/04493-X.

Iese, V., Kiem, A. S., Mariner, A., Malsale, P., Tofaeono, T., Kirono, D. G.C., ... & Iona, N. (2021). Historical and future drought impacts in the Pacific islands and atolls. *Climatic Change*, 166(1-2), 452. https://doi.org/10.1007/s10584-021-03112-1.

Ingold, T. (1993). The temporality of the landscape. *World Archaeology, 25(2) Conceptions of Time and Ancient Society*,152–174.

Ingold, T. (2000). *The perception of the environment: Essays on livelihood, dwelling and skill*. London: Routledge.

Ingold, T. (2007). Earth, Sky, Wind, and Weather. *Journal of the Royal Anthropological Institute*, 19–38.

Ingold, T. (2008). Bindings against Boundaries: Entanglements of Life in an Open World. *Environment and Planning a: Economy and Space*, 40(8), 1796–1810. https://doi.org/10.1068/a40156.

Ingold, T. (2011). *Being Alive: Essays on Movement, Knowledge and Description*. Abingdon, Oxon, N.Y.: Routledge.

Ingold, T., & Vergunst, J. L. (2008). Introduction. In T. Ingold & J. L. Vergunst (Eds.), *Anthropological studies of creativity and perception. Ways of walking: Ethnography and practice on foot* (pp. 1–19). Aldershot, Farnham: Ashgate.

IPCC. (2007). IPCC Fourth Assessment Report (AR4): Climate Change 2007: Impacts, Adaptation and Vulnerability. Contribution of Working Group II to the Fourth Assessment Report of the Intergovernmental Panel on Climate Change. Cambridge University Press.

James Paul, & Steger, M. B. (2016). Globalization and Global Consciousness: Levels of Connectivity. In R. Robertson & D. Buhari-Gulmez (Eds.), *Global connections. Global culture* (pp. 21–39). Farnham, Surrey, Burlington, VT: Ashgate Publishing.

James, S. (n.d.). *Food Security in Port Vila, Vanuatu*. Retrieved from https://library.sprep.org/sites/default/files/food-security-port-vila.pdf.

Jensen, C. B. (2021). *Practical Ontologies Redux*. Berlin: Humboldt-Universität zu Berlin. https://doi.org/10.18452/22974.

Jetnil-Kijiner, K. (2014). *United Nations Climate Summit Opening Ceremony – A poem to my Daughter.* https://www.kathyjetnilkijiner.com/united-nations-climate-summit-opening-ceremony-my-poem-to-my-daughter/ [accessed 06/10/2021].

Johnson, S., & Lenge, B. (2012). *2009 National Population and Housing Census Youth Monograph. Young people in Vanuatu: An analysis of the situation of young people from the 2009 Population and Housing Census*. Port Vila: Vanuatu National Statistics Office. Retrieved from https://www.youthpolicy.org/national/Vanuatu_2009_Youth_Monograph_Report.pdf.

Jolly, M. (1999). Another time, another place. *Oceania*, 69 (4), 282–299.

Jolly, M. (2018). 1. Horizons and Rifts in Conversations about Climate Change in Oceania. In W. Anderson, M. Johnson, B. Brookes, W. Anderson, B. Brookes, & M. Johnson (Eds.), *Pacific Futures: Past and Present* (pp. 17–48). University of Hawaii Press. https://doi.org/10.1515/9780824877422-003.

Keck, V. (1998). Introduction. In V. Keck (Ed.), *Explorations in anthropology. Common Worlds and Single Lives: Constituting Knowledge in Pacific Societies* (pp. 1–32). Oxford, New York: Berg.

Kelman, I. (2019). Pacific island regional preparedness for El Niño. *Environment, Development and Sustainability*, 21(1), 405–428. https://doi.org/10.1007/s10668-017-0045-3.

Kempf, W. (2019). Tsunami Warnings: Cultural Conceptualizations of Climate Change Impacts in Kiribati. *Journal De La Société Des Océanistes*. (149), 245–256. https://doi.org/10.4000/jso.10877.

Kempf, W., & Hermann, E. (2014). Uncertain Futures of Belonging: Consequences of Climate Change and Sea-level Rise in Oceania. In E. Hermann, W. Kempf, & T. van Meijl (Eds.), *Movement, Place-making and Multiple Identifications* (pp. 189–213). New York, Oxford: Berghahn.

Klenk, N., & Meehan, K. (2015). Climate change and transdisciplinary science: Problematizing the integration imperative. *Environmental Science & Policy*, 54(2), 160–167. https://doi.org/10.1016/j.envsci.2015.05.017.

Klepp, S., & Chavez-Rodriguez, L. (2018). Governing climate change: The power of adaptation discourses, policies and practices. In S. Klepp & L. Chavez-Rodriguez (Eds.), *Routledge advances in climate change research. A Critical Approach to Climate Change Adaptation: Discourses, Policies, and Practices*. London, New York: Routledge earthscan from Routledge.

Klöck, C., & Fink, M. (2019). Dealing with Climate Change on Small Islands: Towards Effective and Sustainable Adaptation? In C. Klöck & M. Fink (Eds.), *Dealing with climate change on small islands: Towards effective and sustainable adaptation* (pp. 1–15). Göttingen: Göttingen University Press. https://doi.org/10.17875/gup2019-1209.

Knox, H. (2020). *Thinking Like a Climate: Governing a City in Times of Environmental Change*. Duke University Press. https://doi.org/10.1215/9781478012405.

Kraemer, D. (2013). *Planting Roots, Making Place: An Ethnography of Young Men in Port Vila, Vanuatu*. London, London School of Economics. (PhD thesis).

Kraemer, D. (2020). Planting Roots, Making Place: Urban Autochthony in Port Vila Vanuatu. *Oceania*, 90(1), 40–54. https://doi.org/10.1002/ocea.5239.

Krause, F. (2021). Now what? Repositioning anthropology vis-à-vis climate change activism. *Social Anthropology*, 29(1), 229–231.

Krebs, J., & Bach, S. (2018). Permaculture—Scientific Evidence of Principles for the Agroecological Design of Farming Systems. *Sustainability*, 10(9), 3218. https://doi.org/10.3390/su10093218.

Kuehling, S. (2017). "We Die For Kula" – An Object-Centred View of Motivations and Strategies in Gift Exchange. *The Journal of the Polynesian Society*, 126(2), 181–207.

Kumar, L. (2020). *Climate Change and Impacts in the Pacific*. Cham, Switzerland: Springer International Publishing. https://doi.org/10.1007/978-3-030-32878-8.

Kusenbach, Margarethe (2003). Street phenomenology: The go-along as ethnographic research tool. *Ethnography* 4(3), 455–485.

La Cadena, M. d., & Blaser, M. (Eds.). (2018). *A World of Many Worlds*. Duke University Press.

La Puig de Bellacasa, M. (2017). Matters of Care: Speculative Ethics in More Than Human Worlds. *Posthumanities* 41. Minneapolis, London: University of Minnesota Press.

Lannoy, J. d. (2004). *Through the Vale of Darkness: History in South Malakula, Vanuatu* (PhD thesis). University of Oxford, Oxford.

Larcom, Jo. C. & Beierle, J. (2002). *Malekula* (OO12). Human Relations Area Files, INc, New Haven, Conn. Retrieved from https://ehrafworldcultures-yale-edu.emedien.ub.uni-muenchen.de/document?id=oo12-000 [accessed 07/10/2021].

Lata, S. & Nunn, P. (2012). Misperceptions of climate-change risk as barriers to climate-change adaptation: a case study from the Rewa Delta, Fiji. *Climatic Change*, Vol. 110 (1/2), 169–186.

Latour, B. (2017). *Kampf um Gaia: Acht Vorträge über das neue Klimaregime* (A. Russer & B. Schwibs, Trans.). Berlin: Suhrkamp.

Law, J. (2015). What's wrong with a one-world world? *Distinktion: Journal of Social Theory*, 16(1), 126–139. https://doi.org/10.1080/1600910X.2015.1020066.

Layard, J. (1942). *Stone Men of Malekula: Vao*. London: Chatto & Windus.

Lazrus, H. (2012). Sea Change: Island Communities and Climate Change. *Annual Review of Anthropology*, 41(1), 285–301. https://doi.org/10.1146/annurev-anthro-092611-145730.

Lazrus, H. (2016). Shifting Tides: Climate Change, Migration, and Agency in Tuvalu. In S. A. Crate & M. Nuttall (Eds.), *Anthropology and Climate Change: From Actions to Transformations* (pp. 220–227). New York, London: Routledge.

Le Dé, L., Rey, T., Leone, F., & Gilbert, D. (2018). Sustainable Livelihoods and Effectiveness of Disaster Responses: A Case Study of Tropical cyclone Pam in Vanuatu. *Natural Hazards*, 91(3), 1203–1221. https://doi.org/10.1007/s11069-018-3174-6.

Filho, Leal W. (Ed.). (2013). *Climate Change and Disaster Risk Management*. Berlin, Heidelberg: Springer Berlin Heidelberg.

Lebel, L. (2013). Local knowledge and adaptation to climate change in natural resource-based societies of the Asia-Pacific. *Mitigation and Adaptation Strategies for Global Change*, *18*(7), 1057–1076. https://doi.org/10.1007/s11027-012-9407-1.

Lebot, V. (1992). Genetic Vulnerability of Oceania's Traditional Crops. *Experimental Agriculture*, 28(3), 309–323. https://doi.org/10.1017/S0014479700019906.

Lebot, V., & Siméoni, P. (2015). Community Food Security: Resilience and Vulnerability in Vanuatu. *Human Ecology*, 43(6), 827–842. https://doi.org/10.1007/s10745-015-9796-3.

Lebot, V., Malapa, R., & Sardos, J. (2015). Farmers' selection of quality traits in cassava (Manihot esculenta Crantz) landraces from Vanuatu. *Genetic Resources and Crop Evolution*, 62(7), 1055–1068. https://doi.org/10.1007/s10722-014-0209-z.

Lee, J., & Ingold, T. (2007). Fieldwork on foot: Perceiving, routing, socializing. In S. Simon Coleman & P. Collins (Eds.), *Locating the field: space, place and context in anthropology* (pp. 67–85). Oxford.: Berg.

Lind, C. (2014). Why the Future is Selfish and Could Kill: Contraception and the Future of Paama. In W. Rollason (Ed.), *Pacific perspectives: Vol. 2. Pacific futures: Projects, politics and interests* (1st ed., pp. 71–95). New York NY u.a.: Berghahn Books.

Lindstrom, L. (2011). Naming and Memory on Tanna, Vanuatu. In E. Hermann (Ed.), *Changing Contexts, Shifting Meanings: Transformations of Cultural Traditions in Oceania* (pp. 141–156). Honolulu: University of Hawaii Press.

Lindstrom, L. (2017). Respek and Other Urban Vila Keywords. *Journal De La Société Des Océanistes*. (144–145), 23–36. https://doi.org/10.4000/jso.7849.

Long, N. J., & Moore, H. L. (2012). *Sociality: New Directions*. *WYSE Series in Social Anthropology*. New York, NY: Berghahn Books.

Long, N. J., & Moore, H. L. (Eds.) (2012). *Wyse series in social anthropology: Vol. 1. Sociality: New directions*. New York: Berghahn.

Luhrmann, T. (2010). 9. What Counts as Data? In J. Davies & D. Spencer (Eds.), *Emotions in the Field: The Psychology and Anthropology of Fieldwork Experience* (pp. 212–238). Stanford University Press. https://doi.org/10.1515/97808047 74260-012.

Lynch, J., & Crowley, T. (2001). *Languages of Vanuatu: A new survey and bibliography. Pacific linguistics: Vol. 517*. Canberra: Pacific Linguistics Research School of Pacific and Asian Studies Australian National Univ.

Mackinem, M. B., & Higgins, P. (2007). Tell Me about the Test. *Journal of Contemporary Ethnography*, 36(3), 223–251. https://doi.org/10.1177/08912416062 87417.

Maclellan, N. (2015). *Yumi stap redi long klaemet jenis. Lessons from the Vanuatu NGO Climate Change Adaptation Program*. Oxfam Australia. Retrieved from https://www2.pazifik-infostelle.org/uploads/vanuatu_adaptation_p rogram_final.pdf [accessed 07/10/2021].

Malinowski, B. (1922). *Argonauts of the western Pacific: An account of native enterprise and adventure in the archipelagoes of Melanesian New Guinea. Studies in economics and political science: Series of monographs*. London: Routledge.

Malinowski, B. (1935). *Coral gardens and their magic: A study of the methods of tilling the soil and of agricultural rites in the Trobriand Islands*. London: Allen & Unwin.

Mallon, S. (2010). Against Tradition. *The Contemporary Pacific*, 22(2), 362–381.

Manner, H. I., & Thaman, R. R. (2013). Agriculture. In M. Rapaport (Ed.), *Environment and Society, Revised Edition. The Pacific Islands* (pp. 341–354). University of Hawai'i Press.

Marino, E., & Schweitzer, P. (2016). Speaking Again of Climate Change: An Analysis of Climate Chage Discourses in Northwestern Alaska. In S. A. Crate & M. Nuttall (Eds.), *Anthropology and Climate Change: From Actions to Transformations* (pp. 200–209). New York, London: Routledge.

Massey, D. (1997) 'Spatial disruptions', in S. Golding (ed.), *The eight technologies of otherness* (pp. 218–25). London: Routledge.

Massey, D. B. (2005). *For space*. London, Thousand Oaks, Calif: Sage.

Mbow, C., C. Rosenzweig, L.G. Barioni, T.G. Benton, M. Herrero, M. Krishnapillai, E. Liwenga, P. Pradhan, M.G. Rivera-Ferre, T. Sapkota, F.N. Tubiello, Y. Xu (2019): Food Security. In P.R. Shukla, J. Skea, E. Calvo Buendia, V. Masson-Delmotte, H.-O. Pörtner, D.C. Roberts, P. Zhai, R. Slade, S. Connors, R. van Diemen, M. Ferrat, E. Haughey, S. Luz, S. Neogi, M. Pathak, J. Petzold, J. Portugal Pereira, P. Vyas, E. Huntley, K. Kissick, M. Belkacemi, J. Malley, (eds.), *Climate Change and Land: an IPCC special report on climate change, desertification, land degradation, sustainable land management, food security, and greenhouse gas fluxes in terrestrial ecosystems*. Retrieved from https://www.ipcc.ch/srccl/#home-chapter-5 [accessed 07/10/2021].

McCarter, J., & Gavin, M. C. (2011). Perceptions of the value of traditional ecological knowledge to formal school curricula: Opportunities and challenges from Malekula Island, Vanuatu. *Journal of Ethnobiology and Ethnomedicine*, 7.

McCarter, J., & Gavin, M. C. (2014a). Local Perceptions of Changes in Traditional Ecological Knowledge: A Case Study from Malekula Island, Vanuatu. *AMBIO*, 43(3), 288–296. https://doi.org/10.1007/s13280-013-0431-5.

McCarter, J., & Gavin, M. C. (2014b). In Situ Maintenance of Traditional Ecological Knowledge on Malekula Island, Vanuatu. *Society & Natural Resources*, 27(11), 1115–1129. https://doi.org/10.1080/08941920.2014.905896.

McCarter, J., & Gavin, M. C. (2015): Assessing Variation and Diversity of Ethnomedical Knowledge: A Case Study from Malekula Island, Vanuatu. In *Economic Botany*, 69(3), 251–261.

McDonnell, S. (2020). Other Dark Sides of Resilience: Politics and Power in Community-Based Efforts to Strengthen Resilience. *Anthropological Forum*, 30(1-2), 55–72. https://doi.org/10.1080/00664677.2019.1647828.

McNamara, E., & Prasad, S. S. (2013). Valuing Indigenous Knowledge for Climate Change Adaptation Planning in Fiji and Vanuatu. *Traditional Knowledge Bulletin – Tropical Issues Series*, 1–7.

McNamara, K. E., & Farbotko, C. (2017). Resisting a 'Doomed' Fate: an analysis of the Pacific Climate Warriors. *Australian Geographer*, 48(1), 17–26. https://doi.org/10.1080/00049182.2016.1266631.

McNamara, K. E., & Prasad, S. S. (2014). Coping with extreme weather: Communities in Fiji and Vanuatu share their experiences and knowledge. *Climatic Change*, 123(2), 121–132. https://doi.org/10.1007/s10584-013-1047-2.

McNaught, R., Warrick, O., & Cooper, A. (2014). Communicating climate change for adaptation in rural communities: a Pacific study. *Regional Environmental Change*, 14(4), 1491–1503. https://doi.org/10.1007/s10113-014-0592-1.

Meurer, M. (2021) Rethinking Political Ontology. *Berliner Blätter*, 84, 77–9. https://doi.org/10.18452/22973.

Miller, T. L. (2016). Living Lists: How the Indigenous Canela Come to Know Plants Through Ethnobotanical Classification. *Journal of Ethnobiology*, 36(1), 105–124. https://doi.org/10.2993/0278-0771-36.1.105.

Mimura, N., & Nunn, P. D. (1998). Trends of Beach Erosion and Shoreline Protection in Rural Fiji. *Journal of Coastal Research*, 14(1), 37–46.

Ministry of Agriculture, Livestock, Forestry, Fisheries and Biosecurity – MALFFB (2021). Ministry of Agriculture, Livestock, Forestry, Fisheries and Biosecurity – Home. Retrieved from https://malffb.gov.vu/ [accessed 25/09/2021].

Ministry of Agriculture, Livestock, Forestry, Fisheries and Biosecurity – MALFFB (2022). *2022 Vanuatu National Agriculture Census. Volume 1 – Main Tables Report (Provisional)*. Port Vila: Vanuatu Bureau of Statistics.

Mitchell, J. (2004). 'Killing time' in a postcolonial town: Young people and settlements in Port-Vila, Vanuatu, In: Victoria S. Lockwood (Ed.), *Globalization and culture change in the Pacific Islands*, (pp. 358–376). Upper Saddle River, N.J., Pearson Education.

Mitchell, J. (2021). 'Awakening the Stones': The Nieri Performance, Gardens and Regeneration in Tanna, Vanuatu. *Anthropological Forum*, 31(4), 433–449. https://doi.org/10.1080/00664677.2021.2004878.

Mitchell, J., Niras, J., & Niefeu, L. (2020). Cultivating Wellbeing: Young People and Food Gardens on Tanna, Vanuatu. *Engaged Scholar Journal: Community-Engaged Research, Teaching, and Learning*, 6 (1), 1–17.

Moesinger, A. (2019). Influence of socio-economic stressors on interpretations of climate change on Takuu Atoll, Papua New Guinea. *Journal De La Société Des Océanistes*. (149), 224–234. https://doi.org/10.4000/jso.11312.

Mollison, B. (2004). *Permaculture: A designers' manual* (2. ed.). Tagari.

Mondragón, C. (2004). Of winds, worms and Mana: The traditional calendar of the Torres Islands, Vanuatu. *Oceania*, 74(4), col. 289–308.

Mondragón, C. (2006). Time and the Expression of Temporality in the Torres Islands, Vanuatu. *Revista Etnològic De Catalunya*, 28, 8–19.

Mondragón, C. (2014). Seasonal Environmental Practices and Climate Fluctuations in Island Melanesia. Agroforestry, Marine Tenure and Sea Level Rise in Vanuatu. In F. Angleviel & M. Abong (Eds.), *Portes océanes: Vol. 26. La Mélanésie – Actualités et Études: Foncier et Développement Durable: Année 2014, Tome 2* (pp. 131–152). Paris: Harmattan.

Mondragón, C. (2015). Concealment, Revelation and Cosmological Dualism: Visibility, Materiality and the Spiritscape of the Torres Islands, Vanuatu. *Cahiers D'anthropologie Sociale*, 11, 38–51.

Mondragón, C. (2018). Forest, Reef and Sea-Level Rise in North Vanuatu: Seasonal Environmental Practices and Climate Fluctuations in Island Melanesia. In D. Nakashima, I. Krupnik, & J. T. Rubis (Eds.), *Indigenous Knowledge for Climate Change Assessment and Adaptation* (Vol. 4, pp. 23–40). Cambridge University Press. https://doi.org/10.1017/9781316481066.003.

Morel, K., Léger, F., & Ferguson, R. S. (2019). Permaculture. In Brian F. *Encyclopedia of Ecology* (Vol. 99, pp. 559–567). Elsevier. https://doi.org/10.1016/B978-0-12-409548-9.10598-6.

Mucke, P., Kirch, Lotte & Walter, J. (2019). *World Risk Report 2019*. Berlin, Bochum: Bündnis Entwicklung Hilft and Ruhr University Bochum – Institute for International Law of Peace and Armed Conflict (IFHV). Retrieved from https://weltrisikobericht.de/download/1243/ [accessed 04/10/2020].

Mückler, H. (2010). Vanuatu. In A. Dittmann, W. Gieler, & M. Kowasch (Eds.), *Die Außenpolitik der Staaten Ozeaniens: Ein Handbuch; von Australien bis Neuseeland, von Samoa bis Vanuatu* (pp. 161–170). Paderborn: Schöningh.

Munn, N. D. (1986). *The fame of Gawa: A symbolic study of value transformation in a Massim (Papua New Guinea) society* (1. paperback printing). Durham: Duke Univ. Press.

Nakayama, M., Drinkall, S., & Sasaki, D. (2019). Climate Change, Migration, and Vulnerability: Overview of the Special Issue. *Journal of Disaster Research*, 14(9), 1246–1253. https://doi.org/10.20965/jdr.2019.p1246.

National Advisory Committee on Climate Change (NACCC). (2007). *National Adaptation Programme for Action (NAPA), Port Vila, Republic of Vanuatu*. Retrieved from https://www.adaptation-undp.org/resources/naps-least-developed-countries-ldcs/vanuatu-national-adaptation-programme-action-napa [accessed 13/04/2020].

National Advisory Board on Climate Change and Disaster Risk Reduction, Government of Vanuatu (NAB) (2021a). *El Niño-Southern Oscillation* (ENSO). Retrieved from https://www.nab.vu/climate-change-projects/glossary/el-ni%C3%B1o-southern-oscillation-enso [accessed 20/09/2021].

National Advisory Board on Climate Change and Disaster Risk Reduction, Government of Vanuatu (NAB). (2021b). *National Advisory Board*. Retrieved from https://www.nab.vu/ [accessed 20/09/2021].

Neurath, J. (2018). Fricciones ontológicas en las colaboraciones entre huicholes y ambientalistas. *Relaciones Estudios De Historia Y Sociedad*, *156*, 167–194. https://doi.org/10.24901/rehs.v39i156.317.

Newell, J. (2018). Weathering Climate Change in Samoa: Cultural Resources for Resilience. In T. Crook & P. Rudiak-Gould (Eds.), *Pacific Climate Cultures* (pp. 88–105). Warsaw, Poland: De Gruyter Open.

Nightingale, A. J., et al. (2020). Beyond Technical Fixes: climate solutions and the great derangement. *Climate and Development*, *12*(4), 343–352. https://doi.org/10.1080/17565529.2019.1624495.

Nombo, P., Leach, J., & Anip, U. (2021). Drawing on Human and Plant Correspondences on the Rai Coast of Papua New Guinea. *Anthropological Forum*, 31(4), 352–376. https://doi.org/10.1080/00664677.2021.1990012.

O'Reilly, J., Isenhour, C., McElwee, P., & Orlove, B. (2020). Climate Change: Expanding Anthropological Possibilities. *Annual Review of Anthropology*, 49(1), 13–29. https://doi.org/10.1146/annurev-anthro-010220-043113.

Orlove, B. (2009). The Past, the Present and Some Possible Futures of Adaptation. In W. N. Adger, I. Lorenzoni, & K. L. O'Brien (Eds.), *Adapting to Climate Change: Thresholds, Values, Governance* (pp. 131–163). Cambridge: Cambridge Univ. Press.

Orlove, B., Lazrus, H., Hovelsrud, G. K., & Giannini, A. (2014). Recognitions and Responsibilities: On the Origins and Consequences of the Uneven Attention to Climate Change around the World. *Current Anthropology*, 55(3), 249–275. https://doi.org/10.1086/676298.

Ourbak, T., & Magnan, A. K. (2018). The Paris Agreement and climate change negotiations: Small Islands, big players. *Regional Environmental Change*, 18(8), 2201–2207. https://doi.org/10.1007/s10113-017-1247-9.

Pascht, A. (2019). Klaemet jenj worlds. Approaching climate change and knowledge creation in Vanuatu. *Journal De La Société Des Océanistes*. (149), 235–244. https://doi.org/10.4000/jso.11257.

Pascht, A. (forthcoming). *Encountering Climate Change concepts and practices in Vanuatu*.

Pascht, A., & Dürr, E. (2017). Introduction. In E. Dürr & A. Pascht (Eds.), *Environmental Transformations and Cultural Responses: Ontologies, Discourses, and Practices in Oceania* (pp. 103–124). New York, s.l.: Palgrave Macmillan US.

Pascoe, S. (2018). Interrogating scale in the REDD+ assemblage in Papua New Guinea. *Geoforum*, 96(4), 87–96. https://doi.org/10.1016/j.geoforum.2018.08.007.

Pascoe, S. (2021). Stealing Air and Land – The Politics of Translating Global Environmental Governance in Suau, Papua New Guinea. *Conservation and Society*, 19(1), 34. https://doi.org/10.4103/cs.cs_19_125.

Pearce, E. (2012). Dual and plural in languages of Vanuatu. *Linguistic Typology*, 16, 191–232.

Perumal, N. (2018). "The place where I live is where I belong": community perspectives on climate change and climate-related migration in the Pacific island nation of Vanuatu. *Island Studies Journal*, 13(1), 45–64. https://doi.org/10.24043/isj.50.

Pierce, C. (1999). The Changing Coastline at Mele Beach, Vanuatu. *Geography*, 84(2), 149–163.

Piggoott-McKellar, A. E., Nunn, P., McNamara, K. E., & Sekinini, S. T. (2015). Dam(n) Seawalls: A Case of Climate Change Maladaptation in Fiji. In W. Leal Filho (Ed.), *Climate Change Management. Climate change in the Asia-Pacific region* (pp. 69–84). Cham, Switzerland: Springer.

Pink, S. (2009). *Doing Sensory Ethnography*. Los Angeles, Calif.: Sage.

Pink, S. (2012). *Situating everyday life: Practices and places* (1. publ). Los Angeles: Sage. https://doi.org/10.4135/9781446250679.

Pollock, N. (2017). Diversification of Foods and their Values: Pacific Foodscapes. In E. Gnecchi-Ruscone & A. Paini (Eds.), *Tides of Innovation in Oceania* (pp. 261–293). Canberra: ANU Press. https://doi.org/10.22459/TIO.04.2017.08.

Powell, K. (2010). Making Sense of Place: Mapping as a Multisensory Research Method. *Qualitative Inquiry*, 16(7), 539–555. https://doi.org/10.1177/1077800410372600.

Power, S., Delage, F., Chung, C., Kociuba, G., & Keay, K. (2013). Robust twenty-first century projections of El Niño and related precipitation variability. *Nature*, 502(7472), 541–545. https://doi.org/10.1038/nature12580.

Pritchard, M. (2017). *Yumi Stap Redi long Klaemet Jenis.: Ex-Post Evaluation Report – Vanuatu NGO Climate Change Adaptation Program*. Port Vila. Retrieved from https://www.nab.vu/sites/default/files/documents/OXF020%20Ex-Post%20Evaluation%20PRINT.pdf [accessed 23.08.2021].

Radcliffe, C., Rihai, N., Parissi, C., & Raman, A. (2018). More than a political slogan: The value of "kastom" in extension for sustainable agricultural in Vanuatu. *Rural Extension and Innovation Systems Journal*, 14(1), 91–100. https://search.informit.org/doi/10.3316/informit.563546973739721.

Red Cross Red Crescent Climate Centre. (2021). *El Niño complicates Cyclone Pam recovery.* Retrieved from https://www.climatecentre.org/1676/el-nino-complicates-cyclone-pam-recovery/_(accessed 20/07/2021).

Reenberg, A., Birch-Thomsen, T., Mertz, O., Fog, B., & Christiansen, S. (2008). Adaptation of Human Coping Strategies in a Small Island Society in the SW Pacific – 50 Years of Change in the Coupled Human-Environment System on Bellona, Solomon Islands. *Human Ecology*, 36(6), 807–819. https://doi.org/10.1007/s10745-008-9199-9.

Regenvanu, R. (2005). The Changing Face of"Custom" in Vanuatu (The Pacific in the 21st Century Formation of New Culture and Identity). *People and Culture in Oceania, 20, 37–50.*

Regenvanu, R. (2010). *The traditional economy as source of resilience in Vanuatu.* Retrieved from http://milda.aidwatch.org.au/sites/default/files/Ralph%20Regenvanu.%20Traditional%20economy%20as%20a%20source%20of%20resistance%20in%20Vanuatu.pdf [accessed 07/10/21].

Rey, T., Le De, L., Leone, F., & Gilbert, D. (2017). An integrative approach to understand vulnerability and resilience post-disaster. *Disaster Prevention and Management: An International Journal*, 26(3), 259–275. https://doi.org/10.1108/DPM-07-2016-0137.

Richmond, N., & Sovacool, B. K. (2012). Bolstering Resilience in the Coconut Kingdom: Improving Adaptive Capacity to Climate change in Vanuatu. *Energy Policy*, 50(0), 843–848. https://doi.org/10.1016/j.enpol.2012.08.018.

Rio, K. M. (2007a). Denying the Gift: Aspects of Ceremonial Exchange and Sacrifice on Ambrym Island, Vanuatu. *Anthropological Theory*, 7(4), 449–470. https://doi.org/10.1177/1463499607083429.

Rio, K. M. (2007b). *The Power of Perspective: Social ontology and agency on Ambrym Island, Vanuatu*. New York: Berghahn Books.

Rio, K. M. (2009). Subject and Object in a Vanuatu Social Ontology: A Local Vision of Dialectics. *Journal of Material Culture*, 14(3), 283–308. https://doi.org/10.1177/1359183509106422.

Robbins, J. (2004). *Becoming Sinners: Christianity and Moral Torment in a Papua New Guinea Society*. University of California Press.

Robbins, J. (2007). Continuity thinking and the problem of Christian culture. Belief, Time, and the Anthropology of Christianity. *Current Anthropology*, 48(1), 5–17.

Robin, C. (2002). Outside of houses. *Journal of Social Archaeology*, 2(2), 245–268. https://doi.org/10.1177/1469605302002002397.

Rodman, M. C. (1992). Empowering Place: Multilocality and Multivocality. *American Anthropologist*, 94(3), 640–656.

Rollason, W. (2014). Introduction: Pacific Futures, Methodological Challenges. In W. Rollason (Ed.), *Pacific perspectives: Vol. 2. Pacific futures: Projects, politics and interests* (1st ed., pp. 1–27). New York NY u.a.: Berghahn Books.

Rollason, W. (Ed.). (2014). *Pacific futures: Projects, Politics and Interests* (1. ed.). New York NY u.a.: Berghahn Books.

Roncoli, C., Crane, T., & Orlove, B. (2009). Fielding Climate Change in Cultural Anthropology. In S. A. Crate & M. Nuttall (Eds.), *Anthropology and Climate Change: From Encounters to Actions* (pp. 87–115). Walnut Creek, Calif.: Left Coast Press.

Rosengren, D. (2018). Science, Knowledge and Belief. On Local Understandings of Weather and Climate Change in Amazonia. *Ethnos*, 83(4), 607–623. https://doi.org/10.1080/00141844.2016.1213760.

Rousseau, B. (2012). Provincialising Lakatoro: Orienting sociality through a state institution in Vanuatu. *Australian Journal of Anthropology*, 23(2), 197–211. https://doi.org/10.1111/j.1757-6547.2012.00181.x.

Rubow, C. (2013). The Mixed response to Climate Change in The Cook Islands. In K. Hastrup & M. Skrydstrup (Eds.), *Routledge studies in anthropology: Vol. 8. The Social Life of Climate Change Models: Anticipating Nature* (pp. 57–76). New York: Routledge.

Rubow, C. (2018). Woosh – Cyclones as culturalnatural whirls: The receptions of climate change in the Cook Islands. In T. Crook & P. Rudiak-Gould (Eds.), *Pacific Climate Cultures: Living Climate Change in Oceania* (pp. 34–44). Warsaw: De Gruyter.

Rudiak-Gould, P. (2011). Climate Change and Anthropology: The Importance of Reception Studies. *Anthropology Today*, 27(2), 9–12.

Rudiak-Gould, P. (2012). Promiscuous corroboration and climate change translation: A case study from the Marshall Islands. *Global Environmental Change*, 22(1), 46–54. https://doi.org/10.1016/j.gloenvcha.2011.09.011.

Rudiak-Gould, P. (2013). "We Have Seen It with Our Own Eyes": Why We Disagree about Climate Change Visibility. *Weather, Climate, and Society*, 5(2), 120–132. https://doi.org/10.1175/WCAS-D-12-00034.1.

Rudiak-Gould, P. (2016). Climate Change Beyond the "Environmental". The Marshallese Case. In S.A. Crate and M. Nuttall (Eds.), *Anthropology and Climate Change. From Actions to Transformations* (pp. 261–270). New York, London: Routledge.

Russell, P., & Horvat, C. (2023). Extreme South Pacific Phytoplankton Blooms Induced by Tropical Cyclones. *Geophysical Research Letters*, 50(5), Article e2022GL100821. https://doi.org/10.1029/2022GL100821.

Salmond, A. (2014). Transforming translations (part 2): Addressing ontological alterity. *HAU: Journal of Ethnographic Theory*, 4(1), 155–187. https://doi.org/10.14318/hau4.1.006.

Salmond, A. (2017). Epilogue: Re-building ships at sea: Ontological innovation in action. In E. Dürr & A. Pascht (Eds.), *Environmental Transformations and Cultural Responses: Ontologies, Discourses, and Practices in Oceania* (pp. 215–226). New York, s.l.: Palgrave Macmillan US.

Sardos, J., Muller, S., Duval, M.-F., Noyer, J.-L., & Lebot, V. (2016). Root crops diversity and agricultural resilience: a case study of traditional agrosystems in Vanuatu (Oceania). *Agriculture and Human Values*, 33(3), 721–736. https://doi.org/10.1007/s10460-015-9657-0.

Schank, R. C., & Abelson, R. P. (1977). *Scripts, Plans, Goals, and Understanding: An Inquiry Into Human Knowledge Structures. Artificial Intelligence Series*. Hoboken: Taylor and Francis.

Schneider, K. (2012). *Saltwater Sociality: A Melanesian Island Ethnography*. New York: Berghahn Books.

Schorch, P., & Pascht, A. (2017). Reimagining Oceania through Critical Junctures: Introduction, *Oceania* 87(2), 114–123.

Schütz, A. J. (1969). Nguna grammar. *Oceanic linguistics Special publication*: Vol. 5. Univ. of Hawaii Press.

Scott, M. W. (2007). Neither 'new Melanesian history' nor 'new Melanesian ethnography': Recovering emplaced matrilineages in southeast Solomon Island. *Oceania*, 77(3), 337–354.

Secretariat of the Pacific Community (SPC) Land Resources Division. (2010). *SPC/GIZ Coping with Climate Change in the Pacific Island Region*. Retrieved from https://lrd.spc.int/spcgiz-coping-with-climate-change-in-the-pacific-island-regionq [accessed 30/11/2020].

Seggern, J. von. (2021). Understandings, Practices and Human-Environment Relationships – A Meta-Ethnographic Analysis of Local and Indigenous Climate Change Adaptation and Mitigation Strategies in Selected Pacific Island States. *Sustainability*, 13(1), 11. https://doi.org/10.3390/su13010011.

Sillitoe, P. (2010). Trust in Development: Some Implications of Knowing in Indigenous Knowledge. *The Journal of the Royal Anthropological Institute*, 16(1), 12–30. https://doi.org/10.2307/40541802.

Siméoni, P., & Lebot, V. (2012). Spatial Representation of Land Use and Population Density: Integrated Layers of Data Contribute to Environmental Planning in Vanuatu. *Human Ecology*, 40(4), 541–555. https://doi.org/10.1007/s10745-012-9487-2.

Sjöberg, J. (2020). Ethno Science Fiction: Projective Improvisations of Future Scenarios and Environmental Threat in the Everyday Life of British Youth. In P. e. a. Salazar, S. Pin, A. Irving & J. Sjöberg (Eds.), *Anthropologies and futures. Researching Emerging and Uncertain Worlds* (pp. 171–188). London: Routledge.

Snead, J. E., Erickson, C. L., & Darling, J. A. (Eds.) (2010). *Landscapes of Movement: Trails, Paths, and Roads in Anthropological Perspective*. Philadelphia, Pa.: University of Pennsylvania Press. https://doi.org/10.9783/9781934536537.

Sökefeld, M. (2007). Interaktionspartner im Vergleich: Ali Hassan und Mohammad Abbas in Gilgit. *EthnoScripts: Analysen und Informationen aus dem Institut für Ethnologie der Universität Hamburg*, 8(2), 7–29.

Stein, F. (Ed.). (2019). The Cambridge Encyclopedia of Anthropology. Facsimile edition, *The Open Encyclopedia of Anthropology*. Online: https://www.anthroencyclopedia.com/entry/anthropocene.

Stodulka, T. (2024). "Tasting the Soil and Mobilizing the Future: Pedagogies of Hope in Timor-Leste's Permaculture Youth Camps." *American Behavioral Scientist*. doi:10.1177/00027642241246691.

Strathern, M. (1980). No Nature, No Culture: The Hagen Case. In C. MacCormack & M. Strathern (Eds.), *Nature, Culture and Gender* (pp. 174–222). Cambridge Univ. Press.

Strathern, M. (1988). *The Gender of the Gift: Problems with Women and Problems with Society in Melanesia. Studies in Melanesian anthropology: Vol. 6*. Berkeley, Cal.: Univ. of California Press.

Strathern, M. (1992). Parts and wholes: refiguring relationships in a postplural world. In A. Kuper (Ed.), *Conceptualising society* (pp. 75–106). London: Routledge.

Taylor, J. P. (2008). *The other side: Ways of being and place in Vanuatu. Pacific islands monograph series: Vol. 22*. Honolulu: University of Hawai'i Press.

Tcherkézoff, S. (2003). A Long and Unfortunate Voyage towards the 'Invention' of the Melanesia/Polynesia Distinction 1595–1832. *The Journal of Pacific History*, 38(2), 175–196.

Teaiwa, T. (2007). To island. In G. Baldacchino (Ed.), *A world of islands: An island studies reader* (p. 514). Charlottetown, Canada, Luqa, Malta: Institute of Island Studies, University of Prince Edward Island and Agenda Academic.

Teaiwa, K. (2018). Our rising sea of islands: Pan-Pacific regionalism in the age of climate change. *Pacific Studies*, 41(1-2).

The Guardian (2023). 'We are very vulnerable': cyclone-hit Vanuatu pins climate hopes on UN vote. Retrieved from https://www.theguardian.com/world/2023/mar/28/we-are-very-vulnerable-cyclone-hit-vanuatu-pins-climate-hopes-on-un-vote?CMP=share_btn_url [accessed 09/02/2025].

Timon, T., Kaunda, C. J., & Hewitt, R. R. (2019). Re-envisioning Tangintebu Theological College in the context of climate change: An emerging model of coconut theological education and ministerial formation. *HTS Teologiese Studies / Theological Studies*, 75(1), 507. https://doi.org/10.4102/hts.v75i1.5169.

Tong, A. (2014). *Statement by H.E President Anote Tong*, 69th Unga, New York, 26 September 2014. Retrieved from https://www.un.org/en/ga/69/meetings/gadebate/pdf/KI_en.pdf [accessed 07/10/2021].

Tsing, A. L. (2005). *Friction: An ethnography of global connection*. Princeton, N.J.: Princeton University Press.

Turunen, J., Čeginskas, V. L. A., Kaasik-Krogerus, S., Lähdesmäki, T., & Mäkinen, K. (2020). Poly-space: Creating new concepts through reflexive team ethnography. In T. Lähdesmäki, E. Koskinen-Koivisto, V. L. A. Čeginskas, & A-K. Koistinen (Eds.), *Challenges and Solutions in Ethnographic Research: Ethnography with a Twist* (pp. 3–20). London: Routledge. Retrieved from https://www.taylorfrancis.com/books/e/9780429355608 [accessed 10/09/2021].

United Nations, Office of the High Representative for the Least Developed Countries, Landlocked Developing Countries and Small Island Developing States (UN). (2021). *Small Island Developing States*. Retrieved from https://www.un.org/ohrlls/content/about-small-island-developing-states [accessed 20/09/2021].

Vandeputte-Tavo, L. (2013). "Bislama in the Educational System? Debate Around the Legitimacy of a Creole at School in a Post-Colonial Country." *Current Issues in Language Planning* 14 (2): 254–69. doi:10.1080/14664208.2013.837217.

Vanuatu Bureau of Statistics and the Pacific Community. (2022). *Vanuatu 2020 National Population and Housing Census*. Retrieved from https://vbos.gov.vu/sites/default/files/2020_Vanuatu_National_Population_and_Housing_Census_-_Analytical_report_Volume_2.pdf [accessed 15/01/2025].

Vanuatu National Statistics Office. (2017). *Vanuatu 2016 Post-TC Pam Mini-Census Report*: Volume 1. Retrieved from https://vnso.gov.vu/images/Public_Documents/Census_Surveys/Census/2016/2016_Mini_Census_Main_Report_Vol_1.pdf [accessed 25/08/2021].

Vanuatu Project Management Unit. (2024). *Facts about Vanuatu. Government of Vanuatu*. https://vpmu.gov.vu/index.php/about-vpmu/facts-about-vanuatu [accessed 06/10/2024].

Walshe, R. A., Chang Seng, D., Bumpus, A., & Auffray, J. (2017). Perceptions of adaptation, resilience and climate knowledge in the Pacific. *International Journal of Climate Change Strategies and Management*, 10(2), 303–322. https://doi.org/10.1108/IJCCSM-03-2017-0060.

Walter, A., Lebot, V., & Sam, C. (2007). *Gardens of Oceania. ACIAR monograph: Vol. 122*. Canberra: Australian Centre for International Agricultural Research.

Walworth, M., Dewar, A., Ennever, T., Takau, L., & Rodriguez, I. (2021). Multilingualism in Vanuatu: Four case studies. *International Journal of Bilingualism*, 15(2). https://doi.org/10.1177/13670069211023132.

Warrick, O. (2011). *Local Voices, Local Choices? Vulnerability to Climate Change and Community-Based Adaptation in Rural Vanuatu. University of Waikato*, Waikato. (Ph thesis).

Warrick, O. (2021). *Climate change and social change: vulnerability and adaptation in rural Vanuatu*. SPREP Data Set. Waikato: The University of Waikato Retrieved from https://pacific-data.sprep.org/dataset/climate-change-and-social-change-vulnerability-and-adaptation-rural-vanuatu-olivia-warrick [accessed 7.10.21].

Weightman, B. (1989). *Agriculture in Vanuatu: A historical review*. Cheam, Surrey: British Friends of Vanuatu.

Weiner, J. F. (1991). *The Empty Place: Poetry, Space, and Being Among the Foi of Papua New Guinea*. Bloomington: Indiana University Press.

Weiner, J. F. (2002) 'Between a Rock and a Non-Place: Towards a Contemporary Anthropology of Place', *Reviews in Anthropology*, 31(1), 21. https://doi.org/10.1080/00988150212934.

Weisser, F., Bollig, M., Doevenspeck, M., & Müller-Mahn, D. (2014). Translating the 'adaptation to climate change' paradigm: the politics of a travelling idea in Africa. *The Geographical Journal*, 180(2), 111–119. https://doi.org/10.1111/geoj.12037

Wentworth, C. (2017). Good Food, Bad Food, and White Rice: Understanding Child Feeding Using Visual-Narrative Elicitation. *Medical Anthropology*, 36(6), 602–614. https://doi.org/10.1080/01459740.2017.1336621.

Wentworth, C. (2020). Unhealthy Aid: Food Security Programming and Disaster Responses to Cyclone Pam in Vanuatu. *Anthropological Forum*, 30(1-2), 73–90. https://doi.org/10.1080/00664677.2019.1647830.

West, P. (2006). *Conservation is our government now: The politics of ecology in Papua New Guinea. New ecologies for the twenty-first century.* Duke University Press.

Westoby, R., McNamara, K. E., Kumar, R., & Nunn, P. D. (2020). From community-based to locally led adaptation: Evidence from Vanuatu. *AMBIO*, 49(9), 1466–1473. https://doi.org/10.1007/s13280-019-01294-8.

Wewerinke-Singh, M., & Salili, D. H. (2020). Between negotiations and litigation: Vanuatu's perspective on loss and damage from climate change. *Climate Policy*, 20(6), 681–692. https://doi.org/10.1080/14693062.2019.1623166.

Whitaker, J. A. (2018). Imagination and the Poetics of Being and Becoming an Other in Amazonia. *Anthropology of Consciousness*, 29(1), 120–131. https://doi.org/10.1111/anoc.12090.

Whitaker, J. A. (2020). Climatic and Ontological Change in the Anthropocene among the Makushi in Guyana. *Ethnos*, 85(5), 843–860. https://doi.org/10.1080/00141844.2019.1626466.

Whitington, J. (2016). What Does Climate Change Demand of Anthropology? *PoLAR: Political and Legal Anthropology Review*, 39(1), 7–15. https://doi.org/10.1111/plar.12127.

Widlock, T. (2008). The Dilemmas of Walking: A Comparative View. In T. Ingold & J. L. Vergunst (Eds.), *Anthropological studies of creativity and perception. Ways of walking: Ethnography and practice on foot* (pp. 51–66). Aldershot, Farnham: Ashgate.

Willie, G. (2019). Slow Food Festival. *Vanuatu Daily Post, July 16, 2019.* Retrieved from https://www.dailypost.vu/news/slow-food-festival/article_6d7bfeac-94de-5524-a6bf-f98c9d92969e.html [accessed 19/01/2021].

Wit, S. d., Pascht, A., & Haug, M. (2018). Translating Climate Change. Anthropology and the Travelling Idea of Climate Change – Introduction. *Sociologus*, 68(1), 1–20. https://doi.org/10.3790/soc.68.1.1.

Woonton, N. (2018). Climate Vulnerable Forum 2018 – *Three-point Q and A with Hon Ralph Regenvanu, Minister of Foreign Affairs, International Cooperation and External Trade, Vanuatu at the UN Climate Change Conference.* Retrieved from https://www.sprep.org/news/three-point-q-and-a-with-hon-ralph-regenvanu-minister-of-foreign-affairs-international-cooperation-and-external-trade-vanuatu [accessed 11/12/2020].